T0391805

Disruption?

Disruption?

The Senate during the Trump Era

Edited by

SEAN M. THERIAULT

OXFORD

UNIVERSITY PRESS

OXFORD
UNIVERSITY PRESS

Oxford University Press is a department of the University of Oxford. It furthers
the University's objective of excellence in research, scholarship, and education
by publishing worldwide. Oxford is a registered trade mark of Oxford University
Press in the UK and certain other countries.

Published in the United States of America by Oxford University Press
198 Madison Avenue, New York, NY 10016, United States of America.

Library of Congress Cataloging-in-Publication Data
Names: Theriault, Sean M., 1972– editor.
Title: Disruption? : the Senate during the Trump era / Sean M. Theriault.
Description: New York : Oxford University Press, 2024. | Includes index.
Identifiers: LCCN 2024005745 (print) | LCCN 2024005746 (ebook) |
ISBN 9780197767832 (hardback) | ISBN 9780197767849 (paperback) |
ISBN 9780197767863 (epub)
Subjects: LCSH: United States. Congress. Senate. |
United States. Congress. Senate—Rules and practice. | Trump, Donald, 1946—Influence. |
Political parties—United States. | Legislative bodies—United States. |
United States—Politics and government—21st century.
Classification: LCC JK1161 .D57 2024 (print) | LCC JK1161 (ebook) |
DDC 328.73/071090512—dc23/eng/20240216
LC record available at https://lccn.loc.gov/2024005745
LC ebook record available at https://lccn.loc.gov/2024005746

DOI: 10.1093/oso/9780197767832.001.0001

Contents

Acknowledgments

In spring 2021, the Dirksen Center started out a call for an editor of a book on the Senate during the Trump era with this prescient sentence: "One does not have to pick a side to know that the Mitch McConnell-led Senate played a pivotal role in politics and policymaking over the last four years—with lasting impact on the institutional role of the upper chamber." As a student of the Senate, I found the call tantalizing. I was eager to work on my application.

When Tiffany White (the Executive Director of the Dirksen Center) and Frank Mackaman (the Historian at the Dirksen Center) called to let me know that they had chosen my application, I was both honored and terrified. The "honored" part is easy to understand; perhaps less so the "terrified" part. My grant proposal included what I thought would be the dream team of authors I would try to assemble. Putting their name on an application is far different than getting them to agree to join me in this enterprise. But agree they did, and almost every one of them enthusiastically. It has been a joy to work with such a great team of authors coming from the political arena, the think tank world, and several disciplines within the academy. I was excited they were so responsive to the initial invitation and most grateful for how they followed through on their commitment, which allowed me to follow through on mine. In particular, I want to thank Larry Evans and Annelise Russell for helping me talk through the themes of the book multiple times. Even though they did not contribute chapters, Alison Craig and Dan Palazzolo played the same role.

Tiffany White, Chris Kaergard, and Frank Mackaman from the Dirksen Center were partners at every step of the way in the development of this project. While Tiffany and I came at this project from different perspectives, we were always implementing the same game plan using our distinct yet complimentary skill sets. Besides for being wickedly smart, detail-oriented, and unfailingly trusting, Tiffany is a joy of a person. Her smile lights up a room, which is a useful quality to have when discussing the Senate during the Trump years. I am grateful for all the support that the Dirksen Center Board of Directors, the Senior Advisor, and the National Advisory Council gave to this project. I can assure you without it, this book would not exist.

I am thankful to the Kluge Center at the Library of Congress, particularly Travis Hensley and Michael Stratmoen, for hosting a one-day workshop on this book in May 2022. It was only in hearing all the 15-minute presentations by the authors on that day that I knew that we had a book. Within a few months of getting the grant for the book, I contacted Dave McBride, my acquisition publisher at Oxford University Press to see if he also might be interested in working on this book with me. I was delighted with his initial enthusiasm and thrilled that he was willing to be a part of the one-day conference. I am grateful for his support and all the professionals at Oxford who have helped get this book across the finish line.

The manuscript received two generous reviews from Oxford filled with good suggestions. Special thanks to Rob Oldham for carefully reading and commenting on the full manuscript. He saved more than a couple of authors from getting a date or roll-call tally wrong. The authors also got beneficial comments from Dave Barker, Sarah Binder, Michelle Chin, Alison Craig, Matt Green, Cheyenne Lee, and Ira Shapiro, who all attended the one-day conference in DC. Alison Craig, Dan Palazzolo, and Molly Ritchie graciously commented on various chapters at professional conferences. As always, special thanks to Anthony Bristol (who had to endure all of my heightened neuroses in putting this book together), my mom (who always has my back), and my dad (who fortunately knew about the project but regrettably did not see its completion).

I, along with my partners at the Dirksen Center and my fellow authors, dedicate this book to Frank Mackaman. We do so not only for all his years of service to the Dirksen Center, but also for all his years of service to those interested in studying Congress. At the risk of embarrassing him—and as a result possibly even straining my relationship with him—let me expound a bit upon both.

Even while he was finishing up his PhD from the University of Missouri, Frank started working at the Dirksen Center. He left for a few years, but his heart remained in Pekin, he returned in relatively short order. In total he spent more than 30 years at the Dirksen Center. During that time, the Center funded nearly 500 research projects, representing a collective investment of more than $1.1 million. With that funding, legions of PhD students completed dissertations that helped them get jobs, assistant professors turned ideas into papers into articles so that they could get tenure, associate professors developed manuscripts that eventually became books so that they could get promoted, and professors continued their research agendas so that their institutions didn't too abruptly show them the exit door. Without Frank and the Dirksen Center, we would know less about Congress whose problems most assuredly would have worsened, which would have imperiled our democracy.

It is hard to separate out what the Dirksen Center is and what Frank contributed because he is so woven into its fabric. Over the years, the Center (I think Frank would approve of me shining the spotlight on it and not him) constructed a building, digitized the Dirksen collection, acquired the Bob Michel and Ray LaHood collections, created "Congress in the Classroom" for social studies teachers from around the country, and co-founded the Bradley University's Institute for Principled Leadership and its annual symposiums. And the Center accomplished all of this while it has maintained its total independence, which makes it the only institution of its kind in the country.

From the earliest conversations that Frank and I had about this project, his enthusiasm, support, and kindness were apparent. He read each chapter, extensively commented on them, drafted most of the introduction, and sent me thoughtful emails even during difficult days for me personally. I knew Frank before I started working on this project, but one of the best results of it (in addition, obviously, to this book!) was getting to know him and his thoughtfulness and intelligence better. Very early in his career, Frank edited a book, *Understanding Congressional Leadership*, whose authors included Dave Brady, Joe Cooper, Roger Davidson, Chuck Jones, Bird Loomis, Chris Deering, Steve Smith, Larry Dodd, Bruce Oppenheimer, and Barbara Sinclair, most of whom were still early in their career. It was an amazing collection of authors writing on such an important and interesting topic. As Tiffany commented in an email to me about Frank: "The bookends of his career are, appropriately, actual books!" My only hope is that Frank is half as proud of his association with this book as he must have been in putting that book together now more than 40 years ago.

It should go without saying (but permit me to say it), the opinions expressed in this book are solely those of the authors of the chapters, and certainly not Frank, Tiffany, the Dirksen Center, the Kluge Center, or even me.

I can assure you that some of the authors said things that I would not have said. In some instances, I tried on multiple occasions to get them to tone it down. But, in the end, I was grateful for those particularly spicy sentences. It was the freedom that the Dirksen Center gave me that I in turn gave the authors that led to what I hope the reader finds as interesting of a read I did (even on my tenth pass).

Contributors

Christina Bellantoni (Director, Annenberg Media Center, University of Southern California) https://annenberg.usc.edu/faculty/journalism/christina-bellantoni Christina has worked for more than 20 years in journalism, including political editor at PBS NewsHour, editor-in-chief at *Roll Call*, and assistant managing editor for politics at the *Los Angeles Times*.

Joseph Crespino (Jimmy Carter Professor of History, Emory University) https://history.emory.edu/people/bios/faculty-bios/crespino-joseph.html Joe is the author of four books and many articles. His book, *Strom Thurmond's America* (2012), won multiple awards. His most recent book, *Atticus Finch: The Biography—Harper Lee, Her Father, and the Making of an American Icon* (2018), received much public acclaim.

Christopher Bertram (Fellow at the Center for Congressional and Presidential Studies and the Cofounder of the Program on Legislative Negotiation, American University) https://www.american.edu/spa/faculty/cbertram.cfm Chris has more than 30 years of experience in the executive and legislative branches of the federal government. He held senior staff positions in the US Senate and House of Representatives, including most recently as Staff Director of the House Transportation and Infrastructure Committee. His executive branch experience includes a presidential, Senate-confirmed appointment as an Assistant Secretary of Transportation and serving in senior roles at the White House Office of Management and Budget and the Federal Aviation Administration (FAA).

Lee Drutman (Senior Fellow, Political Reform Program, New America) and author of "Breaking the Two-Party Doom Loop") https://www.newamerica.org/our-people/lee-drutman/ Lee has written two books, *The Business of America is Lobbying*, which won the 2016 Robert A. Dahl Award for scholarship of the highest quality on the subject of democracy, and *Breaking the Two-Party Doom Loop: The Case for Mulitparty Democracy in America*. In 2021, he was named one of Washington's Most Influential People by The *Washingtonian*.

C. Lawrence Evans (Newton Family Professor of Government, The College of William and Mary) https://www.wm.edu/as/government/faculty-directory/evans_l.php Larry is the author of three books and dozens of articles about the US Congress, as well as a former coeditor of the *Legislative Studies Quarterly* and chair of the Legislative Studies Section of the American Political Science Association. His most recent book, *The Whips: Building Party Coalitions in Congress*, won the 2019 Fenno Prize, awarded to the best book on legislatures published in 2018.

William G. Howell (Sydney Stein Professor in American Politics, Harris School of Public Policy, the University of Chicago) https://harris.uchicago.edu/direct ory/william-howell Will is the author of seven books and dozens of articles. He has won numerous awards, including the Legacy Award for the book, essay, or article published at least 10 years prior that has made a continuing contribution to the intellectual development of the fields of the presidency and executive politics (*Power without Persuasion*), the William Riker Award for the best book in political economy published in the last three years (*The Wartime President*, co-authored with Saul Jackman and Jon Rogowski), the D. B. Hardeman Prize for the best book on a congressional topic (*While Dangers Gather*, coauthored with Jon Pevehouse), and the Richard E. Neustadt Award for the best book on American Presidency (*While Dangers Gather*, coauthored with Jon Pevehouse).

Frances Lee (Professor of Politics and Public Affairs, Princeton University) https:// politics.princeton.edu/people/frances-lee Frances is the author of seven books and dozens of articles. Her books have won a variety of awards including the Gladys M. Kammerer Award for the best publication on the topic of American national policy in the preceding year (*The Limits of Party: Congress and Lawmaking in a Polarized Era*—coauthor with James M. Curry), the Fenno Prize for the best book in legislative studies (*Beyond Ideology*), and the D. B. Hardeman Prize for the best book published on a congressional topic (*Beyond Ideology* and *Sizing up the Senate*—coauthored with Bruce I. Oppenheimer).

Niels Lesniewski (Chief Correspondent, White House and Congress for CQ Roll Call) https://www.rollcall.com/author/niels-lesniewski/ Niels has filled various roles at CQ Roll Call since 2007. He is currently the chief correspondent for the White House and Congress.

Frank H. Mackaman (Emeritus Historian, The Dirksen Congressional Center) Frank is the author of several books and articles about congressional and presidential history. His most recent book (coedited with Sean Q. Kelly) was an edited volume titled, *Robert H. Michel: Leading the Republican House Minority*.

Terry M. Moe (William Bennett Munro Professor of Political Science, Stanford University) https://politicalscience.stanford.edu/people/terry-moe Terry has written 12 books and dozens of articles on the presidency and public bureaucracy. His most recent book, *Presidents, Populism, and the Crisis of Democracy* (co-authored with William G. Howell), was published in 2020. He was awarded the 2020 Legacy Award for a book, essay, or article published at least 10 years prior to the award that has made a continuing contribution to the intellectual development of the field of the presidency for his article, "The Politicized Presidency." In 2001, Terry was awarded the Herbert Simon Award for contributions to the scientific study of the bureaucracy.

Bettina Poirier (Director, Program on Legislative Negotiation, American University) https://www.wcl.american.edu/community/faculty/profile/poirier/bio Before directing the Program on Legislative Negotiation at American University, Bettina was a long-time Hill staffer, including ten years as the Staff Director and Chief Counsel for the Committee on Environment and Public Works in the US Senate.

Molly E. Reynolds (Senior Fellow, The Brookings Institution) https://www.brookings.edu/experts/molly-e-reynolds/ Molly, the author of *Exceptions to the Rule: The Politics of Filibuster Limitations in the U.S. Senate*, studies Congress with an emphasis on how congressional rules and procedures affect domestic policy outcomes.

Donald A. Ritchie (Historian Emeritus of the United States Senate) In addition to serving in the Senate Historical Office from 1976 to 2015, Don has published many books, including *Press Gallery: Congress and the Washington Correspondents* and *The Congress: A Very Short Introduction*.

Annelise Russell (Assistant Professor, Martin School of Public Policy and Administration, the University of Kentucky) https://martin.uky.edu/annelise-russell Annelise, the author of *Tweeting is Leading: How Senators Communicate and Represent in the Age of Twitter*, has also written a handful of articles on congressional decision-making and communication.

Sean M. Theriault (University Distinguished Teaching Professor, Government Department, The University of Texas at Austin) Sean is the author of five books and dozens of articles. His more recent book, *The Great Broadening: How the Vast Expansion of the Policymaking Agenda Transformed American Politics* (coauthored by Bryan Jones and Michelle Whyman) won the 2020 Fenno Prize, awarded to the best book on legislatures published in 2019.

Craig Volden (Professor, Batten School of Leadership and Public Policy, University of Virginia) https://batten.virginia.edu/people/craig-volden Craig, codirector of the Center for Effective Lawmaking, is the author of several books and dozens of articles. His most recent book (coauthored with Charles Shipan), *Why Bad Policies Spread (and Good Ones Don't)*, was published in 2021. His 2014 book, *Legislative Effectiveness in the United States Congress* (coauthored by Alan E. Wiseman) won the Fenno Prize for the best book on legislatures and the Gladys M. Kammerer Award for the best book on US national policy published.

James Wallner (Lecturer, Department of Political Science, Clemson University, and Senior Fellow, R Street Institute) https://www.rstreet.org/team/james-wallner/ James has extensive experience on Capitol Hill serving in various capacities, including as the Legislative Director for Senators Jeff Sessions and Pat Toomey and as the Executive Director of the Senate Steering Committee under the chairmanships of Senators Pat Toomey and Mike Lee. He was also the Group Vice President for Research at the Heritage Foundation.

Alan E. Wiseman (Cornelius Vanderbilt Chair, Department of Political Science, Vanderbilt University) https://my.vanderbilt.edu/alanwiseman/ Alan, codirector of the Center for Effective Lawmaking, is the author of two books and dozens of articles. His more recent book, *Legislative Effectiveness in the United States Congress* (coauthored by Craig Volden) won the Fenno Prize for the best book on legislatures and the Gladys M. Kammerer Award for the best book on US National policy published.

Julian E. Zelizer (Malcolm Stevenson Forbes, Class of 1941 Professor of History and Public Affairs, Princeton University) https://history.princeton.edu/people/julian-e-zelizer Julian is the author or editor of 25 books and dozens of articles. In 2020, he published *Burning Down the House: Newt Gingrich, The Fall of a Speaker, and the Rise of the New Republican Party*, which the *New York Times* recognized as 100 "Notable Books" in 2020. Beyond his scholarly research, he is a frequent commentator in the international and national media on political history and contemporary politics.

Introduction

Disruption? The Senate during the Trump Era

Frank H. Mackaman and Sean M. Theriault

The genesis for *Disruption? The Senate during the Trump Era* occurred in December 2020 when C. Lawrence Evans, Newton Family Professor of Government at the College of William and Mary, posted a lengthy analysis on Facebook of the Senate floor exchange between Mitch McConnell and Chuck Schumer on potential votes for overriding a veto on a defense bill and the $2,000 stimulus proposal. In that particular moment, the interplay of the Senate and then President Trump was at a critical moment. In the end, Congress overrode Trump's veto; the only one of his presidency. In a proposal to the Dirksen Congressional Center's Board of Directors, the one of us who at the time worked at the Center argued that "it will require sustained scholarly research to understand precisely the dynamics behind the Republican conference's machinations during the Trump presidency." The Board subsequently approved an initial grant of $25,000 to the other one of us to put together a book on how the US Senate evolved during the Trump presidency.[1]

The media coverage of Trump would leave the consumer with the perspective that everything changed either on the day Trump road down the golden escalator at Trump Tower to announce his candidacy (June 16, 2015), on the day that Trump won the presidential contest (November 8, 2016), or on the day that he was sworn into office (January 20, 2017). No one doubts that Trump was cut from a different cloth than his predecessors. The media, though, offers only the first pass at history. The authors in this volume—some of whom come from the media—offer a more measured examination of Trump and the influence he had on an ever-evolving Senate. While the president may have been unique, the personalities in play may have been new, and the technologies and the strategies surrounding them may been

---

[1] The Board later approved an additional $50,000 for the project.

Frank H. Mackaman and Sean M. Theriault, *Introduction* In: *Disruption?* Edited by: Sean M. Theriault, Oxford University Press. © Oxford University Press 2024. DOI: 10.1093/oso/9780197767832.003.0001

innovative, some things persisted even in this new landscape. Let us emphasize one of these by historical example that bears repeating throughout this volume: who leads matters.

As the first session of the 86th Congress drew to a close in September 1959, Everett McKinley Dirksen (R-Illinois), the Senate's minority leader, dictated a letter to his counterpart, Senate Majority Leader Lyndon Baines Johnson (D-TX). "Dear Lyndon," Dirksen began, "The end of the [s]ession is somewhat like the end of an act in a play. It marks but a fragment of time and brings not only reflection on what has transpired but curiosity as to what lies ahead."[2] Dirksen was about to complete his first term as his party's leader in the Senate. He had marshaled his beleaguered and outnumbered Republican troops (the Democrats held a 65-to-35 seat majority) to combat the Democrats in a series of legislative battles including housing bills; mutual security, rural electrification, and highway construction funding; US participation in a new Inter-American Development Bank; and extension of the military draft.

As *Congressional Quarterly* put it at the beginning of the session, "There was no question that a partisan battle of panoramic scope was in store." In the end, *CQ* counted only two major accomplishments in the longest session since 1951—an act admitting statehood for Hawaii and a "tough" labor reform law (the Landrum-Griffin Act).[3] Partisan gridlock, then as now, hampered legislative productivity. The party majorities split on 50 percent of the 1959 roll calls, up from 42 percent in 1958. The average Democratic member and the average Republican member voted with their party majority 75 percent of the time and against it only 16 percent of the time. Despite their nearly two-to-one majorities in the House and Senate, the Democrats made "only token progress" toward the balance of their legislative goals. Similarly, they granted just 40 percent of President Dwight Eisenhower's requests.[4]

Dirksen acknowledged the fraught politics of the session in his missive to Johnson: "We have differed but always with high respect for each other's viewpoint," he suggested. "We have fought—gently, I hope—but always with understanding. We have asserted our various party causes, but always in

---

[2] Dirksen to Johnson, September 12, 1959, Everett M. Dirksen Papers, Alpha File 1959, Johnson.

[3] Mayhew (2005) reports only one additional major piece of legislation passed in 1959 (the National Housing Act of 1959). He includes only two additional major enactments in the second session of the 86th Congress: Civil Rights Act of 1960 and the Kerr-Mills Assistance Program. According to Mayhew, the 86th Congress had the fewest number of major enactments in his dataset, which encompassed the 80th to the 117th Congresses.

[4] *CQ Almanac* 1959 (Washington, DC: Congressional Quarterly Press, 1960), 61, 126.

good grace." Dirksen concluded: "We have shared a high mutual pride in the Senate and in a common effort to make it and keep it what it is and always has been—the greatest free, independent, undominated legislative body in the world."

Partisanship tempered by "high respect," "understanding," and "grace"— terms no one would use to describe the Senate during the Trump years.

Johnson replied two days later. "Of the leaders with whom I have served, there have been none who can wield the partisan stiletto with quite the gusto and the zest that you do." He then added, "But even though the stiletto cuts deep, it never stings."[5] In his letter, Johnson recalled for Dirksen a lesson the Texan had learned as a neophyte in Congress: "I was told that no leader can be very useful unless he has friendships on the other side of the aisle." Dirksen agreed when he noted that "our friendship has deepened and become a nourishing force in pursuing our respective duties."

These private letters, never meant for publication, speak volumes about the relationship between these two leaders of competing political parties. Even as they disagreed, often pointedly, they respected one another, and they cherished their institution. Although the Senate was not particularly productive at that moment, Dirksen and Johnson were building a relationship that would bear much fruit before they both would leave Washington, DC.

The Dirksen-Johnson relationship proved enduring over the next decade as the two leaders worked together to pass landmark legislation during John Kennedy's New Frontier and Johnson's Great Society. In those cases, neither leader, even Johnson then as president, put partisan advantage over the national interest. A calculation few believe party leaders make today.

Partisanship in 1959 looked nothing like the virulent political chauvinism that infects the Senate today—now the stiletto stings. Contrasting the Senate during the first year of Eisenhower's last congress with the first year of the Trump administration shows how much the Senate has changed. In 2017, a majority of Republican senators opposed a majority of Democratic senators on 76.0 percent of the roll-call votes, the highest percentage in CQ's 66 years of gathering the data. On those votes, Democrats voted with each other an average of 92 percent of the time and Republicans voted with each other 97 percent of the time, which is also an all-time high (the next closest was 94 percent in 2003). While the Senate was embroiled in this partisan morass, it was not clear at all that Schumer and McConnell were exchanging private

---

[5] Johnson to Dirksen, September 14, 1959, Everett M. Dirksen Papers, Alpha File 1959, Johnson.

letters that would become the bedrock of a future Senate that would accomplish great legislation down the road.

That the Senate changed from the Johnson-Dirksen era to the McConnell-Schumer era is not in doubt. Why the Senate changed, and Donald Trump's role in that change, is an entirely different question; and one that we take up in this volume.

To answer the question of how much President Trump disrupted the Senate, we brought together what we think is the most diverse set of Senate observers ever assembled in an edited volume. Our authors range from former Senate staffers (Ritchie, Poirier, Bertram, and Wallner) to journalists (Lesniewski and Bellantoni) and historians (Mackaman, Ritchie, Crespino, and Zelizer) to political scientists (Theriault, Evans, Reynolds, Lee, Volden, Wiseman, Russell, Wallner, Howell, and Moe). What made this collaboration so fruitful was that all of the authors, while skilled in the tools of their own particular professions, appreciated the contributions made by those outside their field. The intermingling of the different professions started even before the collaboration on this project. One of the Senate staffers now has her desk in a university, and more than a few of the political scientists at one point collected paychecks from the federal government when they worked in Congress. Another political scientist cut her teeth in politics at *Congressional Quarterly*, and a journalist has been the featured speaker at an academic conference.

The Chapters

Not unsurprisingly, such a learned, thoughtful, and conscientious group of scholars arrived at different answers.

Donald Ritchie, who served in the Senate Historical Office from 1976 until he retired as the Senate Historian in 2015, makes the important point that while the Senate has changed, the rules have not. As both parties transformed from having both liberal and conservative wings, majority parties reinterpreted the rules to achieve the goals that historical precedence would have forbidden. Because both parties engaged in this behavior before Trump's election in 2016, Ritchie argues that the Senate's behavior during the Trump administration was more a culmination than a disruption.

In Chapter 2, Joseph Crespino, the Jimmy Carter Professor of History at Emory University, also looks to history to glean insight into the modern

Senate. He shows that senators were disruptors far before Trump moved into the White House. By recounting Strom Thurmond's filibuster of the 1957 Civil Rights bill, which remains the longest one-person speech in Senate history, Crespino argues that if senators of Thurmond's era had the individual powers of senators today, it is likely that far fewer of the landmark laws ever would have been enacted.

C. Lawrence Evans takes us back even further—all the way back to the US Constitution—in Chapter 3. He argues that the disruption that we saw in the Senate during the Trump era is rooted in bicameralism. By analyzing the 2017 tax reform battle, he shows how the Trump administration used the structural incongruities grounded in apportionment and chamber procedures to disrupt the Senate.

In Chapter 4, Molly Reynolds, Senior Fellow at the Brookings Institution, examines how the Senate's long-standing trends in the legislative process interacted with an unpredictable president. She explains that the unorthodox lawmaking, which has long historical roots, became even more unorthodox. While she argues that much of what was on display during Trump's term was present before his election, his actions still drove the Senate's evolution in important ways.

In the best example of the intermingling of professions, Frances Lee, a professor of political science at Princeton University, wrote a chapter with Bettina Poirier and Chris Bertram, who now both hang their hats in the Program on Legislative Negotiation at American University. Prior to their current appointments, Poirier served many years in the Senate, including 10 years as the Staff Director and Chief Counsel for the Committee on Environment and Public Works, and Bertram worked for more than 30 years in the Senate, House, and executive branch, including a stint as Assistant Secretary of Transportation in the Obama administration. In their chapter, they show how a Democratic-led House, a Republican-led Senate, and the Trump White House came to pass a set of sweeping COVID-aid measures on a wholly bipartisan basis. They draw on concepts from scholarship on negotiation to explain how agreements were reached on these massive legislative packages.

In Chapter 6, Craig Volden, professor in the Batten School of Leadership and Public Policy at the University of Virginia, and Alan Wiseman, the Cornelius Vanderbilt Chair in political science at Vanderbilt University, show how Democratic senators achieved success even while they were both a minority party and a party opposite the president. The particular set of circumstances of the Trump White House, the Republican drive for judicial appointees, and the drive for solutions during the pandemic created the space for Democrats to achieve legislative success where few expected it.

James Wallner, a lecturer in the Department of Political Science at Clemson University and the former Executive Director of the Republican Senate Steering Committee, argues that rank-and-file senators empowered their party leaders to make nearly all the important decisions off the Senate floor, not only during the Trump years but also before then (and even after). As such, Trump did not have nearly the consequence in the Senate that many believe (including some of the other authors in this volume).

In Chapter 8, Julian Zelizer, the Malcolm Stevenson Forbes Class of 1941 Professor of History and Public Affairs at Princeton University, argues that the uneasy personal relationship between President Trump and Senate Majority Leader Mitch McConnell was made functional by their mutual desire to win at all costs. He argues that McConnell sacrificed the goals of governance and preserving democratic institutions on the altar of partisanship by weaponizing every conceivable process and norm to maintain legislative power.

Niels Lesniewski, the chief correspondent for the White House and Congress at CQ Roll Call, documents the unprecedented actions Donald Trump took and shows how few constraints the Senate put on him. He argues that the Senate often found itself either unequipped or uninterested in responding to Trump's pushing of the envelope.

In Chapter 10, Annelise Russell, an assistant professor at the Martin School of Public Policy and Administration at the University of Kentucky, who cut her political teeth at Congressional Quarterly before going to graduate school, shows how Senate communication strategies were transformed by growing dependence upon Twitter and Trump's use of the platform. She explains how senators adapted to the Twitter environment where news is always being made, and Trump made misinformation common and facts debatable. She argues Trump was an accelerant speeding the development of a combustible communication climate rather than the creator of it.

Lee Drutman, Senior Fellow in the Political Reform Program at New America, takes a step back in examining the Senate's legitimacy crisis. He argues that the Senate no longer serves as the second sober thought that the founders envisioned. Even as democracies around the globe are curtailing the power of their upper chambers, the Senate continues to flex its powers, and the gridlock it imposes on the entire system will likely persist for the foreseeable future.

In Chapter 12, Christina Bellantoni, the director of the Annenberg Media Center at the University of Southern California and formerly the political editor at the PBS NewsHour and editor-in-chief at *Roll Call*, wears both her journalist and academic hat in documenting how the Senate has changed since she started her career in Washington, DC. In the end, she argues that many of the fibers that kept the institutional fabric of the Senate together were cut during the Trump years.

The final substantive chapter showcases presidency scholars—William Howell, the Sydney Stein Professor of American Politics at the University of Chicago, and Terry M. Moe, William Bennett Munro Professor of Political Science at Stanford University—putting the Senate into the broader American political system context. They chronicle the many unilateral actions Trump took in the face of congressional disinterest, dysfunction, and even opposition. They argue that Congress's own pathologies often make legislators incapable of overturning any presidential action, even those with which they vehemently disagree.

In the conclusion, one of us assesses the Senate since Trump moved out of the White House. It is clear that the Senate has not snapped back to its pre-Trump contours, but rather continues to wrestle with the norms, rules, and procedures disrupted by Trump's four years in the White House. Perhaps the hangover is made more severe as Trump still dominates the coverate in news cycle after news cycle.

The Lessons

All the authors agree that Trump mattered; though they might heartily disagree over the extent to which he mattered. Over the development of this book, we argued in person at a one-day conference hosted by the Kluge Center in the Library of Congress and at two panels in professional conferences. Those arguments continued over several nice dinners and in email threads that connected us even over distance and time. While the varying perspectives vindicated the Dirksen Center's board in seeking an examination of this subject and the collection of perspectives that one of us assembled, the team of authors in this volume are more unified in arguing that Trump mattered than they are divided in how much he mattered. Beyond the explicit question of analyzing, measuring, and arguing about Trump's disruption, the authors weave through their various chapters four prevalent themes.

First, the Senate matters. To each of the authors, the Senate is more than just a second chamber of the legislative branch. It is the one institution in the national government with compromise written into its rules. While the president can change policy with the stroke of his pen and a unified majority in the House can pass legislation on a party-line vote, the Senate requires support from both parties in all but the rarest of circumstances. As James Madison, though himself never a senator, said at the Constitutional Convention, the "use of the Senate is to consist in its proceedings with more coolness, with more system, and with more wisdom" than the House of Representatives. So the authors, admittedly with varying degrees, recognize the uniqueness and peculiarities of the Senate. Drutman argues that ultimately the Senate mattering could be—and in his opinion should be—the Senate's downfall. While Howell and Moe think the Senate's peculiarities undermine its relevance, Bellantoni and Ritchie suggest that these features are what make the Senate so interesting and so important.

Second, history matters. None of the authors think the Senate changed only because of President Trump. What preceded his victory in the 2016 election—and, perhaps even what caused it—has its roots at least as far back as the politics of Strom Thurmond (Crespino) or even the Constitution (Evans). Wallner might say that Obama almost seamlessly handed off the baton to Trump in understanding the effect that presidents can have. Without dissent, all the authors recognize that what came before Trump in the Republican Party (Zelizer and Russell) and in the Senate (Bellantoni) shaped the impact he had on how it operated during his four years in the White House.

Third, rules matter. While the Senate rules were unchanged under Trump (Ritchie), the manner and frequency with which they were used and abused did change (Reynolds and Liesnewski), though not always for obstructionism (Volden and Wiseman and Lee, Poirier, and Bertram). Senate rules can constrain behavior, but they do not force any one set of actions; rather, they permit a range that can be influenced by those like the Senate Democrats inside the chamber (Volden and Wiseman) or like Trump outside the chamber (Russell and Bellantoni).

Fourth, who leads matters. Whether being led by the Great Triumvirate (John C. Calhoun, Daniel Webster, and Henry Clay), Czar Thomas Reed, the Senate Four (Nelson Aldrich, William Allison, Orville Platt, and John

Spooner), Johnson and Dirksen, or McConnell and Schumer, leaders have discretion in the actions they take. Lyndon Johnson's leadership in the Senate during the Eisenhower administration made a difference, as did his relationship with Everett Dirksen during his own. And so it is the case with Mitch McConnell during the Trump administration and his relationship with Chuck Schumer. While the authors may disagree about how leadership mattered and the extent to which it mattered, no author doubts that the combination of Trump-McConnell-Schumer produced different outcomes than some other set of leaders. At the same time, no author is naïve enough to think that any two party leaders in today's Senate could mirror the mutual affection between Dirksen and Johnson if they wanted to stay on the job. In today's Senate, indeed, the stiletto stings because a sufficient number of senators in both parties demand that it do so.

We hope that the readers of this volume find answers to their questions about how the Senate operates today while providing some evidence and arguments for those questions that remain open.

Reference

Mayhew, David R. 2005. *Divided We Govern: Party Control, Lawmaking, and Investigations, 1946–2002*, 2nd ed. New Haven, CT: Yale University Press.

1

The Changing Senate's Unchanging Rules

Donald A. Ritchie

Introduction

The US Senate during the presidencies of Donald Trump and Joseph Biden bears little resemblance to the institution that Biden joined in 1973. Then there were no women senators nor women staff in prominent positions and few minorities. The Senate's chief computer was collectively reserved for mass mailings. Reporters in the press gallery still telegraphed their stories to their newspapers. No television cameras recorded debates in the Senate chamber.

Campaign finance laws regulated and limited contributions to candidates. The Senate met five days a week and on an occasional Saturday. Six-year terms encouraged senators to move their families to Washington for the months that Congress was in session, providing opportunities to socialize with each other during off-hours.

A half century later, a quarter of the senators were women, and women and minorities held key staff positions. Digital electronics dominated office work, communications, and the media. Television lights brightened the Senate Chamber from twilight to high noon. The Supreme Court had disabled most campaign finance restrictions, interpreting monetary contributions as a form of free speech, and causing senators to engage in perpetual fund raising. The congressional workweek shrank to Tuesdays through Thursdays, and more members left their families back in their home states, providing less time and opportunity to legislate or socialize.[1]

Politically, the Senate underwent an even more sweeping transformation. Biden first took his seat in an institution that Democrats had controlled for 36 of the previous 40 years. Most senators from the South were Democrats,

---

[1] Donald A. Ritchie, "Changes in the Senate Since the 1960s," US Capitol Historical Society, August 22, 2012, C-SPAN, https://www.c-span.org/video/?307706-1/senate-1960s

Donald A. Ritchie, *The Changing Senate's Unchanging Rules* In: *Disruption?* Edited by: Sean M. Theriault, Oxford University Press. © Oxford University Press 2024. DOI: 10.1093/oso/9780197767832.003.0002

among them the archconservative James Eastland of Mississippi. Senate Republicans included such ardent liberals as Jacob Javits of New York. Both parties were internally divided between their liberal and conservative wings, which created what political scientists have described as "four-party politics." Liberals would join forces against conservatives, with both sides vying for those in the middle. Almost all votes were bipartisan. A straight party-line vote would have made headlines (Burns 1963).

Over the next five decades, Democrats and Republicans split control of the Senate equally, with the majority switching back and forth about every six years. The South seceded from the Democratic Party and conservative Republicans expelled liberals as RINOs (Republican in name only). As conservative Democrats and liberal Republicans traded party affiliations, the reshuffling created unprecedented levels of unity within the congressional party conferences, whose members began voting together more than ninety percent of the time. Bipartisan votes now made headlines (Barone 2019).

During the "four-party" era, shifting coalitions prompted compromise and cooperation, but internal cohesion has removed much of the parties' incentive to work together. Instead of needing to pacify dissident factions, the leader of a united conference could focus on a common adversary—the other party. Minority parties aimed to win back control in the next election, and unless the issue was of transcendent nature, they saw little reward in bipartisan collaboration.

The only significant part of the Senate that had not changed was its standing rules.

Business as usual was highly unlikely after such a dramatic shakeup of the political parties, and recent majority leaders have had to struggle to keep the institution functioning. The Senate rule that has caused the most anguish and generated the most calls for reform concerns cloture, the mechanism for ending debate and permitting a vote. The history of Senate treatment of filibusters and cloture reflects the difficulty in changing the formal rules and reveals the alternative tactics that leaders have employed.

The Constitution authorizes each chamber of Congress to write its own rules. The Senate and House operating under similar rules, but the larger House gradually adjusted its procedures to permit a majority to act more efficiently. It has always been easier for the House to revise its rules since its entire membership stands for election every two years. Newly elected majorities can adopt whatever rules suit their purposes. By contrast, since only a third of the senators run in each election, a quorum always carries over into the next congress. The Senate has therefore defined itself as a continuing body that does not revise its rules at the beginning of each congress.

The Senate Rules

In its more than two centuries of operation, the US Senate has conducted only seven general revisions of its rules, the last taking place between 1979 and 1983. Technically, a simple majority can rewrite the rules, but since revisions are debatable, it takes a two-thirds vote to cut off debate, which means that substantial rules changes can occur only after a broad bipartisan consensus has been reached.

The rules have traditionally given more muscle to the minority, which in the Senate can be the minority party, a faction within either party, or a single senator. These rules better fit the compromise-seeking, coalition-building, logrolling, horse-trading days of the past than they do the polarized politics of the present. As the Senate grew polarized, minority parties repeatedly and effectively employed the standing rules to impede the majority. Such recalcitrance prompted the majority to devise creative efforts to enable Senate business to proceed.

While the Senate's rules remain seemingly immutable, the institution also operates under a myriad of precedents that can override the rules. A notable instance occurred in 1995, when the presiding officer declared an amendment by Senator Kay Bailey Hutchinson (R-Texas) out of order because Senate rules prohibit legislating on an appropriations bill. Senator Hutchinson appealed, and a majority supported her. Presiding officers were then obligated to allow legislative amendments on appropriations bills, despite their violating the standing rules. Four years later, Majority leader Trent Lott (R-Mississippi) engineered a vote to overturn the precedent and return to the rules. "I learned painfully what a mistake that was," he admitted. "We should not be legislating on appropriations bills." The incident serves as an example of the tactics that leaders have employed to alter Senate procedures by precedent if not by rule, depending upon how irritated the majority has become and how arbitrarily it is willing to act.[2]

The rules of the Senate are unique to the Senate. The House of Representatives, state legislatures, and parliaments around the world operate

---

[2] Trent Lott's remarks in the *Congressional Record*, 110th Cong., 1st sess., S10076.

by majority rule, whereas Senate rules make it difficult for a majority to end debate and force a vote. The Senate did not adopt a cloture rule to cut off debate until 1917. Even then, its two-thirds requirement was difficult to achieve—until the grueling 60-day filibuster in 1964 ended with a successful cloture that enabled passage of the Civil Rights Act. Yet even some who fought hardest against the filibuster at the time conceded its value. Charles Ferris, who directed the Senate Democratic Policy Committee, believed that the length and intensity of the filibuster had been an asset. "That's why the law was so well accepted in the end," he asserted in an oral history, because white Southerners "knew their senators had fought it for so long and the bill passed after a most deliberate debate."[3]

The turbulent 1970s produced two significant changes in Senate procedures. In the wake of Watergate and President Richard Nixon's refusal to spend appropriated funds, Congress passed the Congressional Budget and Impoundment Control Act of 1974, which included reconciliation, a provision to restrict the time allotted for debating budget bills. Intended to reconcile differences between the Budget and Appropriations committees, reconciliation's ability to dodge filibusters by setting a 20-hour limit on debate and permitting passage by a simple majority has made it a tempting tactic to push controversial legislation through the Senate. But to prevent its misuse the Senate in 1985 adopted the "Byrd Rule," sponsored by Senator Robert C. Byrd (D-West Virginia), which bans extraneous provisions. The Senate parliamentarian is authorized to decide whether any provisions of the legislation fall under these restrictions (known as a "Byrd bath"), tempering an otherwise powerful parliamentary tool.[4]

The other critical change was a revision of the Senate's cloture rule. Reformers advocated what they called the "constitutional option," a theory that—like the House—the Senate could rewrite its rules by majority vote at the beginning of a congress. Liberals promoted it to derail filibusters against civil rights bills. But the Senate never carried out the "constitutional option" because senators usually reached compromises to deflect it.

At the start of the 94th Congress in 1975, Senator James Pearson (R-Kansas) moved to reduce cloture from two-thirds (67) to three-fifths (60).

[3] "Charles D. Ferris: Staff Director, Senate Democratic Policy Committee (1963–1977)," Oral History Interviews, April 5, 2004, to September 23, 2009, Senate Historical Office, Washington, DC, 36, 155.

[4] "G. William Hoagland: Staff Director of the Senate Budget Committee, Advisor to the Senate Majority Leader," Oral History Interviews, November 28, 2006, to August 30, 2007, Senate Historical Office, Washington, DC, 19.

Majority Leader Mike Mansfield (D- Montana) objected, but the Senate tabled his point of order. Vice President Nelson Rockefeller, acting against the advice of the parliamentarian, announced that he viewed the tabling as a sign that the Senate regarded Pearson's motion as proper, and he would call for an immediate yea-or-nay vote. But Senator James Allen (D-Alabama) moved that the motion be divided, since it contained distinct and separate clauses. This action permitted debate on the portions of a motion that could not be debated as a whole, creating a "parliamentary tangle" (Byrd 1991).

"So, making a long story short," Senate Parliamentarian Floyd Riddick later explained in his oral history, "they vitiated all of this proceeding," and decided to invoke cloture in "the proper way." The leadership filed a cloture motion on the original bill, which the Senate adopted by 73 to 21—an ample two-thirds majority. Senators then adopted a substitute measure that reduced cloture to three-fifths.[5]

Consider that a member of the minority party took the lead in promoting a reduction of cloture. Consider also that the majority party had 61 senators on its side at the time. Why would the minority give away the store? Because of ideological divisions in 1975 no one expected all Democratic senators to vote together on any issue; neither was Republican unity expected.

The Senate's Changing Precedents

Two years after lowering the bar, the Senate voted cloture on a bill to deregulate natural gas. Liberal senators James Abourezk (D-South Dakota) and Howard Metzenbaum (D-Ohio) immediately launched a "post-cloture filibuster." Determined to defeat the bill, they filed hundreds of amendments that could tie up the Senate with readings, debate, quorum calls, and roll-call votes. After a dozen days and one long night of debate, Majority Leader Robert C. Byrd enlisted Vice President Walter Mondale to declare the amendments dilatory under cloture and therefore out of order. In a matter of minutes, the vice president struck down 33 amendments. As Senator Byrd later described the scene, "Pandemonium broke loose as senators were denied recognition to appeal the chair's rulings declaring the amendment disqualified, and both the vice president and I were severely criticized for

---

[5] "Floyd M. Riddick, Senate Parliamentarian," Oral History Interviews, June 26 to December 4, 1978, Senate Historical Office, Washington, DC, 214–221.

the extraordinary actions we had taken to break the post-cloture filibuster" (MacNeil and Baker 2013; Shapiro 2012; Byrd 1991).

As a new Senate historian, I sat in the galleries that day and witnessed the uproar and Senator Byrd's spirited response to his critics, noting that he broke the protocol that required senators to address the chair rather than each other and swung around with his back to the vice president to confront the protesters. He had been their spear carrier on countless occasions, he reminded them, but not acting would have rendered cloture meaningless. He claimed only to be trying to "keep senators from abusing the Senate." Decades later, when Republicans first contemplated the "nuclear option," they pointed to Byrd's action that day as a "mini-nuclear" precedent, using the chair to reinterpret the rules.[6]

In 1975, senators regarded cloture not as a protection for the minority party but as a tool for the leaders of both parties to exert control over minority factions. It was not unusual for the majority and minority leaders to cosponsor cloture motions. The number of cloture motions filed each congress rose only slowly until 1987, when Democrats had won back control of the Senate and Republicans occupied the White House. Majority Leader Byrd filed more cloture motions while Minority Leader Bob Dole (R-Kansas) reasoned that he needed just 41 votes to prevent Congress from sending President Ronald Reagan legislation he would feel compelled to veto.[7]

When George Mitchell (D-Maine) became majority leader in 1989, House Democrats complained about Senate inaction. Mitchell blamed the gridlock on the record number of filibusters he faced. Reporters contacted the Senate Historical Office for verification. We found quantifying filibusters problematic since the term covers any obstructionism and rarely takes the form famously portrayed in *Mr. Smith Goes to Washington*. Most often it involves objections to unanimous consent agreements, holds, and votes against cloture, which require practically no talking. Since failed cloture votes can be counted, however, they became synonymous with filibusters. In claiming that the minority was conducting a record number of filibusters, Senator

---

[6] Senate Gallery Notes, October 3, 1977; Box 1; Donald Ritchie Files; Office of the Historian; Office of the Secretary of the Senate; Records of the U.S. Senate, Record Group 46; National Archives and Records Administration (NARA), Washington, DC; "W. Lee Rawls: Staff Director to Senators Pete Domenici and Bill Frist," Oral History Interviews, 2009–2010, Senate Historical Office, 110, 137; Martin B. Gold and Dimple Gupta, "The Constitutional Option to Change Senate Rules and Procedures: A Majoritarian Means to Overcome the Filibuster," *Harvard Journal of Law and Public Policy* 28 (January 2005): 206–272.

[7] See Senate Actions on Cloture Motions, http://www.senate.gov.

Mitchell meant that they were defeating a record number of cloture motions (MacNeil and Baker 2013; Arenberg and Dove 2015).

After a reversal of fortune relegated them to the minority in 1995, Senate Democrats began hearing from their House counterparts that it was up to them to stop the Republicans' "Contract with America" because they had more than 40 votes to defeat cloture. "That's when we pointed out to them," said Democratic Secretary Marty Paone, " 'Oh, you mean using the rules that you all wanted us to change two years ago?' And they realized that perhaps there was some utility in the way the Senate was set up."[8]

Over the next two decades, the steady upturn in political polarization snarled the Senate's confirmation of judicial nominations. Republicans blocked some of Bill Clinton's liberal choices, and Democrats similarly dead-ended some of George W. Bush's conservative nominees. One day in 2003, the volatile Senator Ted Stevens (R-Alaska) erupted in the Republican cloakroom. He insisted that as president pro tempore he could march into the chamber, take the chair, and rule that the minority could no longer filibuster judicial nominations. "We can put an end to this now!" Stevens exhorted. The idea attracted support within the Republican conference, but not sufficiently to prevail given their narrow 51–49 majority. Winning four more seats in the next election emboldened majority leader Bill Frist (R-Tennessee) to threaten a "nuclear option" to use a ruling by the chair to reduce cloture on confirmation to a simple majority. Democrats protested loudly and a bipartisan group of centrists crafted a compromise that allowed more nominations to be considered while still reserving the right to filibuster.[9]

Although defused, the nuclear option loomed over the Senate for another decade. Martin Gold, who provided parliamentary advice to the Republican leadership, reasoned that it would take "extreme provocation" and sufficient unity within the majority to work to make the nuclear option work. The minority simply would not permit abolishing the filibuster by a formal change in the Senate's rules.[10]

Democrats reclaimed the congressional majorities during the last two years of George W. Bush's administration. The House churned out legislation

[8] "Martin P. Paone: Senate Democratic Cloakroom Staff to Majority Secretary, 1979–2008," Oral History Interviews, March 11, 2009 to June 2, 2010, Senate Historical Office, Washington, DC, 78.

[9] Jim VandeHei and Charles Babington, "From Senator's 2003 Outburst, GOP Hatched 'Nuclear Option,'" *Washington Post*, May 19, 2005; Robert Novak, "Byrd's 'Nuclear Option,'" *Washington Post*, December 20, 2004

[10] "Martin Gold, Counsel to the Senate Republican Leader, 1979–1982, 2003–2004," Oral History Interviews, Senate Historical Office, Washington, DC, 119.

at a fast pace and grumbled about the Senate's slowness to act. Majority Leader Harry Reid (D-Nevada) confessed that at times he wished he were the Speaker of the House. "The Speaker of the House doesn't have to worry about the minority, they run over everybody," he mused. "That is the way it is set up," in the House, "if one party is in control, they can do anything they want, and in . . . the Senate—if one Party is in control, they can do some things they want but not everything, because the minority has tremendous power in the Senate. I know. I have been in the minority quite a bit."[11]

With Barack Obama's election as president in 2008, Democrats temporarily gained a 60-vote majority in the Senate, which the media optimistically labeled "filibuster proof." That margin enabled them to enact an ambitious agenda without needing Republican support. Then the "tea party" revolt of 2010 cost Democrats their majority in the House and reduced their Senate ranks to 53. Minority Leader Mitch McConnell (R-Kentucky) urged his conference to stand united against Obama's legislative initiatives and nominations, proclaiming his number one goal to limit him to a one-term presidency. Ted Kaufman, who served as Senator Biden's chief of staff before succeeding him as senator from Delaware, identified the strategy as holding up judicial nominees at different points in the process to reduce the overall number that would be confirmed. "There's a rule that was based on the need sometimes to hold a judicial nomination over for a week for a hearing because you need more information," Kaufman explained. "Well, that went out the window in this session. The Republicans just held everyone over."[12]

Republicans also defeated a record number of cloture motions, prompting some Democrats to propose invoking the "constitutional option" at the start of the next congress. Dubious about this tactic, which would require the presiding officer to ignore the rules, Majority Leader Reid contemplated a different strategy: The chair could uphold the rules, be appealed by the majority, and overturned. Normally, this would not work since appeals are debatable and subject to filibuster. But if the point of order was made *after* cloture had been voted upon, it could not be debated. Parliamentarians described this as a procedural sweet spot.[13]

---

[11] *Congressional Record*, 110th Cong., 1st sess., 11937.

[12] "Edward E. (Ted) Kaufman: United States Senator from Delaware and Chief of Staff to Senator Joe Biden, 1973–2010," Oral History Interviews, August 17 to September 27, 2012, Senate Historical Office, Washington, DC, 309.

[13] Mike Allen and Jeffrey H. Birnbaum, "A Likely Script for the 'Nuclear Option,'" *Washington Post*, May 18, 2005; Paul Kane, "Democrats' Young Bucks, Not 'Old Bulls,' Nuked the Filibuster," *Washington Post*, November 24, 2013.

Senator Reid conducted a nuclear test in October 2011. After the Senate voted cloture on a Chinese currency bill, Minority Leader McConnell moved to suspend the rules to allow senators to vote on President Obama's jobs bill. His aim was to embarrass the majority, which had not yet worked out a compromise on the bill. When the chair found the motion permissible, Senator Reid appealed the ruling. Being non-debatable after cloture, his appeal won 51 to 48. Senator McConnell heatedly pointed out that the majority leader had "over-ruled the chair with a simple majority vote and established the precedent that even one single motion to suspend—even one—is dilatory, changing the rules of the Senate." Reid, however, described the adjustment as "a return to order" intended to facilitate the Senate's functioning, not to limit the rights of the minority.[14]

President Obama won a second term in 2012, and Democrats retained control of the Senate in part by securing seats in Republican-leaning states. Legislation moved forward but the president's nominations encountered stiff resistance. By summer 2013, Senator Reid was threatening to detonate the nuclear option unless some compromise was reached to reduce filibusters on nominations. The two parties met in a joint conference in the historic Old Senate Chamber where Henry Clay had once forged compromises. Ninety-eight senators spent three and a half hours talking through their grievances. Cordiality prevailed, and the following morning they reached a deal to confirm a director for the Consumer Financial Protection Bureau—two years after that agency's creation.[15]

That compromise did not last for long. During fall 2013, a notable standoff developed over three vacancies on the Court of Appeals for the District of Columbia Circuit, which is significant because it handles cases regarding federal regulations and because it has served as a springboard to the US Supreme Court. Republicans resisted filling these vacancies, arguing that the court did not have enough business to justify adding three new members. Without those appointments, the court would continue to function with half of its judges having been appointed by Republican presidents.[16]

---

[14] Suspension of the rules requires a two-thirds vote, and the last successful suspension vote occurred in 1941. The move was therefore destined to fail, but it would have allowed Republicans to say that Democrats had voted against the president's jobs bill. Alexander Bolton, "Reid Triggers 'Nuclear Option' to Change Senate Rules, End Filibuster," *The Hill*, October 7, 2011; Congressional Record, 112th Cong., 1st Sess., S63176-17; Harry Reid, "A Return to Regular Order," *Washington Post*, October 11, 2011.

[15] Paul Kane and Ed O'Keefe, "As Senate Nears Filibuster Showdown, Reid Says Republicans Can Still Avoid Fight," *Washington Post*, July 15, 2013.

[16] Jeremy W. Peters, "G.O.P. Filibuster of 2 Obama Picks Sets Up Fight," *New York Times*, October 31, 2013.

The appeals court impasse led the majority leader to announce that he would use the nuclear option to reduce cloture requirements for all nominations below the level of the Supreme Court. Immediately, the phones started ringing in the Senate Historical Office with calls from reporters seeking historical precedents. Before long we found that Democratic senators had given the same explanation for blocking President Bush's nominations to the same court a decade earlier—what goes around comes around. One of the calls came from a reporter for a Russian news agency who wanted to know why the tactic was called a nuclear option, which to him sounded like a remnant from the Cold War.[17]

Senator Reid triggered the nuclear option on November 21, 2013. Having failed to achieve cloture on an appeals court nomination, the majority leader asserted that a majority vote should be sufficient for cloture on nominations. Citing the standing rules, the chair rejected his point of order, and the majority leader appealed. Since the appeal followed the failed cloture motion it was nondebatable. The Senate voted 52 to 48 to uphold Reid's appeal, setting a new precedent. The narrowness of the vote showed that this was as far as the agreement could go. A motion that included Supreme Court nominations would have lost, since not all Democrats agreed.[18]

A "nuclear winter" followed, with routine party-line votes for cloture on nominations followed by overwhelmingly bipartisan votes for confirmation. Senator Reid called it "Groundhog Year" because the Senate kept going through the same motions over and over. The minority would decline to go along until cloture was filed and nothing else could get done for the next 30 hours. Republican senators also conducted an all-night talkathon to protest the nuclear option. Although cloture had already been invoked and the outcome was inevitable, they gained media attention for their cause by holding the floor throughout the night. As a Senate historian I could leave at night even if the Senate stayed late. When I arrived at the cafeteria the next morning, I found a half dozen weary Democratic senators hunched over their coffee. It was a reminder that proposals to force "talking filibusters" can exhaust the majority as much as the minority.[19]

---

[17] Senate Historical Office Log, November 21, December 2, 2013, Box 19, Ritchie Files, NARA.

[18] Paul Kane, "Reid, Democrats Trigger 'Nuclear' Option; Eliminate Most Filibusters on Nominees," *Washington Post*, November 22, 2013.

[19] Noah Bierman and Kimberly Railey, "Congress Back to Business but It's Still Not Working," *Boston Globe*, March 1, 2014; Senate Historical Office Log, December 13, 2013, February 26, 2014, Box 19, Ritchie Files; *Congressional Record*, 113th Cong., 1st sess., S8714.

The exasperated majority leader threatened to keep the Senate in session over the weekend to run out the cloture clock and wrap up lingering nominations, a warning that brought about a compromise and restored harmony just before the holiday break. Under a unanimous consent agreement, senators voted on two nominations that evening, six more the next morning, and scheduled another for the new year. Still, resentments lingered on both sides. Republicans felt mistreated by the majority leader's repeated filing of cloture motion and filling the "amendment tree" to prevent their amendments. (That imagery derived from diagrams of the process of offering amendments, which abstractly resemble tree branches. Only majority leaders can consistently amend their own amendments, thereby filling the tree and preventing other amendments. Leaders use this tactic to exclude "gotcha" amendments that have nothing to do with the bill's content.) Democrats felt mistreated by the minority's repeated objections to unanimous consent agreements and attempts to force them to vote on non-germane issues.[20]

When Senate Republicans won back the majority in 2014, they considered formally revising the rules to lower the cloture bar for Supreme Court nominations, rather than follow the Democrats' path by imposing a new precedent. Republican staff speculated that this might be the only congress where they might achieve the necessary 67 votes to invoke cloture on changing the rules since neither party would be losing anything: Democrats could help confirm their president's last nominees and Republicans could set the stage for the next Republican president. Nothing came of it. Republicans simply left the nuclear option precedent unchallenged. In 2016, President Obama nominated Judge Merrick Garland to the Supreme Court, and the Republican majority declined to hold hearings, declaring the decision should be left to the voters in the election that would be held eight months later—unlike their rush to confirm the nomination of Amy Coney Barrett to the Supreme Court eight days before the next presidential election.[21]

Shortly after Donald Trump took office, he nominated Neil Gorsuch to the Supreme Court. Democrats indicated they would vote against cloture, and Trump encouraged Republicans to "go nuclear." In April 2017, the Republican majority exploded its own nuclear option, establishing a precedent for confirming Supreme Court justices by a simple majority. Senator McConnell argued that ending the filibuster for all nominees would decrease

---

[20] Seung Min Kim, "Senate Reaches Deal on Obama Nominees," *Politico*, December 19, 2013; *Congressional Record*, 113th Cong., 2nd sess., S111.

[21] Senate Historical Office Log, January 26, 2015, Box 19, Ritchie Files, NARA.

partisan tensions and return the Senate to a time when filibusters were not so commonly used to block nominations. "This will be the first and last partisan filibuster of a Supreme Court nomination," he promised. What the media described as a "carefully staged deconstruction" of the Senate rule began with a cloture vote, after which McConnell raised a point of order that the nomination could be advanced with a simple majority. The chair rejected it, but the majority overturned the ruling and established a new precedent. "It was very sanitary," commented Senator Bob Corker (R-Tennessee). "Unemotional. Telegraphed in advance."[22]

Disruption or Culmination?

The nuclear option marked a culmination rather than a disruption. Despite their mutual protests, the two parties had begrudgingly reached a consensus to rationalize the process and end routine filibusters of nominations. Federal offices need to be filled, and the ideological divide between the two parties had grown so wide that neither side was likely to approve of the other party's nominees. It is still possible to slow nominations down, or to derail a nominee if at least a few members of the majority find the candidate unfit. But for the most part nominees are going to reflect the ideology of the incumbent president and are going to be confirmed if the president's party holds the Senate majority.

The question remained whether to reduce cloture for legislation. House members were all in favor of it, claiming that the standing rules have made the Senate a graveyard for their bills. President Donald Trump insisted on an end to filibusters on legislation. "Republican in the Senate will NEVER win if they don't go to a 51 vote majority NOW," he tweeted in 2017. "They look like fools and are just wasting time." But 61 senators from both parties sent a letter notifying Senate leaders of their opposition to eliminating the filibuster for legislation. Republican Majority Leader Mitch McConnell agreed: "It would fundamentally change the way the Senate has worked for a very long time. We're not going to do that," Although angered by the resistance from his own party, Trump changed his mind after Democrats took back the

---

[22] Sean Sullivan, Ed O'Keefe, and Karoun Demirjian, "As Gorsuch Makes Rounds, Trump Talks 'Nuclear' Tactics," *Washington Post*, February 2, 2017; Ed O'Keefe and Sean Sullivan, "Senate Burns Bridge to Clear Gorsuch's Way," *Washington Post*, April 7, 2017.

Senate majority, conceding that it would be "catastrophic" for Republicans if the Democrats ended the filibuster.[23]

Having a narrow majority prevented Democrats from making any dramatic changes. During the evenly divided Senate of the 117th Congress, Democrats lost a cloture vote on voting rights legislation and attempted to suspend the rule. They failed because of the opposition to changing the rules by two Democratic senators and the entire Republican conference.[24]

A polarized Senate can still find ways to solve pressing issues. Take for instance the perennial squabble over raising the debt ceiling, a necessary but unpopular vote for the majority. In 2022 the Republican minority was unwilling to vote to raise the debt ceiling, but also unwilling to trigger a default on the US debt. Instead, Republicans agreed to let Democrats raise the debt ceiling on their own. Party leaders crafted a bill that limited debate, waived points of order, and prohibited amendments, specifying that it could only be used once. Eleven Republicans and every Democrat voted for the bill, even the two Democrats who resisted changing the filibuster rules for voting rights, since this bill was bipartisan and would not create a lasting change. "The point was that the filibuster was set aside to pass a piece of legislation, and the sky didn't fall down," observed reporter Amber Phillips in the *Washington Post*.[25]

Senators have been reluctant to abolish the filibuster because it would erode the individual power of all members—maverick and mainstream alike—to block objectionable items and to exert pressure on administration policies. Veterans who have experienced the frequent rotation of the majority in recent years also appreciate the protection that filibusters offer when they find themselves in the minority. And some worry that reducing the rights of the minority to shape legislation would lead to more extreme policies. Negotiations have tended to force legislation toward the middle of the political spectrum, more in line with public opinion.

For all the Senate's transformation over the past half century, its standing rules remain unchanged. Polarization has prevented any formal revision of

[23] Carl Hulse, "Thanks to President, Senators Finally Find Something to Agree On," *New York Times*, May 4, 2017; Maggie Haberman, "Trump Tells G.O.P. Senator Not to be 'Total Quitters' on Health Bill," *New York Times*, July 30, 2017; Ed Kilgore, "Trump Flip-Flops on the Filibuster," *Intelligencer*, March 22, 2021.

[24] Mike DeBonis, "Manchin, Sinema Join with GOP in Rejecting Attempt to Change Filibuster Rules, Effectively Killing Democratic Voting Bill," *Washington Post*, January 19, 2022.

[25] Amber Phillips, "Why Manchin and Sinema Waived the Filibuster for the Debt Ceiling but Won't for Voting Rights," *Washington Post*, January 18, 2022.

the rules, prompting majorities to set new precedents to alter their interpretation. Strong-arm tactics by the majority are unlikely to reduce acrimony and restore comity, but the Senate must continue to function. Both parties have stood on both sides of the debate. The staff of the two conferences joke about exchanging playbooks when the majority switches, knowing that senators' positions on the rules can reverse overnight with their party's political fortunes. The majority and minority will see things from where they stand. Neither side is ready to abandon the filibuster on legislation yet, but the more that a minority refuses to engage, it may provoke the majority to force a change. The minority will protest vigorously, before preserving that change once it returns to the majority. The Senate would be a very different place, but then it already is.[26]

References

Arenberg, Richard A. and Robert B. Dove. 2015. *Defending the Filibuster: The Soul of the Senate* (Bloomington: Indiana University Press).

Barone, Michael. 2019. *How America's Political Parties Change (And How They Don't)* (New York: Encounter Books), 59–89.

Burns, James M. 1963. *The Deadlock of Democracy: Four-Party Politics in America* (Englewood Cliffs, NJ: Prentice-Hall).

Byrd, Robert C. 1991. *The Senate, 1789–1989: Addresses on the History of the United States Senate* (Washington, DC: Government Printing Office).

Gold, Martin B. and Dimple Gupta, 2005. "The Constitutional Option to Change Senate Rules and Procedures: A Majoritarian Means to Overcome the Filibuster." *Harvard Journal of Law and Public Policy* 28: 206–272.

MacNeil, Neil and Richard A. Baker. 2013. *The American Senate: An Insider's History* (New York: Oxford University Press).

Shapiro, Ira. 2012. *The Last Great Senate: Courage and Statesmanship in Times of Crisis* (New York: Public Affairs).

---

[26] Senate Historical Office Log, February 10, 2014, Box 19, Ritchie Files, NARA.

2

The Filibuster and the Trump Senate

The View from the Mid-Twentieth Century American South

Joseph Crespino

Introduction

The US Senate is practically alone among legislative bodies in the world in the length to which it goes to protect the rights of the minority. This protection can be seen in the equal representation of all states regardless of population, and it inheres in the Senate principle of unlimited debate. Any minority group of senators, or even a single senator, can block a vote on any issue simply by refusing to end debate. Since roughly the 1850s, when Senate observers adopted a Dutch word meaning "pirate" to describe the process of obstructing Senate business to prevent action on a bill, this practice has come to be called a filibuster.

It is difficult to measure the frequency of filibusters, because obstruction can take myriad forms. A filibuster can be, as is most commonly imagined, a lengthy, one-person speech, heroic or dastardly depending on the senator and the issue. It can be an organized campaign of speeches by a minority group of senators, such as the campaign waged by southern senators against the 1960 and 1964 civil rights bills. But it can also be any action or inaction that delays or obstructs the timely execution of duties of the Senate as a whole. In recent years, the practice of obstruction has become so ornate that the mere threat of a filibuster is enough to stimy progress. Individual senators can write to the majority leader informing him (and, eventually, her) of their intention to filibuster an action if it is brought to the floor. The frequency of this practice, which can be initiated by as little as an email, has led to calls for a return to the "speaking filibuster" as one possible reform of Senate rules (Warwo and Schickler 2006; Binder 2010; Reynolds 2017; Lau 2021).

Joseph Crespino, *The Filibuster and the Trump Senate* In: *Disruption?* Edited by: Sean M. Theriault, Oxford University Press. © Oxford University Press 2024. DOI: 10.1093/oso/9780197767832.003.0003

The easiest way to measure the frequency of filibusters is to count the number of times that senators vote to end debate on a subject, a procedure known as cloture (Senate Rule 22). It is itself a relatively modern invention, adopted only in 1917, and first utilized two years later when more than two-thirds of senators voted to end debate on the Treaty of Versailles.

Cloture votes taken in the Senate since the adoption of Rule 22 shows an unmistakable trend (see Figure 2.1). They were rare in the four decades following the adoption of cloture. Beginning in the 1970s, cloture votes, and the filibusters that prompted them, have become a regular part of Senate life. The truly disturbing spike in the practice began during the Obama administration. The numbers are stark, yet they do not even account for the most egregious forms of Republican obstruction, such as Senate Majority Leader Mitch McConnell's unprecedented refusal to grant a hearing to Obama's Supreme Court nominee, Merrick Garland. Yet Democrats have been eager participants in the accelerating trend of Senate obstruction. Cloture was invoked more times during the Trump presidency than in any presidency in US history, despite the fact that he served only four years.

In order to appreciate the modern usage of the filibuster, it is important to understand its historical development. Throughout the twentieth century, the filibuster was notorious for its use by southern senators in stifling the progress of civil rights for African Americans. Yet the record of cloture votes

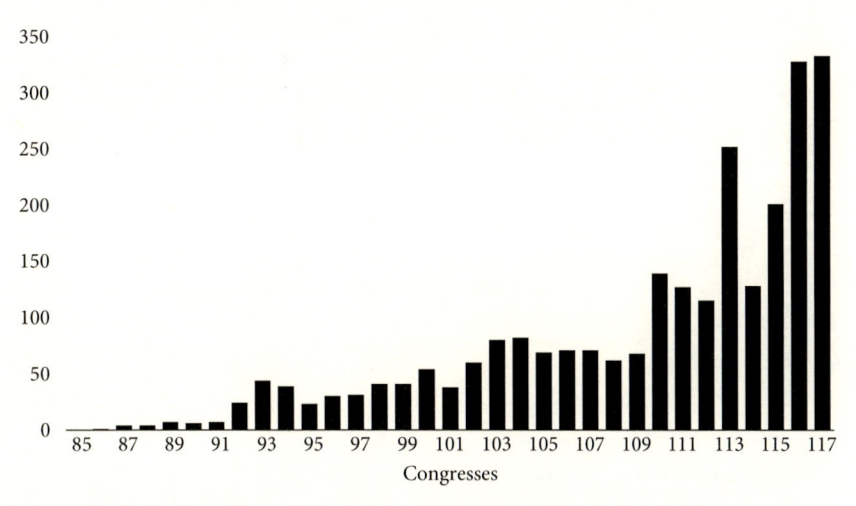

Figure 2.1 The Number of Cloture Motions Filed, 85th to 117th Congress (1957–2023)

Source: https://www.senate.gov/legislative/cloture/clotureCounts.htm.

alone speak to the very different attitudes and practices that surrounded the filibuster in that era compared to our own. A look back at perhaps the most famous southern filibuster against civil rights legislation—Strom Thurmond's record-breaking 24 hour and 19-minute speech in opposition to the 1957 Civil Rights bill—reveals how dramatically the filibuster, the US Senate, and American politics have changed in the interim.

The differences that have developed since the 1970s owe in part to the very different rules and norms governing the filibuster, which have transformed the power of individual senators to obstruct Senate business. The sort of obstruction that Strom Thurmond pursued in the 1950s and 1960s, Jesse Helms continued and accelerated in the 1970s and 1980s (Link 2008). By the 1980s and 1990s, as Theriault (2013) has shown, a hyperpartisan politician outside the Senate like Newt Gingrich could drastically impact tactics and strategies within the body (see also, Zelizer 2020). Donald Trump has played a similarly outsized role since he emerged on the political scene. Trump himself has displayed a characteristically shameless attitude toward the filibuster. He urged Senate Republicans to get rid of it when they held the majority. When they were in minority, he warned that ending the filibuster would be "catastrophic for the Republican Party."[1]

The partisan influence of figures like Gingrich and Trump has been accelerated and amplified by the vastly altered media landscape of recent decades in which cable television and social media allow individual senators to justify their obstruction to their most ardent supporters. Senators today cannot only block legislation more easily, they also have vastly increased powers to shape political narratives justifying their obstruction, thereby polarizing broader issues and raising money for their next campaign. All of this would have been unimaginable to senators from Strom Thurmond's era.

Filibuster Fights in the 1950s

Over the course of Senate history, members have used the filibuster to block all sorts of legislation. The issue in 1917 that compelled senators to finally

---

[1] Quoted in John Bresnahan, Burgess Everett, and Sarah Ferris. 2018. "Trump to GOP: Dump the Filibuster Before Schumer Does," *Politico* (https://www.politico.com/story/2018/06/26/donald-trump-kill-the-filibuster-677151; accessed on June 1, 2023). See also Dominik Mastrangelo. 2021. "Trump: Ending the Filibuster would be "Catastrophic" for Republican Party," *The Hill* (https://theh ill.com/homenews/senate/544275-trump-getting-rid-of-filibuster-would-be-catastrophic-for-rep ublican-party/; accessed on June 1, 2023).

adopt the cloture rule involved a small group of senators' opposition to American involvement in World War I. Since roughly the turn of the twentieth century until the 1960s, though, the filibuster has been associated most closely with actions by southern senators to opposed civil rights measures. Southerners successfully filibustered a voting rights bill in 1891, for example. Its defeat hastened the widespread disfranchisement of African Americans in the South and helped usher in the Jim Crow era. The alteration of Senate rules in 1917 gave civil rights forces hope that they might be able to defeat the entrenched southern minority. In 1922, in the wake of horrific acts of racial violence following World War I, civil rights supporters in Congress mounted the first, most impressive campaign for civil rights in the twentieth century. The Dyer Anti-Lynching bill, named for Missouri Congressman Leonidas Dyer, passed in the House of Representatives only to die a slow death in the Senate at the hands of southern obstructionists. Calls for anti-lynching legislation were renewed in the late 1930s, following a disturbing rise in lynchings during the Depression years. Once again, organized opposition by southern senators turned back the efforts (Jenkins and Peck 2010; Jenkins, Peck, Weaver 2010).

World War II transformed American racial politics, providing African Americans new opportunities to fight for change. War time service emboldened a rising generation of African Americans. NAACP membership grew ten-fold in the 1940s. Postwar violence against returning veterans in the South lead President Truman to form the President's Committee on Civil Rights, which issued a landmark study in 1947 that would become a blueprint for civil rights reforms in the following two decades. The following year President Truman desegregated the United States military. At the same time, Supreme Court decisions, beginning with *Smith v. Allwright* (1944), which outlawed the white primary, transformed southern electoral politics. The full force wouldn't be felt until 1965 with the Voting Rights Act, but in southern cities like Atlanta, the Black vote became a potent force. By the early 1950s, the court's rulings on equality in higher education created new opportunities for African Americans and new momentum for reform. This momentum culminated in the Supreme Court's 1954 decision striking down segregation in southern public schools (Norrell 2005).

Up until the mid-1950s, civil rights reforms had come through the executive and judicial branches. Many members of Congress felt the urgency to take legislative action. Significant factions in both parties believed it was in their electoral interest to do so. With the Great Migration, African American votes in electorally rich northern industrial states had become a critical swing vote. The 1956 election results had shown as much. The following year, leaders in both parties were eager to pass a civil rights bill. How to get any such legislation past the entrenched Southern Caucus was the question.

By 1957, not even the Southern Caucus was immune to escalating pressures for change. The head of the caucus, Georgia Senator Richard Russell, renowned for his keen political barometer, felt them exquisitely. Fellow senators from around the nation sought his advice in their own campaigns. In 1957, Russell had two concerns that were intimately connected with the civil rights legislation being discussed in the Senate. First, he knew how small his caucus of reliable votes against civil rights measures had become. He could no longer be sure that his two Tennessee colleagues—Estes Kefauver and Albert Gore—would line up with their fellow southerners. He feared that a protracted filibuster against a civil rights bill with significant support in both parties could lead his Senate colleagues to amend Senate rules to make cloture easier to invoke, thus imperiling the southern position even more. Second, Russell knew that his protégé and fellow southerner, Senator Lyndon Johnson of Texas, had national political aspirations. He made sure his fellow caucus members knew all of the advantages to their region in having a fellow southern Democrat in the White House. Russell knew that if Johnson as majority leader could pass civil rights legislation, the first bill of its kind since the Reconstruction era, he could transcend his southern roots, establish his bona fides as a national leader, and position himself as the leading Democrat going into the 1960 presidential primaries.

The greatest hurdle that Johnson and Russell faced was in weakening the civil rights bill enough to convince their fellow southerners that it wasn't in their interests, or the South's interests, to filibuster it. Johnson successfully maneuvered to kill portions of the bill that granted the attorney general powers to initiate civil lawsuits against discrimination in schools, housing, and other public areas. He also diluted voting rights provisions in the bill through the adoption of a jury trial amendment. This provision guaranteed that white southern officials accused of violating the rights of black southerners would be tried by a jury of their peers, which, in the South in the 1950s, still meant an all-white jury. A successful prosecution in such a scenario was all but unimaginable.[2]

---

[2] The most exhaustive account of the history and politics of the 1957 Civil Right Act, particularly as they concern Lyndon Johnson, can be found in Robert A. Caro, *The Years of Lyndon Johnson, Vol. 3: Master of the Senate* (New York: Alfred A. Knopf, 2002). For a more general overview, see Keith M.

The jury trial amendment represented a huge win for Richard Russell and the Southern Caucus. They received support for the measure from populist western Democrats who resented the power of judges to quell labor disputes, as well as from conservative Republicans who backed the right of trial by jury as one of the oldest, most fundamental rights dating back to English common law. Even some liberal Democrats voted in favor of the jury trial amendment, including the young Massachusetts Senator John F. Kennedy, his eye no doubt on currying southern sympathy in anticipation of his own run for the presidency in 1960.

With the jury trial amendment in place, the civil rights bill went back to the House of Representatives. There, civil rights forces were able to slightly alter the jury trial amendment. It allowed judges to try minor criminal contempt cases without a jury, yet it guaranteed a new trial, by jury, if the penalty imposed was more than $300 or 45 days in prison. The provision would have little real impact, given the unlikelihood of judges hearing a case without a jury when doing so would make it likely that the case would have to be tried twice. It was largely a face-saving measure for civil rights supporters in the House (Crespino 2012).

Most members of the Senate's Southern Caucus recognized it as much in a meeting the next day to discuss the revised bill. A memo written by a member of Majority Leader Johnson's staff warned the southerners that the South stood "right on the brink of disaster." Invoking the specter of a change in Senate rules making cloture easier to invoke, the memo argued that with an objection at this late date the South could lose "not only the ability to have any impact on civil rights legislation but any influence it has in Congress at all." Russell laid out the case to his colleagues in simple, unemotional terms. All the members agreed that a filibuster at this stage would be unwise.

Or at least that was the way that *Time* magazine reported the meeting. One member of the Southern Caucus, South Carolina Senator Strom Thurmond, would later dispute that account. He claimed that the only thing that he had agreed to in that meeting was that "an organized extended debate would not be held." Public pressure for a filibuster was intense. The day after the caucus meeting, Thurmond had breakfast with his fellow South Carolina Senator Olin Johnston and the powerful South Carolina Congressman Mendel Rivers. Later that day, Rivers explained to South Carolina newsmen how he

Finley, *Delaying the Dream: Southern Senators and the Fight Against Civil Rights, 1938–1965* (Baton Rouge, LA: Louisiana University Press, 2008).

had implored the state's two senators to filibuster the bill. Telegrams urging a filibuster poured into the offices of all the southern senators.

Thurmond was closely attuned to the reaction. When the compromise bill returned to the Senate for consideration, he made sure that he was on the Senate floor. In an attack uncoordinated with his fellow southerners, he moved to send the bill to the Judiciary Committee, chaired by Mississippi's James Eastland, the notorious graveyard for civil rights legislation. His motion was easily defeated. The next day he went back to Richard Russell to urge him to reconvene the southerners so that they might reconsider the decision not to filibuster. Russell held firm with the caucus's earlier decision. He told Thurmond that unless a majority of southerners contacted him to convene another meeting, then "each senator would follow his own course" (Crespino 2012). This last point was the one that Thurmond would emphasize later when defending his decision to filibuster.

Thurmond took the Senate floor at 8:54 p.m. on the evening of Wednesday, August 28, and did not relinquish it until 9:12 p.m. the following day. He began by reading, in alphabetical order, the election statutes of each of the forty-eight states. About two hours in, Everett Dirksen passed the word: "Boys, it looks like an all-nighter" (Crespino 2012). Around 1:00 a.m., Barry Goldwater of Arizona, as part of a coordinated plan, asked Thurmond to yield for an insertion in the *Congressional Record*, allowing him to steal away for his only bathroom break (Goldwater himself, it should be noted, voted in favor of the 1957 Civil Rights bill; his assistance to Thurmond in this instance was due likely to the friendship the two forged as the Senate's foremost Cold War hawks). During the course of his speech, Thurmond read listlessly at times from the nation's founding documents, including the Declaration of Independence, the Bill of Rights, and Washington's Farewell Address. By midday Thursday, his voice had become so faint that California Senator William Knowland, sitting on the other side of the chamber, asked him to speak up. Thurmond asked Knowland to move closer. Knowland declined, saying he was "well satisfied" with his seat (Crespino 2012). Thurmond passed the existing record for the longest Senate speech, held by Senator Wayne Morse of Oregon, in the seven o'clock hour. Winding down roughly two hours later he drew a laugh, unwittingly, when he closed by saying that he expected to vote against the bill, a point that by then was obvious to all.

Thurmond's harshest critics were his fellow southerners, who had the most to lose from his dramatics. "Oh God, the venomous hatred of his Southern colleagues," recalled an aide to Lyndon Johnson. "I'll never forget Herman Talmadge's eyes when he walked in on the floor of the Senate that day and saw Strom carrying on that performance." Talmadge and other caucus members were incensed that after months of coordinated effort by every southern senator, exertions that had effectively neutered the legislation, Thurmond was promoting himself as a lone warrior manning barricades that had been abandoned by his fellow southerners. It was grandstanding of the worst sort, said Georgia's Talmadge, the author of a book titled *Segregation and You* and a man who knew a lot about political grandstanding. Richard Russell delivered one of the most impassioned speeches of his long career, calling Thurmond's performance an act of "personal political aggrandizement" and touting the Caucus's success in preserving segregation. "I would gladly part with what remains of [this] life," he intoned melodramatically, "if this would guarantee the preservation of a civilization of two races of unmixed blood in the land I love" (Crespino 2012).

Russell and Talmadge were right, of course. Thurmond's filibuster was entirely a political stunt. But it was a well-considered one. Why Thurmond was willing to risk alienation from his fellow southerners owed to a number of political liabilities that he hoped to shore up. One had to do Thurmond's consistent unwillingness to back the Democratic presidential ticket, dating back to his run on the Dixiecrat presidential ticket in 1948. To establishment southern Democrats like Russell and other members of the Southern Caucus, the foolhardy Dixiecrat movement had been a gift to Republicans that had significantly weakened Democratic control in the South. Thurmond had refused to endorse the Democratic ticket in either 1952 or 1956. The Southern Caucus presented the 1957 civil rights bill as essentially Republican legislation. One of Thurmond's closest advisors was privately amazed at how far President Eisenhower and other Republicans had gone in backing the civil rights bill. This advisor urged Thurmond to get pictures of himself speaking against the civil rights bill, because he would need them in future campaigns against South Carolina Democrats who would accuse Thurmond of backing anti-South Republicans.

With his one-man filibuster, Thurmond went one better. He could get photographs of himself speaking against the bill alongside other caucus members. But his caucus loyalty would not be enough to stem the criticisms of him aiding Republican presidential candidates. Congress was going to pass some kind of civil rights law, and Thurmond needed to show not that he was loyal to the caucus, but that he was loyal to the South. So as negotiations wore on, the more that caucus members acted as if the deal had already gone down, the more Thurmond got worked up over the deal that caucus members had settled for. And as he did, he opened up room to counterattack Richard Russell and other establishment southern Democrats. Thurmond had to run for reelection to the Senate in 1960, and he was already eyeing a potential challenger in South Carolina Governor George Bell Timmerman, who had made a name for himself in leading segregationist southerners at the 1956 Democratic National Convention. Timmerman called a press conference after the compromise on the jury trial amendment passed in the House, warning that South Carolina's senators must "stand and fight or step aside and let there be elected men with political courage who will" (Crespino 2012).

If Thurmond's speech is one of the most famous anti-civil rights filibusters, it was also one of the least effective. Only two hours after Thurmond ended his filibuster, the Senate passed the civil rights bill. Thurmond joined all the members of the Southern Caucus, of course, in voting against it. As a one-person filibuster, Thurmond's filibuster was fundamentally different from the organized, coordinated ones that the southerners waged, and lost, against civil rights legislation in 1960 and, most famously, in 1964. It remains today as curious bit of Senate trivia, a relic of a different age in the US Senate and the nation's history. Yet reconsidering it in light of the current Senate rules and norms is instructive. To do so, we must first understand the differences in the rules and norms between Thurmond's day and the present.

The Evolving Filibuster

Two important changes came in the 1970s. Both were adopted as progressive reforms intended to reduce gridlock. First, in 1975, the Senate voted to amend Rule XXII to lower the vote threshold needed to invoke cloture from two-thirds of senators present and voting to three-fifths of the full Senate. The change enshrined the 60-vote supermajority that is now effectively required to pass any meaningful legislation. Second, the Senate adopted a "two-track" system for scheduling business on the floor. Under this system, when a senator indicates to leadership his or her intention to filibuster a bill, the majority leader simply puts that issue aside and proceeds with other business until the majority in favor of the bill can successfully negotiate the necessary 60 votes to invoke cloture. The advantage of the two-track system is that it allows the Senate majority to proceed with business as usual; a single filibustering senator cannot obstruct the entirety of Senate business to protest a single issue. The disadvantage is that it gives individual senators enormous power to obstruct specific bills. Senators do not need to hold the floor with lengthy, exhaustive speeches, as with the "talking filibuster" that Strom Thurmond waged. Indeed, most do not even take the floor at all to even discuss measures they oppose. All they need to do is to indicate their intention to filibuster to have the issue put aside (Barnes et al. 2021). The two-track system also makes cloture votes a less accurate measure of filibusters.

The rule changes have coincided with a dramatic increase in the use of the filibuster. Lowering the bar to end them has meant that filibusters have become much more common. Yet this seems to have had more to do with the changing nature of American political parties than with the decision to lower the bar for cloture. As late as the 1960s, the Democratic Party contained both the most liberal (typically from the northeast) and conservative (typically southern) senators. Republicans, though not as schizophrenic as Democrats, also had a relatively high degree of ideological diversity. Beginning in the 1960s, however, and expanding rapidly in the two decades that followed, Republicans and Democrats aligned more strictly along ideological lines, conservative and liberal. Strom Thurmond's switch from the Democratic to the Republican Party would be as good a starting point as any to mark the beginning of this process. Since roughly the 1980s, the Senate has been narrowly divided and highly contested. With Senate control changing frequently over such a short span filibusters became a much more common tool that the minority used to check the power of a majority that a senator and his or her party hoped very much wouldn't be in the majority in two years' time.

In this context, the filibuster has evolved into an everyday tool to frustrate political opponents and position oneself and one's party for the next round of elections. Because the two-track system gives individual senators power to block specific proposals or appointments, there is little incentive for reform. Senators relish their power. It helps them get into the news, build a public profile, raise money, and positions themselves for their next election.

Another factor that has exacerbated the impact of the filibuster involves the mundane act of Senate scheduling. Only so much time exists in a given congress, and the work of the Senate has become enormously complex. At the same time, the demands of electoral politics and the lack of regulations governing campaign finance, dictate that senators spend enormous amounts of time raising money for their next campaign. Here we see the impact of one of the cultural shifts in the Senate chronicled by Don Ritchie in this volume.

All of Congress works on a Tuesday to Thursday schedule, allowing members four days out of the week to travel the country to meet with lobbyists, constituents, and potential donors. The complexity of Senate work, in combination with a compressed calendar and the two-track system makes obstruction absurdly simple. Surely this is one of the most basic reasons for the historic rates of obstruction in the Trump Senate.

Filibuster Reform (or The Talking Filibuster)

Senators could reform the filibuster in a variety of ways. One potentially promising measure would be to use a sliding scale for cloture based on the size of the majority. Another would put the onus on the minority party to maintain 41 votes for continuing a filibuster rather than on the majority for invoking cloture. The proposal that has received perhaps the most attention—and, on its face, would seem the most logical—would be to force senators to return to a "talking filibuster." In a 2021 study published by the Brookings Institute, the authors cite Strom Thurmond's 1957 filibuster as an example of how forcing senators to speak on the floor can serve as a useful check on obstruction. Thurmond spoke for as long as anyone ever has in Senate history, but, because he could not share the burden of speaking with any of his fellow southern senators, even he had his limits. The authors do admit that a talking filibuster is unlikely to be painful enough to truly weaken the filibuster in its current form. With a Senate calendar as crowded as it is, teams of senators could coordinate speaking schedules relatively easily. More consequentially, a talking filibuster can backfire on the majority party. Forcing senators to hold the floor to maintain a filibuster would mean abandoning the "two-track system." A minority team of filibustering senators working together could shut down the entire work of the body, blocking not only the legislation under discussion but scores of other nominations, appointments, and other bills vital to the majority party's agenda (Barnes et al. 2021).

A talking filibuster by itself would be weak medicine given how dysfunctional the Senate has become under the modern filibuster. Imagine, for example, what havoc Strom Thurmond might have been able to cause back in 1957 had current filibuster rules and norms been in place. In truth, it's hard to imagine, because so many things were different back then, not just about Senate rules and norms, but about the culture and practices of the Senate and American politics and society more generally. Yet even a rough sketch is instructive.

Had Richard Russell been operating in today's political environment, it's almost impossible to imagine that he would have ever been able to gain unanimity among Southern Caucus members around the strategy of allowing a watered-down civil rights bill to pass without a filibuster. In the 1950s, loyalty to the caucus meant a tremendous amount to southern senators. The caucus was the most prominent node in a larger network of Democratic officials at the national and state levels, descending all the way down to the "courthouse gangs" in rural counties who controlled local politics, often in nefarious ways. In the desperately poor Jim Crow South, with malapportioned state legislatures that favored rural interests, a highly disfranchised voting population that excluded almost all African Americans and a great number of poor whites, this network controlled all aspects of electoral politics. They recommended the best people to run political campaigns and staff offices in Washington and the state capitol. They also provided access to the newspaper editors and journalists whose columns could make or break political careers. Most importantly, they controlled campaign funds at a time when the idea of raising money from sources outside the party, much less self-financing a campaign, would have gotten a person laughed out of a meeting. In 1957, when Richard Russell proposed a strategy on legislation as hotly anticipated as the 1957 civil rights bill, smart senators who wanted to stay in the good graces of the Democratic establishment both in Washington and back home went along. That's what Strom Thurmond did, until the very end of the process. Only at the last minute, when he spied an opportunity to better position himself against an upcoming opponent and immortalize his name in the Senate history books, did he step out on his own.

A variety of developments in the 1960s weakened the power of this political network. Television had a huge impact. So did the 1962 Supreme Court decision that forced the reapportionment of southern legislatures. The heaviest blow came from the 1965 Voting Rights Act. But changes in Democratic Party rules, economic growth, the rise of a truly competitive Republican Party, and countless other modernizing forces all were important in ending the Jim Crow era in southern politics.[3]

---

[3] The literature on this subject is large, but three important works that have informed my thinking are Earl and Merle Black, *Politics and Society in the South* (Cambridge, MA: Harvard University Press, 1987) and *The Rise of Southern Republicans* (Cambridge, MA: Harvard University Press, 2002), and Robert Mickey, *Paths Out of Dixie: The Democratization of Authoritarian Enclaves in America's Deep South, 1944–1972* (Princeton, NJ: Princeton University Press, 2015).

Comparing the 1950s to Today's Senate

If today's conditions existed in 1957, southern senators would have had far greater ability to operate independently from the Southern Caucus. Senators have their own fundraising networks. Some finance their own campaigns. Social media gives them an enormous platform that they can use to shape political narratives and communicate broadly. Under the current filibuster system, Thurmond could have blocked the bill without ever having to take the Senate floor. Of course, Lyndon Johnson as majority leader and Richard Russell as caucus leader would have used every power at their disposal to pressure Thurmond to fall in line with his fellow southerners. Perhaps they would have called Thurmond's bluff and force him to actually speak, just as they did in 1957. There's nothing in Senate rules today that prevent the majority from temporarily abandoning the two-track system, when forcing a senator to hold the floor would be to their advantage.

What we do know is that Thurmond, had he been operating in the current environment, would have had enormous opportunities to take the offensive against Johnson and Russell. In 1957, Thurmond had no good way to advance his argument that the House compromise was a bad deal for the South. He tried to draw attention to himself by sending the compromise bill to the Judiciary Committee when it came back from the House, but it received little notice in the press. After that, the only way to sway public opinion, and by extension, his fellow southerner senators, was to pursue his one-man filibuster. Thurmond had no cozy relationships with influential journalists or columnists, either in South Carolina or at the regional or national level, who could have articulated the logic of continued obstruction. Quite the opposite, he had a number of entrenched foes back home, like the influential newspaper owner Wilton Hall of Anderson, South Carolina, who had been sworn enemies ever since Thurmond had led the Dixiecrat walkout in 1948. Such newsmen were tightly connected to the Jim Crow Democratic network.

If operating in today's environment, Thurmond could have used social media to paint Richard Russell and other members of the Caucus as having abandoned the cause of the South (this was what Southern House members were doing at the time). He could have tweeted out the video of himself standing alone on the Senate floor to meet the bill when it returned from the House floor, futilely trying to send it to the Judiciary Committee. He could have pinned a Twitter thread explaining in detail all the ways that the House compromise on the jury trial amendment imperiled the ability of white southerners to hold fair and honest elections. Another thread could have exposed the alleged corruption that motivated Russell and the Southern Caucus in the first place, the fact that Russell was willing to let pass the most significant civil rights legislation since Reconstruction all as part of a scheme to position Johnson for the 1960 Democratic presidential nomination. If it were happening today, it would be easy to imagine that a hastily formed PAC might put together videos amplifying all the racist, southern nationalist tropes of the Lost Cause, juxtaposing the 1957 legislation with the "Force Bills" and other civil rights legislation that "Radical Republicans" had imposed upon the prostrate South in the nefarious days of Reconstruction. Thurmond could have retweeted such fare daily, ramping up the pressure on his fellow southerners to join him in his filibuster.

If the filibuster existed in 1957 as it exists today, it's reasonable to assume that there never would have been a 1957 Civil Rights bill. That bill, diluted though it was, was an historic milestone, the first civil rights bill that Congress passed since the Reconstruction era. It established the US Commission on Civil Rights, an independent, bipartisan, fact-finding federal agency that investigated, reported on, and made recommendations regarding civil rights issues in the United States. One of that agencies first initiatives was to investigate voting records in Montgomery, Alabama. A circuit judge in Alabama revived his failing political career by publicly defying the commission's request for records, threatening to "jail any commission agent who attempts to get the records." No agent was ever jailed, and the commission got the records it wanted, despite all the bluster from George Wallace. In December 1958, 26 African American witnesses testified in the Fifth Circuit Courtroom in Montgomery, Alabama, to how they were denied the right to vote.[4]

That testimony and those records were part of a mountain of evidence that the commission marshalled to keep up the pressure for change. In 1960, Congress passed another civil rights bill, this time over a coordinated southern filibuster that lasted 125 hours. The bill strengthened aspects of the 1957 bill and adopted Civil Rights Commission recommendations to criminalize interference with a court order for desegregation and establish federal penalties for crossing state lines to engage in the bombing or burning of schools or churches (Berry 2009). Four years later, despite a 57-day filibuster

---

[4] Quoted in Berry, 2009, 10–16. For more on how Wallace quietly turned over the records while maintaining public defiance, see Dan T. Carter, *The Politics of Rage: George Wallace, the Origins of the New Conservatism, and the Transformation of American Politics* (New York: Simon and Schuster, 1995), pp. 99–105.

coordinated by the southern caucus, civil rights forces managed for the first time to invoke cloture on civil rights legislation. At the conclusion of the vote, Senate Minority Leader Everett Dirksen famously quoted from the diary of Victor Hugo: "Stronger than all the armies is an idea whose time has come" (Mann 2007).

The irony of Strom Thurmond's 1957 filibuster is that instead of showing how the filibuster was used to frustrate the will of the majority, it actually reveals how, at least in this one instance, the Senate operated as one of its originators, James Madison, imagined that it should, with "more cool-ness . . . [and] more system" (Reynolds 2017). Civil rights advocates did not get what they wanted in the 1957 legislation. Federal power to fully enforce the right to vote for southern Blacks would not come until 8 years later, with the passage of the 1965 Voting Rights Act. But white southerners didn't get what they wanted either. The creation of a permanent Commission on Civil Rights would be a bitter pill to swallow, the aftertaste becoming all the more unpalatable, year after year, as southern African Americans bravely testified before commissioners of the ongoing civil rights abuses that they faced.

The Senate, as it operates today can no longer play the cooling role that it did in 1957. The power that individual senators have under the current filibuster to obstruct reasonable legislation has become too great. And the power to justify that obstruction for the narrow band of voters that are crit-ical for senators to win the next party primary—thereby polarizing debates for their own partisan, political purposes—has become standard practice in American politics. The record of obstruction in the United Senate during the Trump administration, as it was during the Obama administration and is currently under the Biden administration, makes clear that democracy demands reform. When will the time for that idea come?

References

Barnes, Mel, Norman Eisen, Jeff Mandell, and Norman Ornstein. September 13, 2021. "Filibuster Reform is Coming—Here's How." Governance Studies at Brookings. https://www.brookings.edu/research/fiilibuster-reform-is-coming-heres-how/.

Berry, Mary Frances. 2009. *And Justice for All: The United States Commission on Civil Rights and the Continuing Struggle for Freedom in America*. New York: Knopf.

Binder, Sarah A. 2010. *The History of the Filibuster*. Brookings, https://www.brookings.edu/testimonies/the-history-of-the-filibuster/.

Black, Earl and Merle Black. 1987. *Politics and Society in the South*. Cambridge, MA: Harvard University Press.

Caro, Robert A. 2002. *The Years of Lyndon Johnson, vol. 3: Master of the Senate*. New York: Alfred A. Knopf.

Carter, Dan T. 1995. *The Politics of Rage: George Wallace, the Origins of the New Conservatism, and the Transformation of American Politics*. New York: Simon and Schuster.

Crespino, Joseph. 2012. *Strom Thurmond's America*. New York: Hill and Wang.

Finley, Keith M. 2008. *Delaying the Dream: Southern Senators and the Fight Against Civil Rights, 1938–1965*. Baton Rouge: Louisiana University Press.

Jenkins, Jeffrey A., Justin Peck, and Vesla M. Weaver. 2010. "Between Reconstructions: Congressional Action on Civil Rights, 1891–1940." *Studies in American Political Development* 24 (1): 57–89.

Lau, Tim. 2021. *The Filibuster Explained*. Brennan Center for Justice, https://www.brennancenter.org/our-work/research-reports/filibuster-explained.

Link, William. 2008. *Righteous Warrior: Jesse Helms and the Rise of Modern Conservatism*. New York: St. Martin's Press.

Mann, Robert. 2007. *When Freedom Would Triumph: The Civil Rights Struggle in Congress, 1954–1968*. Baton Rouge: Louisiana State University Press, 2007.

Mickey, Robert. 2015. *Paths Out of Dixie: The Democratization of Authoritarian Enclaves in America's Deep South, 1944–1972*. Princeton, NJ: Princeton University Press.

Norrell, Robert J. 2005. *The House I Live In: Race in the American Century*. New York: Oxford University Press.

Reynolds, Molly E. 2017. *Exceptions to the Rule: The Politics of Filibuster Limitations in the U.S. Senate*. Washington, DC: The Brookings Institution.

Theriault, Sean. 2013. *The Gingrich Senators: The Roots of Partisan Warfare in Congress*. New York: Oxford University Press.

Wawro, Gregory J. and Eric Schickler, 2006. *Filibuster: Obstruction and Lawmaking in the U.S. Senate*. Princeton, NJ: Princeton University Press.

Zelizer, Julian. 2020. *Burning Down the House: Newt Gingrich, the Fall of a Speaker, and the Rise of the New Republican Party*. New York: Penguin Press.

3

Trump's Senate: A Bicameral Perspective

C. Lawrence Evans

Introduction

Considerable perspective can be shed on the US Senate during the Trump presidency by juxtaposing the internal operations and electoral environment of the chamber with those of the House. To what extent did the central features of the Senate during this remarkable era derive from structural features of the Senate itself, such as apportionment by state and the filibuster, as opposed to the burgeoning political polarization that characterized the nation as a whole and the governing style of the Trump White House? When we consider the Senate and House together, what was most striking about the era on Capitol Hill, continuity or change?

Bicameralism is perhaps the defining feature of Article I of the US Constitution. Senators, of course, are no longer selected by state legislatures, but two centuries after the foundational decisions of 1789, important structural differences between the two chambers endure. The House and Senate can be distinguished by their respective apportionment schemes (states in the Senate, population in the House); different term lengths (six years in the Senate, two years in the House); the dual representation of constituencies on the Senate side (two representatives per state); chamber size (100 versus 435); the Senate's prerogatives over the confirmation of judges and executive branch nominees and over treaties; and the House's responsibility to originate tax legislation.

The best scholarship indicates that these differences have consequences for representational relationships, internal congressional processes, and the contents of legislation (Fenno 1982; Baker 2008). Considerable evidence has been marshaled, for example, that the Senate's larger constituency and smaller chamber size make campaigns for the body more visible, expensive, and competitive. Evidence also shows that the legislative and representational decisions of senators vary over the six-year term—a temporal

C. Lawrence Evans, *Trump's Senate: A Bicameral Perspective* In: *Disruption?* Edited by: Sean M. Theriault, Oxford University Press. © Oxford University Press 2024. DOI: 10.1093/oso/9780197767832.003.0004

variance that is much less pronounced on the House side of the Capitol. Due to the smaller membership and broader policy portfolios of individual senators, committees traditionally have been less critical in that chamber. The prerogatives and resources extended to the Senate majority leadership are far less extensive than are the formal powers of their House counterparts. The modern House has nothing like the filibuster, where individual senators can bring the chamber to a halt absent the 60 votes necessary for cloture. According to traditional narratives, congressional life just feels different depending on the two sides of Capitol Hill—the Senate more deliberative and personal, the House quicker to act and more partisan.

Senate-House differences should matter the most when the array of preferences varies systematically across chambers (Cutrone and McCarty 2008). When important interests are not distributed evenly across states, policy preferences within the House and Senate may diverge because of the respective apportionment schemes. Differences in constituency size also matter. Size and diversity often increase together, creating incentives for senators to consider a broader array of interests than do House members as they form positions. Apportionment and size also combine to shape the funding formulas included in House and Senate legislation. Allocations to small states tend to be larger than they would be based on population or other objective indicators of need, in part because the votes of small state senators are necessary to build winning coalitions on the floor (Lee and Oppenheimer 1999). Due to the six-year term, only one-third of the Senate is up for re-election at any point in time, whereas the entire House confronts the voters every two years. As a result, the chambers may respond in different ways to electoral shifts like the rise of Trump.

On the other hand, for several reasons such claims about bicameral difference may need to be qualified, especially during the Trump years. American politics has taken on an increasingly national cast characterized by rampant partisan polarization across the entire nation. Beginning in the mid 1990s, the policy agendas embraced by state legislative parties have grown more homogeneous and polarized across the nation, and it no longer is the case that activists in one part of the country differ substantially from their co-partisan in other areas (Hopkins, Schickler, and Azizi 2022). Congressional districts and states now tend to tilt firmly toward the Democratic or the Republican Party, and fewer battleground constituencies are at play in either chamber. Electorally, subunits of the nation tend to respond in similar ways to the same national-level forces.

One consequence is that the internal operations of the two chambers have evolved in similar directions. In both chambers, committees have become less autonomous, and more decisions are made behind closed doors at the party leadership level. Legislative agendas across the Capitol have grown more "budgetized," with major decisions made via massive reconciliation bills and omnibus spending packages, rather than piece-meal via discrete measures. The ability of rank-and-file members to offer amendments on the House and Senate floors has been curtailed. And in both chambers, message politics is rife, with the two parties increasingly focused on advancing and publicizing policy positions that appeal to the relevant party base. Centralization and party teamsmanship are pervasive throughout the bicameral system (Curry and Lee 2020). In short, the extent to which bicameralism continued to shape congressional lawmaking during the Trump era is an open question.

Constituencies

I begin with the constituencies that contemporary senators and House members represent. From 2016 to 2020, election outcomes were closely related to population density and the prevalence of voters of color. Other factors mattered—education levels, economics, and so on. But population density and the presence of minority voters were key, with higher levels of both associated with Democratic Party strength (Sides, Tesler, and Vavreck 2019). I summarize the distribution of Senate and House constituencies during 2019–2020 for five measures that capture aspects of population density: percent urban, percent suburban, percent exurban, percent micropolitan, and percent rural (see Table 3.1). Here, "urban" refers to citizens living in the named cities of metropolitan statistical areas (MSAs). "Suburban" is for people residing in central counties within an MSA, but who cannot be categorized as urban. "Exurban" is for residents of noncentral counties who also are not city dwellers. "Micropolitan" is for people living outside the MSA's, but in areas that include an urban cluster of between ten and fifty thousand residents—essentially large towns in parts of the country that are not metropolitan. And rural is for the areas that remain. Similar evidence is also provided for the percent of Black voters within a constituency, and Trump's portion of the two-party vote in 2016.[1]

---

[1] The distinctions based on population density derive from calculations made by *Daily Kos*, and I rely on them instead of the simpler categories provided by the Census Bureau because the *Daily Kos* approach better reflects the complexities of partisan polarization. The *Daily Kos* typology resembles categorization schemes developed by the U.S. Office of Management and Budget, the Department of Housing and Urban Development, and the organization *City Lab*, and is predictive of partisan leanings and electoral outcomes. For background, consult https://www.dailykos.com/stories/2020/10/15/1967942/-Our-new-model-tells-you-how-urban-suburban-and-rural-every-congressional-district-is

Table 3.1 Demographic Composition of the House and Senate, 2019–2020

Category	Chamber	1st	5th	10th	25th	Med	75th	90th	95th	99th
Urban%	Senate	9.6	11.2	13.2	19.9	27.0	32.6	40.7	47.3	49.8
	House	0	0	0	9.3	22.3	43.0	71.8	88.5	100
%Suburban	Senate	9.3	11.0	16.0	26.7	40.7	55.2	70.1	79.7	90.3
	House	0	3.7	11.5	26.7	46.1	70.7	93.5	100	100
%Exurban	Senate	0	0	0	1.7	6.0	10.1	13.6	16.6	18.9
	House	0	0	0	0	0	9.8	20.1	27.7	45.1
%Micropolitan	Senate	0	0	1.4	6.3	12.7	18.5	29.6	34.3	44.7
	House	0	0	0	0	0	15.9	29.0	37.3	51.2
%Rural	Senate	0	0	.1	2.5	6.7	17.9	26.5	28.4	34.6
	House	0	0	0	0	0	8.4	19.0	27.3	47.8
% Black	Senate	.35	.85	.96	3.1	6.8	15.0	27.4	32.0	37.9
	House	.5	1.0	1.7	3.3	7.0	16.0	30.3	51.2	60.7
% Trump 2016	Senate	32.6	34.8	37.1	44.0	51.9	61.1	67.1	69.8	75.7
	House	9.2	17.4	22.1	36.3	51.8	61.7	69.0	74.0	80.1

Source: Daily Kos: https://docs.google.com/spreadsheets/d/1fTy-lAIn8zuZd0HfFGP_nrJTwazjc1zS_pcMGHOfmZQ/edit#gid=0

The rows of Table 3.1 show the distribution of constituencies for the Senate and House across these dimensions. The median, of course, is the constituency at the 50th percentile within the relevant distribution—for that chamber, half of the constituencies (again, states for the Senate and districts for the House) fall below and half above. As the table indicates, the median Senate constituency is 27 percent urban and the median House district 22.3 percent, a modest difference. Chamber medians for the other factors that capture population density have analogous deviations. Interestingly, the medians for Black residents and Trump support were almost the same. But we also need to consider chamber differences at the extremes, which are captured by the lower and upper ends of the distribution and here the differences by chamber are telling. The column labeled 25th percentile, for instance, is for the constituency located at that point in the distribution—about one-fourth of the other constituencies fall below and about three-quarters fall above. The column labeled 75th is for the district or state with only one-quarter above and three-quarters below, and so on through the distributional scale. Notice that the most heavily urbanized House districts (95th percentile and above) are almost completely comprised of city dwellers, while the most urbanized states were more mixed. At the other end of the scale, the least urbanized House districts included no urban voters, while the Senate end featured states where many residents still lived in major cities. Similar deviations in the House and Senate distributions for the other categories are apparent, as well as for the incidence of African Americans and levels of Trump support. The most extreme House districts are very extreme, the outlier Senate constituencies, much less so.

The systematic differences that exist in the composition of House districts and states have consequences for the partisan makeup of Congress as shown by the size of the Democratic margin as a percent of the full membership for each chamber from 1969 to 2020 (see Figure 3.1). In 2019, midway through the Trump administration, there were 235 Democrats and 200 Republicans in the House, and the size of the Democratic margin as a percent of the chamber was 35/435, or about 8 percent.[2] That year, the Senate was comprised of 45 Democrats, 53 Republicans, and two independents who caucused with the Democrats for organizational purposes. If we treat the two independents as Democrats, the Democratic margin as a percent

---

[2] On opening day of the 116th Congress, the seat for North Carolina 9th was unfilled, but soon would be held by a Republican, so that district is included in the GOP total here.

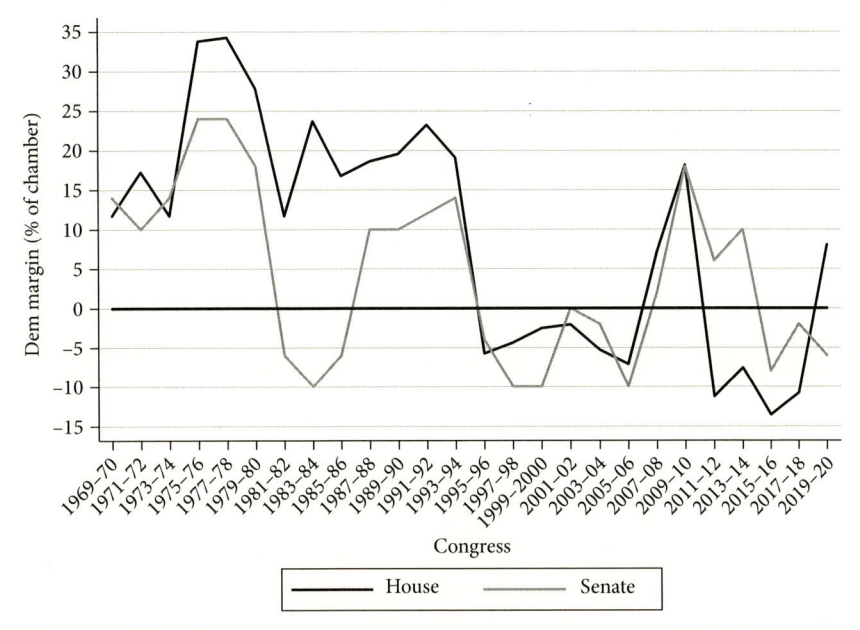

Figure 3.1 Party Margins in the House and Senate (Percent of Chamber)

of the chamber was −6/100, or −6 percent. During the 1970s, the magnitude of the Democratic majorities that characterized the House and Senate were about the same size. From the early 1980s through the emergence of unified GOP of congressional control in 1995, the House tilted more Democratic than was the case for the Senate. From 1995 until 2010, party margins as a percent of the relevant chamber were again very similar across the Capitol. That year, Republicans regained majority status in the House, but Democrats remained as the Senate majority until 2015, and the party margin trends diverged. In 2017, with unified GOP control of Washington, party margins across the chambers were identical. And with the shift to a Democratic House majority during 2019–2020, the balance tilted toward Republicans in the Senate and Democrats in the House.

To some extent, the periodic divergences by chamber are due to geographic differences in party strength (see Figure 3.1). Smaller states are somewhat more likely to include rural areas, and as mentioned rural areas are associated with pro-GOP voting. But as political scientist Jonathan Rodden (2019) has shown, the urban-rural divide also benefits the GOP in the House. Democratic voters tend to be packed into highly urbanized congressional districts, where candidates of that party rack up huge margins. Republicans, in contrast, are spread more evenly across the districts that tilt their way, and fewer GOP votes are "wasted" in House elections.

For additional guidance, consider the quadrants of Figure 3.2, which show the distribution of members across different levels of Trump support at the constituency level for the 115th (2017–2018) and 116th (2019–2020) Congresses. The horizontal axes are broken into intervals of pro-Trump sentiment (0–5 percent, 6–10 percent, and so on). For each quadrant, the vertical axis is the number of members. Not surprisingly, in both chambers Democrats were mostly from constituencies where Trump did not do well, and Republicans were mostly from constituencies where he did.

For the chambers taken as a whole, the median among districts and states was about the same—just under 52 percent. If we break the evidence down by party, as well as chamber, in 2017–2018 the median among House districts represented by a Democrat was 33.7 percent and among Democratic senators it was 44.0. On the GOP side of the aisle, the district median was 60.6 percent and 60.2 percent for Senate constituencies. During 2019–2020 (following the transition to a Democratic House), the Democratic median was 37.8 percent in that chamber and for Democrats in the Senate, 43.8 percent. For Republicans that Congress, the House median shifted to 62.8 percent and the

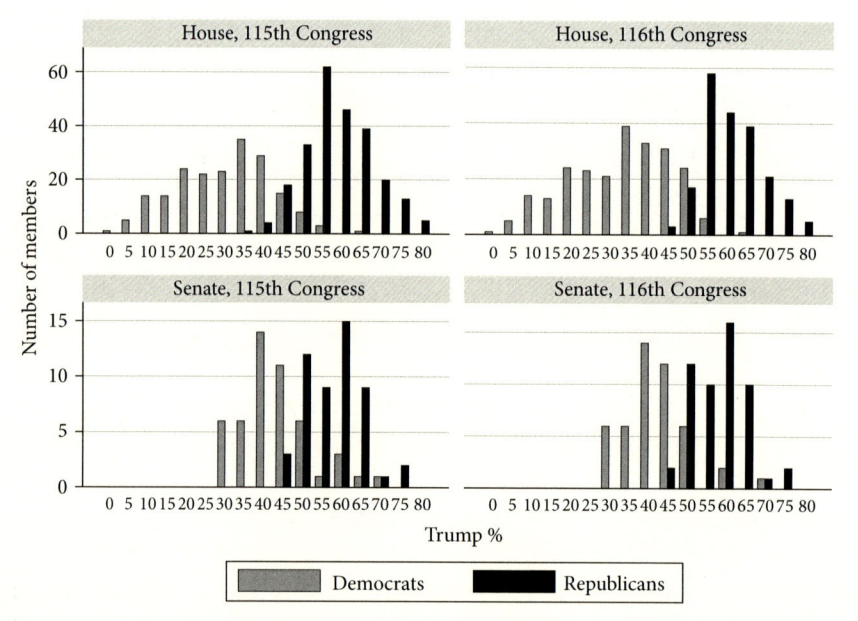

Figure 3.2 Distribution of Members by Trump Percent of Two-Party Vote

Senate median was now 60.2 percent. In terms of partisan-electoral leanings at the constituency level, then, the largest differences by chamber appeared to be for Democrats, as opposed to Republicans.

But once again, we need to weigh the variance around those medians. Clearly, the House includes many districts where the partisan composition (as captured by the Trump vote) is heavily skewed one way or the other, whereas such extremes are less frequent in the Senate. "Extremist" constituencies are especially apparent for House Democrats, where significant portions of the party caucus—largely from heavily urbanized areas with many non-white voters—confronted Trump support at home that was under ten percent. In the Senate, the anti-Trump extreme was comprised of the six Democratic senators from Hawaii, California, and Vermont; states where the GOP presidential standard-bearer still received between 30 and 35 percent of the two-party vote. Significant, albeit smaller differences between the chambers are also apparent among Republicans at the pro-Trump end of the scale, with a larger proportion of the House GOP Conference hailing from constituencies where Trump voting levels were very high than was the case for Senate Republicans.

The staggered nature of Senate elections also mattered. The Senate is divided into three classes, the first two comprised of 33 members and the third of 34, and each federal election year only one class faces the voters. As a result, the partisan leanings of the states with a Senate campaign during a particular year may be very different from the leanings of the states with a Senate campaign two or four years hence. In and of itself, the staggered nature of Senate elections can produce lurches in party margins and representational relationships. If most of the Senate seats up for election are currently held by Democrats, and that year there is a national swing toward the GOP, the result can be a substantial drop in the Democratic margin. An analogous shift toward the GOP would also be apparent in House elections, but because all members are running the loss of Democratic seats as a percentage of the full chamber may be less pronounced. The Democratic party's "exposure" in such a year would be greater on the Senate side of the Capitol (Oppenheimer, Stimson, and Waterman 1986).

Exposure effects were apparent in the Senate during the Trump era. At the beginning of Trump's term, among Class 1 (senators elected in 2012), 25 members were Democrats and only 8 were Republicans. For Class II (senators elected in 2014), the breakdown was 11 Democrats and 22 Republicans. And for Class III (on the ballot in 2016), the mix was 12 Democrats and

22 Republicans. Class I, in other words, tilted strongly Democratic, while the other two were nearly two-to-one GOP. Part of this was due to the states where Senate elections were conducted during each cycle, with more anti-Trump states included in Class 1 than in Classes II or III. Increased sorting by party was also apparent as we move across classes. A few of the Democrats in Class I (2012) hailed from GOP strongholds that voted in high percentages for Trump. The incidence of such Democrats within Class II (2014) was substantially less, and among the Democrats of Class III (2016), the lions' share represented states where Trump did poorly. Several Republicans senators from classes I and II represented swing constituencies based on the Trump measure. For the Republican senators of class III, all were from states that tilted GOP, but a large portion fell in the 50–55 percent area—states where Democrats were a threat on election day.

Lawmaking

Bicameral differences at the constituency level had important implications for legislative behavior and outcomes throughout the Trump era. The most obvious and visible place to begin identifying them is the roll-call record, which I analyze by averaging the party difference score by chamber on floor votes by two-year congress, 1969–2020 (see Figure 3.3). Party difference scores are calculated at the level of the individual roll call and are the absolute value of the difference between the percent of the two main political parties that voted "yes" on that matter. So, if every Republican voted yes and no Democrats did so, then the party difference for the question is the absolute value of 100–0, or 100. If the two parties divide the same way, say 50 percent "yes" within both parties, then the difference score is the absolute value of 50–50, or zero. Thus, the scale ranges from zero (no difference between the parties in how members voted) to 100 (complete divergence based on partisan affiliation).[3] To promote generalization about trends over time and across chambers, Senate roll calls that pertain to treaties and nominations are dropped, and difference scores are averaged by congress and chamber.

In Figure 3.3, average party difference is shown by chamber for all nonunanimous votes (those with more than 90 percent of the membership

---

[3] Party difference scores are perhaps the most straightforward indicator of roll call partisanship and are widely used by congressional scholars (Theriault 2008).

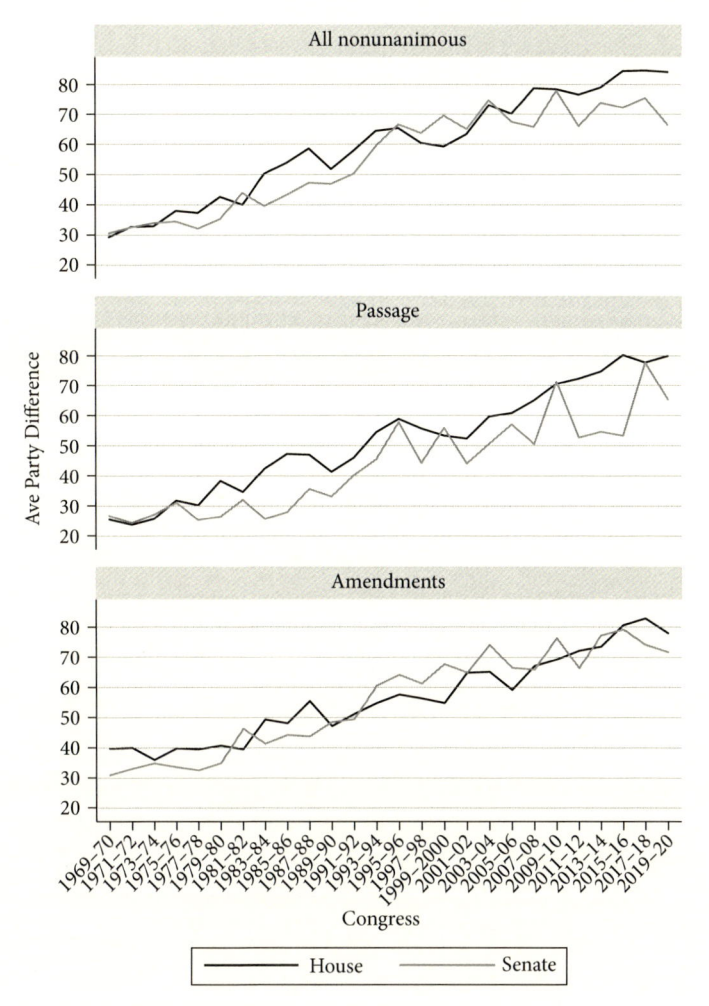

Figure 3.3 Average Party Difference on Roll Calls by Chamber, 1969–2000

was on the same side are excluded), nonunanimous votes that cover entire bills or resolutions (initial chamber passage, conference reports, and veto overrides); and nonunanimous votes on amendments (first- and second-degree amendments, motions to table amendments, and so forth).[4] It is in-structive to consider these three partitions of the roll-call record because

[4] The data about vote type are from Jason Roberts, David Rohde, and Michael H. Crespin. Political Institutions and Public Choice Senate and House Roll-Call Databases, University of Oklahoma. Retrieved from https://ou.edu/carlalbertcenter/research/pipc-votes/.

partisan imperatives may differ across them. Passage roll calls tend to be lopsided and bipartisan because they occur toward the end of the legislative process and reflect the compromises and accommodations necessary to clear the many hurdles that structure lawmaking. Moreover, the choice that members confront on passage is between an entire bill and the outcome that occurs if nothing passes. Members may not particularly like the legislation before them, but still prefer it to what will occur if gridlock obtains. Amendment votes, in contrast, are more likely to concern discrete modifications, and thus may be associated with higher levels of partisanship.

Across all three subsets, the temporal increase in partisan polarization is fully apparent. While amendments were somewhat more partisan than passage votes in the late 1960s and early 1970s, those differences all but disappeared in the decades that followed. Part of this reflects decisions by House and Senate leaders to restrict the floor amendment process. In the House of 2017–2020, open amendment rules were no longer used, and roughly half of measures brought to the floor were subject to rules that were highly restrictive or completely closed.[5] In the Senate, amendment activity has been substantially reduced because the deals necessary to get legislation scheduled typically require that the floor process be highly scripted, with only limited opportunity for rank-and-file members to propose modifications. As a result, significant partisan differences now characterize most subsets of the roll-call record across both chambers. If we focus on nonunanimous votes and passage votes, average levels of partisan difference tend to be somewhat higher in the House than in the Senate, which was also the case for amendment votes during the 1960s and 1970s, and for the Trump years. While both chambers demonstrate substantial partisanship on their floors, the level appears to be somewhat lower in the Senate.

The deviations in party difference across chambers are fully consistent with the patterns we observed at the constituency level. House members are more likely to represent constituencies that fall toward the extreme ends of the scale, and one consequence is higher levels of roll call partisanship there than in the Senate. Cross-chamber differences in procedure and the contents of the House and Senate legislative agendas may also play a role. For the most part, the House is a majority rule institution, and if the backers of a measure can muster 218 votes, they will carry the day on the floor. In the Senate, the

---

[5] And of course, more consensual legislation consider under suspension of the rules cannot be amended.

ability to filibuster and otherwise engage in obstructionism often raises the passage bar to 60 votes, as opposed to 51, which can induce coalition leaders to alter their proposals to foster significant cross-partisan support. Moreover, the roll-call records of each chamber include legislative proposals that are never considered by the other body. Votes in the Senate may be less partisan than is the case for the House because the legislative proposals senators craft aim at avoiding party cleavages in the first place.

For these reasons, additional light can be shed on bicameral difference by focusing on roll calls that occur on questions that also were subject to a vote in the other body—linked roll calls, if you will (Binder 2003). Some questions faced by both chambers have the same or similar language at around the same point in time, and thus allow us to partially control for differences in the Senate and House agendas. A careful review of the roll-call record during the Trump era produces 83 distinct vote pairings, 50 from 2017–2018 and 33 for 2019–2020. In a few cases, the linking of questions across chambers was not perfect, but the underlying politics was still captured by two related votes.[6] For details, consult the appendix to this chapter.[7]

The levels of party difference on paired votes were often similar across chambers. For 21 of the 83 pairs (about one in five), the cross-chamber difference was just three or less on the 100-point scale. But numerous pairs show considerable deviation. On 30 of the items, the cross-chamber deviation was 10 or more. For a significant subset, the deviation was quite large; 25 or more in 15 cases. And for most of the pairs, the party difference was larger in the House than in the Senate. Consider the cluster graph in Figure 3.4, which shows the relationship between House and Senate party difference scores for the paired votes in each Congress. The solid lines are what would occur if the items had identical levels of party differences across chambers. As you can see, many of the pairs are close to the dividing line, especially during 2017–2018. And a disproportionate number of items in both congresses are clustered toward the upper right of the relevant graph, indicating high levels of party voting in both chambers. But many vote pairs diverge substantially from the dividing line. And when such deviations occur, they tend to cluster

---

[6] Excluding the items, in any event, would not substantially alter the generalizations presented in this chapter.

[7] The appendix also denotes the party difference for the votes in each chamber, and the cross-chamber deviation (the difference score for the Senate is subtracted from the score for the House). Within each Congress, items are ordered by the size of that deviation.

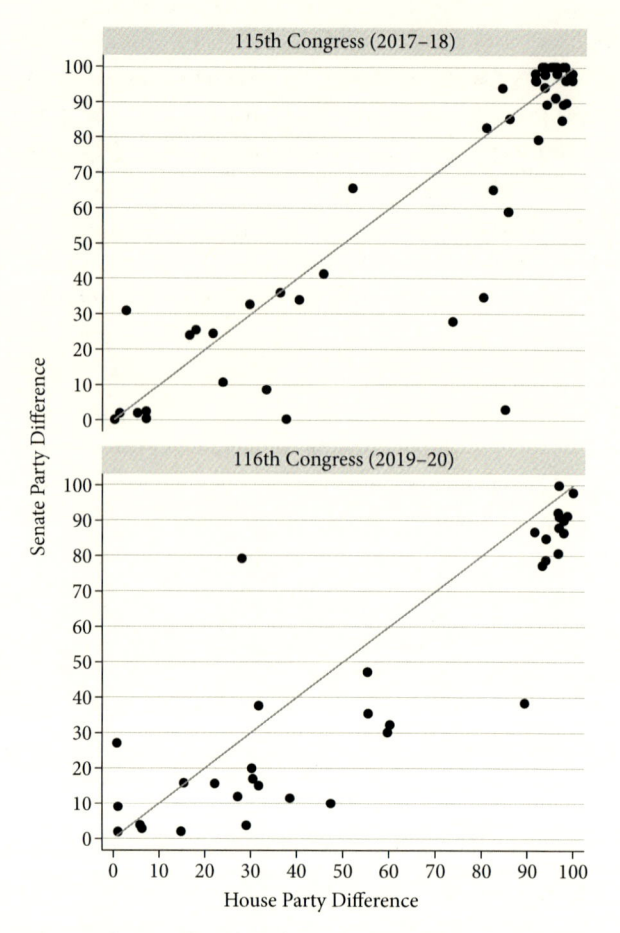

Figure 3.4 Party Difference by Chamber on Linked Votes, 2017–2020

below that line, reflecting levels of partisan difference that are higher in the House than in the Senate.

In other words, the larger number of House districts, as opposed to states, that lean strongly toward one or the other party, is associated with higher levels of partisan behavior—*even after controlling for the contents of the underlying legislation*. Differences in chamber procedures play a role, but the deviations in roll-call partisanship also appear to be rooted in more fundamental differences between the chambers. As mentioned, the partisan leanings of the median constituency across chambers are similar—even when the two political parties are considered separately. Why, then, might the relative absence of extreme constituencies on the Senate side be associated with the patterns apparent in Figure 3.4?

To understand the modern legislative process, we need to look within the two party caucuses in both chambers and consider the degree and form of factionalization (Bloch Rubin 2017; Curry and Lee 2020). Portrayals of lawmaking often prioritize the policy views of the chamber median along some underlying dimension of evaluation. Legislative outcomes, so the argument goes, should tend toward the preferences of that median, or some other legislator made pivotal by the rules of the game (Krehbiel 1998). But within a congress characterized by high levels of team-like behavior on both sides of the partisan aisle, the bargaining that occurs between factions within each party over the construction of proposals is crucial—especially when margins are as tight as 2017–2020. If the majority leadership believes that support from across the partisan aisle will be minimal or none, building near unanimity within the majority caucus or conference is essential, which in turn empowers organized factions within that party. Several dozen House Republicans in the conservative "Freedom Caucus," for example, routinely bargained with GOP leaders as an organized group throughout the Trump presidency. Senate Republicans, in contrast, are somewhat less factionalized because of the smaller proportion of extremist constituencies within the body. Among Democrats, organized factional bargaining is also less apparent in the Senate than in the House. Especially in the House, then, if a faction defects from the party position, the result may be gridlock and an embarrassing loss on the floor. As a result, we need to consider the bargaining and gamesmanship that occurs within parties to understand the voting patterns that emerge.

This point can be clarified by inverting the relationships in Figure 3.4 and calculating *chamber* difference scores by *party* (rather than party difference scores by chamber). More concretely, let chamber difference be the absolute value of the percent of senators voting yes minus the percent of House members voting yes, calculated separately by party and two-year Congress. So, if 50 percent of Senate Republicans voted aye on an item and 50 percent of House Republicans were also in that column, then the chamber difference on the item for the GOP would be the absolute value of 50 minus 50, or zero. The benefits of reconfiguring the evidence in this manner are apparent in Figure 3.5, which plots the chamber difference scores of Republicans and Democrats for 2017–2018 and 2019–2020. Each point represents the

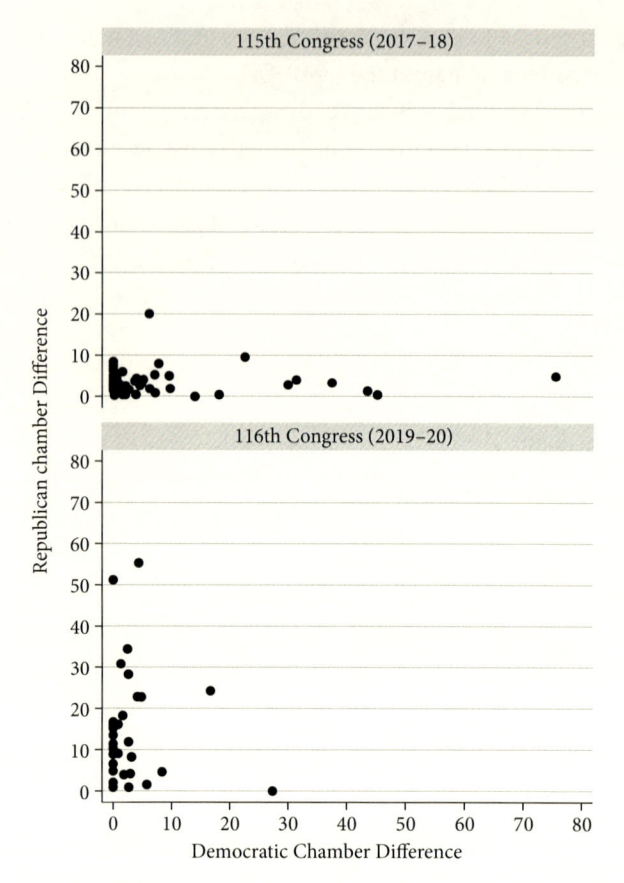

Figure 3.5 Chamber Difference by Party on Linked Votes, 2017–2020

chamber difference combination for the two parties on a particular linked item. Both periods contain a clustering of roll-call pairs near the origin, which indicates that voting patterns for Senate and House members within each party were often similar. Given the close party margins of the day, even small levels of cross-chamber difference within a party can impede its ability to advance a legislative agenda through both chambers. So, the outside portions of clusters near the origin signal potentially important bicameral difference, especially for the partisan majority. But even more striking are the obvious asymmetries that existed across 2017–2018 and 2019–2020. During the first period, the spread for the Democrats is noticeably larger, while for 2019–2020 the more extensive spread is for the GOP. In other words, congressional Democrats regularly produced high levels of interchamber difference during the earlier Congress, while for the latter one Republicans were the party that often exhibited significant interchamber difference.

Why? During 2017–2018, the Republicans held the White House and both chambers of Congress. Their margins were relatively slim—just 51 to 49 in the Senate and 241 to 194 in the House. They could afford to lose some votes in the House, but not in the Senate. With a newly elected Republican in the White House, the bicameral GOP leadership had incentives to work closely together and with the Trump administration and only bring before the full House and Senate proposals capable of uniting the party. Moreover, especially on final passage votes, or issues like appropriations or budget bills where the costs of gridlock can be prohibitively high, Senate Democrats— who are much less likely to represent extremist constituencies than are their House counterparts, were more inclined to vote with the Republicans than were Democrats on the other side of the Capitol. As a result, the levels of interchamber difference were often substantial for the Democrats and seldom that way for the GOP.

In 2019–2020, in contrast, Democrats were now the majority party in the House. As a result, the Trump administration and Senate Republican leaders needed to bargain with the House Democratic leadership to enact legislation. At first, the Senate and House might proceed independently and produce very different measures, but to bring items to the president's desk, substantial compromise was necessary. As Trump and Senate Majority Leader Mitch McConnell struck the necessary bargains with Speaker Nancy Pelosi, Republican House members—especially the Freedom Caucus and other members from the pro-Trump end of the constituency distribution— regularly rebelled and voted no. The legislation that resulted would pass with strong Democratic support in the House, a relatively large bipartisan coalition in the Senate, and a significant number of House Republicans in opposition. Per the figure, the result now was significant chamber difference for Republicans and not much for Democrats. Bicameralism matters, but the effects are conditioned by the underlying partisan and electoral contexts.

Trump Gets a Tax Cut

If we look beyond roll calls, and more carefully at the *process of legislative construction*, the effects of bicameralism are fully apparent even on bills where voting alignments across the two chambers were very similar. Roll call differences are just the tip of the iceberg. A good illustration was one of the most significant legislative enactments of the Trump era, the sweeping tax legislation passed by the Congress in December 2017. The measure constituted the most important overhaul of the tax code in more than three decades. After nearly a year of discussions between the Trump administration and GOP leaders in the House and Senate, the House passed its bill on November 11 without a single Democratic "yes." Thirteen Republican members voted no, primarily from states with relatively high tax rates who were concerned about provisions to roll back the federal deduction for state and local taxes (SALT). The measure was considered subject to a closed rule that precluded amendment votes. On the Senate side, roll calls occurred on the motion to proceed, 10 motions from Democrats to refer the measure to the Finance Committee with instructions for modification, and several motions to waive budget rules as they pertained to amendments. At that point, the chamber passed its version of the legislation on a party-line 51 to 49 vote.[8] Several roll calls concerning conference action occurred in both chambers, culminating in final passage votes on December 20 in both bodies.[9] In the House, the margin was 224 to 201, with all Democrats and 12 Republicans voting no. Once again, the narrow GOP opposition centered in high tax states like New York and New Jersey. In the Senate, the outcome was 51 to 48, cleanly dividing the two parties.

If we just consider the roll-call record, in other words, the party difference scores were high in both chambers. But if we take a closer look at the process through which the House and Senate developed their legislation, systematic and important bicameral effects are apparent. The first flashpoint emerged early in the year, when House Speaker Paul Ryan floated offsetting certain of the tax reductions under consideration by imposing a border adjustment tax. While Ryan's idea enjoyed only limited support among Senate Republicans or in the Trump White House, a coalition of business groups and the agricultural community were strongly opposed. The Speaker backed away from his proposal, at which point several months of intense backroom negotiations ensued between Republicans and the administration to develop a framework for the bill. After the party failed to advance a measure to repeal the Affordable Care Act in the Senate, the stakes became enormous for passing a

---

[8] Only Republican Bob Corker broke with his party on initial passage.
[9] Thomas Kaplan and Alan Rappeport, "Republican Tax Bill Passes Senate in 51–48 Vote," *New York Times*, December 19, 2017, https://www.nytimes.com/2017/12/19/us/politics/tax-bill-vote-congress.html.

tax bill. Absent a legislative win on taxes, Republicans feared they would have little to show for their majority status (Green and Deatherage 2018).

Trump released his own outline of principles for drafting the measure, but it was vague and ran only a single page, reflecting the internal difficulties that Republicans confronted finding common ground. Kevin Brady, chair of the House Ways and Means Committee, which has jurisdiction over the tax code, said that no markup within the panel would occur until Republicans on both sides of the Capitol and key actors within the Trump administration were on the same page. As a result, negotiations occurred between the so-called Big Six, comprised of Speaker Ryan, Majority Leader McConnell, Brady, Senate Finance Chair Orrin Hatch, Treasury Secretary Steven Mnuchin, and Gary Cohn, who directed the National Economic Council for Trump. Perhaps the central disagreement between the chambers at this stage concerned the duration of the proposed tax cuts and whether the revenue losses would be offset elsewhere in the code. House GOP leaders pushed for permanent cuts with offsets to avoid increasing the deficit. But many Republicans on both sides of the Capitol preferred temporary cuts without offsets—essentially the approach used to pass the Bush tax cuts of 2001 and 2003.

Republican leaders unveiled their unified framework at the end of September, and action shifted to drafting legislation within each chamber. The gist of the House and Senate packages were similar—they were operating within the same framework that had been developed across chamber lines. But the two bills had significant differences that reflect the bicameral logic of this chapter.[10] First, the Senate measure included a repeal of the individual mandate portion of the Affordable Care Act. House leaders, in contrast, wanted to proceed with such a repeal on a separate track and leave it out of the tax bill. The two measures also differed in how they treated so-called "pass through" businesses. Pass throughs are firms that do not pay corporate taxes, but instead report income via the individual returns of owners or partners. Often, they are small (sole proprietorships or partnerships, like law practices). As a result, pass throughs are taxed at the individual rather than the corporate rate. The Senate's approach was substantially less generous toward pass throughs than was the case on the House side, and GOP

---

[10] My review of the contrasting tax measures advanced by Senate and House Republicans relies on multiple issue briefs produced by the *Congressional Research Service*. Consult, for example, "The 2017 Tax Revision (P.L. 115-97): Comparison to 2017 Tax Law." Updated February 6, 2018, https://crs reports.congress.gov/product/pdf/R/R45092 . See also "Comparing the Conference Reports with the House and Senate Tax Bills," *Committee for a Responsible Federal Budget*, December 19, 2017, https://www.crfb.org/blogs/comparing-conference-report-house-senate-tax-bills.

conservatives threatened not to support the Senate bill unless more was done for them.[11]

Perhaps more significant was the different way that the House and Senate measures approached the deduction for SALT. The initial position adopted by Senate Republican leaders was to eliminate the deduction entirely. On the House side, GOP leaders also embraced elimination early on—the high tax states that primarily benefited from the break tended to support Democrats. But after Republican members from such states objected to the change House GOP leaders moderated their language in order to prevail on the floor. The Senate also began moving toward the House position to secure adoption in both chambers, even as the Senate was clearly more inclined to end the deduction. Analogous differences existed by chamber in the corporate tax deductions that were the centerpiece of the legislation. Under the Senate bill, the cuts would be implemented beginning in 2019, while the House would implement the reductions immediately in 2018.

The House and Senate also adopted different approaches to the Alternative Minimum Tax (AMT) that provides a floor on taxation. Originally intended to keep wealthy individuals from reducing their tax burdens to absurd levels through the creative use of loopholes, by 2017 it affected over 5 million filers. The Senate package would have left the AMT largely intact, while the inclination on the House side was to repeal it outright. The reductions in individual income rates were more widely publicized. Here, the Senate included more income brackets (seven as opposed the five proposed by House GOP leaders), with a somewhat lower marginal tax rate for millionaires. But the main difference throughout the year were efforts to make the individual tax cuts permanent. The House process was more oriented toward that approach than was the Senate. The House bill also went further to repeal the estate tax, a move that primarily benefited extremely wealthy individuals. Both bills doubled the exemption to $11.18 million for individuals and $22.36 million for married couples, dramatically increasing the number of millionaires who would escape the tax. But the House approach would have repealed estate taxes entirely in 2025.

The deduction that homeowners receive from interest that they pay on mortgages is politically charged and a regular feature of tax reform debates on Capitol Hill. Here, the Senate would have made no changes, but the House

---

[11] Dylan Matthews, "Pass-Through Companies, the Issue that Could Make or Break the Senate Tax Bill, Explained." *Vox*, November 28, 2017. https://www.vox.com/2017/11/28/16709634/pass-thro ugh-republican-tax-bill

proposed that the break be cut in half and only permitted for a filer's primary residence. Along those lines, while the Senate package would not have altered the deductions for student loans and medical expenses, these mostly would have been eliminated under the House GOP approach. Finally, House and Senate Republicans also took divergent approaches to the child tax credit, which obviously benefits families with children. Here, the Senate opted for a more generous approach, doubling the break to $2 thousand per child and only phasing out the reduction for families earning more than $500 thousand in joint income. The House bill also would have increased the deduction, but only to $1.6 thousand per child, with a phaseout at $230 thousand in married income.

In short, although a bicameral accord worked out with the Trump White House set certain parameters on the tax cut debate, the approaches taken by the Senate and House were substantively and politically distinct. In part these differences derive from the size and power of the conservative faction on the House side. The House generally was more oriented toward tax reduction across the board especially for corporate interests and the wealthy than was the case among Senate Republicans. The distinction should not be exaggerated—the thrust of both packages was tax reduction of historic proportions and an outcome that disproportionately benefited the well off, but this was especially pronounced in the House where more GOP members represented homogenously conservative constituencies. Members of the House face the voters every two years, while senators have six-year terms. Not surprisingly, the House pushed for immediate implementation of the business cuts, while Senate Republicans were willing to wait a year.

Senate procedure was another factor behind the divergence. Early on, a decision was made to consider tax reduction as a reconciliation bill—under Senate rules, reconciliation measures cannot be filibustered. Otherwise, GOP leaders would not have been able to advance their package through the chamber. But limits exist on what can be placed in a reconciliation bill. As a result of the "Byrd Rule," provisions cannot be included that would increase the size of the federal budget deficit during "out years," which are beyond the scope of the underlying measure (ten years). If, like their corporate counterparts, the tax reductions for individual income had been permanent, the legislation would have run afoul of the Byrd proviso and been subject to a three-fifths vote in the Senate. Although sentiment to make the income tax cuts permanent was strong in the House, GOP leaders in both chambers embraced language that would sunset these provisions. In addition, to meet the strictures of the rule, Senate leaders needed to come up with offsets to avoid adding to the deficit—imperatives that were less significant on the House side of the Capitol. As a result, they integrated the proposal to end the ACA individual mandate into the tax reduction package. According to the Congressional Budget Office, the repeal would decrease federal expenditures by about $318 billion over ten years, and this savings could be used to offset the revenue reductions elsewhere in the bill. For these reasons, Senate Republicans included the repeal in their version of the tax legislation, and House Republican leaders were forced to follow suit to secure enactment.

The incidence of different taxes across Senate and House constituencies provides further insight into the sources of bicameral difference (see Table 3.2). This table adopts the basic design of Table 3.1, but instead of showing the distribution of population density or race across districts or states, the focus is on the incidence of the taxes upon which the House and Senate bills diverged. Since decision making was highly partisan throughout the fight and largely centered in the Republican majorities of the two chambers, only constituencies represented by the GOP are included in the tabulations. Again, following the basic setup of Table 3.1, the incidence of various taxes is shown for the median House and Senate constituencies, but also the other percentile rankings within each chamber. The entries are measured in dollars per capita within the relevant district or state to promote comparison and are from 2017. So, the state with the least amount of filings for pass through businesses (sole proprietors, partnerships, and so-called S-corps) had total filings of $718 per capita. In contrast, the House district at this end of the scale had pass through filings totally just $504 (again, controlling for population). At the median (50th percentile), the filing totals per capita were over $1,687 in the Senate and a slightly less $1,605 for the House district at the center of that distribution. And at the upper level (the 99th percentile for the relevant chamber), the differences are stark. The state with the highest incidence had filings per capita of $3,093 while the most affected House districts had totals of $7,736. A sizable portion of House Republicans represented districts with massive quantities of pass-through filing, which is one reason why the House approach included more tax relief for these payers than was the case on the Senate side.

When we consider the AMT, the two chamber distributions have striking differences at the upper level. Only a fraction of filers is affected by this tax, but the difference at the top is large—$87 per capita for the highest state, but over five times that amount for House districts at that tail of the distribution.

Table 3.2 Tax Incidence among Senate and House Republicans, 2017

Category	Chamber	1st	5th	10th	25th	Med	75th	90th	95th	99th
Sole proprietor	Senate	718	1003	1169	1395	1687	2083	2327	2414	3093
	House	504	727	868	1097	1605	2199	3396	4626	7736
SALT	Senate	38	66	93	269	713	909	981	1009	1127
	House	24	38	79	344	644	1035	1591	2075	3670
AMT	Senate	21	21	24	33	49	60	68	74	87
	House	12	16	19	25	44	81	141	227	487
Mortgage interest	Senate	363	399	442	523	597	761	857	1019	1290
	House	258	313	362	481	668	1005	1472	1633	2180
Student loans	Senate	25	27	29	33	37	48	59	59	64
	House	20	23	25	31	40	48	56	61	70
Medical deductions	Senate	144	202	224	245	302	359	381	403	406
	House	103	194	214	244	297	360	449	541	658
Child credit	Senate	68	75	76	80	89	106	112	116	140
	House	56	65	73	79	87	100	109	112	129
Total taxes	Senate	3171	3371	3774	4009	4478	4787	5974	6365	6714
	House	2555	2937	3174	3731	4378	6105	8912	10361	15701

Source: US Internal Revenue Service: https://www.irs.gov/statistics/soi-tax-stats-data-by-congressional-district-2017. Cell entries are dollar amounts per capita. Population data are from the 2017 American Community Survey, accessed via Social Explorer.

The House Republicans representing such districts were adamant about repealing the policy, and that was the position adopted by the party in the chamber. On the Senate side, the sentiment for repeal was less pronounced, and they mostly sought to leave the policy alone.

Now compare the distribution of pass-through payers or the AMT within each chamber with the distribution of beneficiaries from the state and local deduction. Again, controlling for population, the state benefiting the least from the SALT deduction paid $38 per capita in state and local income taxes, and for the House district at this end of the distribution the value was $24 per capita. At the median point of each distribution, the values remained similar across chambers. But at the upper end, there were substantial differences. The states with the highest levels were at $1,127 per capita, while for the House end of the distribution that amount was over three times higher. While relatively few Republican senators represented high tax states—mostly these constituencies elected Democrats to the chamber—House Republicans constituted a sizable faction from such areas. Since Speaker Ryan needed their votes, he opted against repealing this tax deduction. And on final passage, the small number of House Republicans who still voted no were largely from such states.

Now consider the entries in Table 3.2 for the mortgage interest tax deduction. The incidence of this loophole across House and Senate constituencies is very different from the distribution of state and local taxes or those targeting pass-through entities and the AMT. For the tax break on home mortgages, the incidence is somewhat higher at the low end of the distributions in the Senate than in the House, and at the upper ends the larger number is for the House. But in this case, the distributions are flatter and do not diverge as much by chamber. The distribution of homeowners with mortgages is relatively even across geographic subsets of the United States. Not surprisingly, both chambers and both parties provided considerable support for maintaining the policy. In the House, the reformist inclinations of the Republican majority led them to favor rolling back this deduction, but only because of the income tax and other reductions for individuals also included in the broader package. The Senate had little interest at all in taking on this loophole.

For student loans, medical deductions, and the child tax credit, the distributions vary somewhat across Senate and House constituencies, but as with mortgages the differences are less pronounced than are those for pass through operations, SALT, or the AMT. Here, the Senate had little interest for rolling back the deductions. Indeed, in the Senate, conservatives such as Mike Lee of Utah pushed for more generous tax benefits for families with children. Perhaps because of average family size and the proportion of married couples with children, the per capita incidence of beneficiaries in Utah is the highest in the nation. And overall, because of the distribution of Republicans across states as opposed to districts, the beneficiary levels for the child tax credit were somewhat higher in the Senate than in the House across the entire distribution. For these reasons, the sentiment to expand the beneficiary base was particularly strong in the Senate, with Lee taking the lead.

Clearly, tax reform in 2017 was a partisan fight, with the GOP mostly united in favor of tax cuts and no support coming from Democrats in either chamber. The parameters were worked out at the leadership level, with Republicans from the Senate and House equally involved. The key roll calls did not exhibit much cross-chamber difference. But when we dig a little deeper and look at the substance of legislative construction, important differences between the chambers are apparent, deviations that are rooted in chamber procedure and constitutionally grounded differences between the Senate and House.

The Enduring Importance of Bicameral Difference

The bottom line? Bicameral difference continued to shape legislation and representation during the Trump era. Senate apportionment appeared to benefit Republicans. But the geographic sorting that characterizes the country as a whole also advantages the GOP in the House. As many scholars have demonstrated, the disproportionate packing of Democratic voters in urban districts made the distribution of Republican voters more efficient for that party in House races. Any advantage to the GOP in Senate campaigns because of the small state bias needs to be considered relative to the alternative. If senators did not represent states, how precisely would seats be allocated in the chamber? An apportionment scheme that resembled the equal population approach of the House would not necessarily produce party margins more representative of the nation.

When we consider the implications for the constituencies that House members and senators represent, the largest differences between the chambers are at the extremes. If constituencies are arrayed based on their partisan-electoral leanings, House districts are much more likely to be at the far ends of the scale. On the Senate side, the geographic constituencies represented by Democrats and Republicans are somewhat less different from one another, with significant consequences for coalition building. Narrow party margins in the House and regular party-line voting mean that the majority leadership cannot afford to lose the support of significant factions within the relevant caucus or conference. As a result, House members from outlier districts have significant bargaining power during the legislative process. This dynamic is less pronounced in the Senate. Chamber rules also reinforce this tendency in important ways. Although the share of the policy agenda that is "fast tracked" and not subject to super majority requirements has expanded in recent decades (Reynolds, 2017), our discussion of linked votes and the landmark tax cuts of 2017 shows how the obstructionist potential of Senate procedure continues to shape decision making and legislative outcomes in both chambers.

During the Trump years, the Senate and House were both buffeted by intense partisan polarization that characterized the country, and that was exacerbated by the agenda and operating style of the Trump White House. But striking and predictable divergences between the Senate and House were still apparent. These divergences, we have seen, were rooted in the longstanding structural differences that distinguish the two chambers and thus are enduring. Most important, the impact of extremist factions on lawmaking appears to be less pronounced in the Senate because of constituency composition and chamber rules. The precise impact of bicameral difference also depended on the political context within which the two chambers operated. For reasons rooted in the evolving partisan configuration on Capitol Hill, for example, Democrats exhibited more Senate-House difference during 2017–2018, while Republicans were the primary source of cross-chamber discord during 2019–2020. Bicameral effects endure, in other words, but generalizations about their impact need to be conditional. And reform advocates need to pay more attention to how the different structural arrangements (e.g., apportionment schemes and internal chamber procedures) interact with one another and with the partisan-electoral context.

From a bicameral perspective, were the Trump years primarily a disruption, or the continuation of longstanding patterns in congressional lawmaking? Disruption certainly characterized the legislative agenda and to some extent the behavior of senators and House members. Trump's Senate was often unsetting and volatile and constituted a clear break from the policy priorities of the past. But lawmaking within the two chambers of Congress continued to differ in predictable ways that were mostly consistent with logical partisan imperatives, recent procedural traditions, and the underlying constitutional framework. To be sure, Trump disrupted the political scene on Capitol Hill and in the nation more generally. But the underlying logic of bicameralism and House-Senate difference was fully apparent throughout this remarkable era.

References

Baker, Ross. 2008. *House and Senate*. 4th ed. New York: Norton.

Binder, Sarah. 2003. *Stalemate: Causes and Consequences of Legislative Gridlock*. Washington: Brookings Institution Press.

Bloch Rubin, Ruth. 2017. *Building the Bloc: Intraparty Organization in the U.S. Congress*. Chicago: University of Chicago Press.

Curry, James M., and Frances E. Lee. 2020. *The Limits of Party: Congress and Lawmaking in a Polarized Era*. Chicago: University of Chicago Press.

Cutrone, Michael, and Nolan McCarty. 2008. "Does Bicameralism Matter." In *Oxford Handbook of Political Economy*. B. Weingast and D. Whitman, eds., New York: Oxford University Press, 180–195.

Fenno, Richard F., Jr. 1982. *The United States Senate: A Bicameral Perspective*. Washington, DC: AEI Press.

Green, Matthew N., and William Deatherage. 2018. "When Reputation Trumps Policy: Party Productivity Brand and the 2017 Tad Cut and Jobs Act," *The Forum* 16: 419–440.

Hopkins, Daniel J., Schickler, Eric, and David L. Azizi. 2022. "From Many Divides, One? The Polarization and Nationalization of American State Party Platforms, 1918–2017." Unpublished paper.

Krehbiel, Keith. 1998. *Pivotal Politics: A Theory of U.S. Lawmaking*. Chicago: University of Chicago Press.

Lee, Frances E., and Bruce I. Oppenheimer. 1999. *Sizing Up the Senate: The Unequal Consequences of Equal Representation*. Chicago, IL: University of Chicago Press.

Oppenheimer, Bruce J., James A. Stimson, and Richard M. Waterman. 1986. "Interpreting U.S. Congressional Elections: The Exposure Thesis." *Legislative Studies Quarterly* 11: 227–247.

Reynolds, M. E. 2017. *Exceptions to the Rule: The Politics of Filibuster Limitations in the U.S. Senate*. Washington, DC: Brookings Institution Press.

Rodden, Jonathan. 2019. *Why Cities Lose: The Deep Roots of the Urban-Rural Political Divide*. New York: Basic Books.

Sides, John, Michael Tesler, and Lynn Vavreck. 2019. *Identity Crisis: The 2016 Presidential Campaign and the Battle for the Meaning of America*. Princeton, NJ: Princeton University Press.

Theriault, Sean M. 2008. *Party Polarization in Congress*. New York: Cambridge University Press.

Appendix

Party Difference by Chamber on Linked Votes, 2017–2020

115th Congress

Issue	House Dif.	Senate Dif.	Deviation
Consolidated appropriations FY18, HR1625	2.7	29.5	−26.9
Immigration (Trump plan), HR2579	51.9	65.9	−13.9
Farm bill, HR2	17.9	25.5	−7.6
Criminal justice reform, S756	16.5	24.0	−7.5
Budget resolution FY18, HCRes71	91.5	98.1	−6.6
CRA/Broadband, SJRes34	93.5	100.0	−6.5
Trump tax cuts, HR1	94.9	100.0	−5.1
CRA/Alaskan wildlife, HJRes69	93.0	97.9	−4.9
CRA/OSHA record keeping, HRes83	95.3	100.0	−4.7
CRA/SEC disclosure	95.6	100.0	−4.4
CRA/Auto lending, SJRes57	93.6	97.9	−4.3
Presidential rescissions, HR3	91.7	96.0	−4.3
CRA/BLM planning HJRes44	96.1	100.0	−3.9
Disaster relief, HR2266	29.6	32.7	−3.1
Flood insurance, S1182	21.6	24.5	−2.8
ACA revision, HR1628	91.6	94.2	−2.7
CRA/Drug testing, HJRes42	97.5	100.0	−2.5
CRA/Fair pay & safe workplaces, HJRes37	98.0	100.0	−2.0
Budget resolution FY17, SCRes3	96.2	98.1	−1.9
CRA/Methane emissions, HCRes71	93.6	94.2	−0.7
Tribal rights S140	80.8	81.3	−0.5
Defense appropriations FY18, HR695	85.8	85.8	0.1
Nuclear weapons amendment, HR5515	94.1	94.0	0.1
Online sex trafficking, HR1865	0.2	0.0	0.2
Consolidated appropriations FY17, HR2244	36.2	36.0	0.2
CRA/State retirement savings, HJRes67	99.0	98.0	1.0
Sanctions/Russia, Iran, North Korea, HR3364	1.3	0.2	1.1
CRA/School accountability, HJRes57	99.6	98.0	1.5
CRA/Family planning, HJRes43	98.1	96.2	1.9
CRA/Private retirement savings, HJRes66	98.2	96.2	2.0
Opioid treatment & prevention, HR6	5.2	2.0	3.2
CRA/Consumer financial protection, HJRes11	99.6	96.2	3.4
CRA/Stream protection	94.0	89.7	4.3
FISA warrants, S139	45.6	41.1	4.5

115th Congress

Issue	House Dif.	Senate Dif.	Deviation
Minibus 1, HR5895	7.1	2.2	4.9
CRA/Guns sales to mentally ill, HJRes40	95.9	89.6	6.3
CR & disaster supplemental, HR601	40.4	34.0	6.4
FAA authorization, HR302	7.1	0.1	7.0
Pain-capable unborn, S2311	97.6	89.6	8.0
DC insurance mandate, HR6147	98.3	89.8	8.5
Defense authorization FY19, HR5515	23.8	12.2	11.7
CR FY18 cloture on House bill, HRHR195	92.2	79.8	12.4
CRA/Teacher preparation, HJRes58	97.3	83.3	14.0
Dodd-Frank reform, S2155	82.3	64.6	17.7
Bipartisan Budget Act, HR1892	33.3	7.5	25.8
CR & disaster supplemental, HR1370	85.6	58.5	27.1
VA overhaul, S2672	37.6	2.2	35.5
Mattis exception, S84	80.2	35.4	44.8
CR Final FY18, HR195	73.5	28.7	44.9
CR FY18, HJRes123	85.1	4.5	80.5

116th Congress (2019-20)

Issue	House Dif.	Senate Dif.	Deviation
Russia sanctions, SJRes2	28.0	79.2	−51.2
FISA reauthorization, HR6172	0.8	26.4	−25.7
Consolidated appropriations (defense), HR1158	1.0	8.7	−7.6
NAFTA overhaul, HR5430	15.4	17.2	−1.8
Criminal robocalls, S151	1.0	2.0	−0.9
Coronavirus 1, HR6074	1.0	1.9	−0.9
9/11 compensation fund, HR1327	5.9	3.8	2.0
CRA/Community reinvestment, HJRes90	100.0	98.0	2.0
Border assistance & security, HR3401	96.7	92.5	4.2
US forces in Yemen, SJRes7	91.6	86.8	4.8
Defense authorizations FY21 passage, HR6395	6.3	1.2	5.0
Minibus cloture on House bill, HR2740	97.0	91.2	5.8
Coronavirus 2, HR6201	22.2	15.7	6.5
Taxpayer funded abortions, S109	98.7	91.6	7.1
Public lands conservation, HR1957	55.4	47.2	8.2
Disaster supplemental FY19, HR268	96.9	88.0	8.9
Iran war powers, SJRes68	94.1	84.9	9.2
CR FY21, HR8337	30.3	20.0	10.3
Defense transfers to Saudi Arabia, SJRes36	97.9	86.5	11.4
Defense authorization FY20, S1790	14.8	1.8	13.0
Disaster supplemental FY19, HR2157	30.5	17.0	13.5

(*continued*)

116th Congress (2019-20)

Issue	House Dif.	Senate Dif.	Deviation
Presidential national emergency 2, SJRes54	94.1	78.8	15.2
Coronavirus relief & omnibus appropriations, HR133	27.2	12.0	15.2
Presidential national emergency 1, HJRes46	93.3	77.4	16.0
CRA/Student loans, HJRes76	96.8	80.8	16.0
Public lands conservation, S47	31.8	15.1	16.7
Consolidated appropriations (domestic), HR1865	55.5	35.6	19.9
Defense authorizations veto override, HR6395	29.1	2.1	27.0
Border assistance & security, HR3401	38.6	11.2	27.4
Balanced Budget Act, HR3877	60.2	32.6	27.6
CR FY20, HR4378	59.7	30.2	29.5
Consolidated appropriations FY19, HJRes31	47.4	10.5	36.9
Minibus 2, HR3055	89.4	38.5	51.0

4

Unorthodox Legislating in Trump's Senate

Molly E. Reynolds

Introduction

Much about Donald Trump's four years in office has been described as "unorthodox"—his phone habits, his debate style, and his approach to record keeping, to name a few.[1] His relationship with Congress might be fairly characterized the same way; as the *New York Times* reporter Maggie Haberman described it in one example, "even after four years in office, Trump failed to grasp basics about Senate vote counting, insisting to me that the minority could block any legislation by skipping votes" (Haberman 2022, 326). But a look back at Congress's own work during the Trump presidency allows us the opportunity not only to explore, in-depth, several forms of legislating we might consider also "unorthodox," but also the chance to unpack what "unorthodox" means in the contemporary Senate. Situating the Senate's Trump era behavior in the broader context of "unorthodox" policymaking also allows us to assess whether the period was uniquely disruptive or a continuation of pre-existing trends.

Unpacking "Unorthodox" Legislating

The notion of "unorthodox lawmaking," or the use of centralized, less committee-reliant, and less open techniques to write and pass bills, often

---

[1] Gloria Borger, Jamie Gangel, and Ashley Semler, "Trump's Unorthodox Phone Habits Complicate January 6 Investigation," *CNN*, February 13, 2022, https://www.cnn.com/2022/02/13/politics/trump-telephone-records-capitol-riot-investigation/index.html; Tamara Keith, "Examining President Trump's Unorthodox Debate Style," *NPR*, September 29, 2020, https://www.npr.org/2020/09/29/918080858/examining-president-trumps-unorthodox-debate-style; Jennifer Jacobs and Gregory Korte, "FBI Probe Renews Focus on Trump's Haphazard Handling of Files," *Bloomberg*, August 9, 2022, https://www.bloomberg.com/news/articles/2022-08-09/fbi-inquiry-renews-focus-on-trump-s-haphazard-handling-of-files.

Molly E. Reynolds, *Unorthodox Legislating in Trump's Senate* In: *Disruption?* Edited by: Sean M. Theriault, Oxford University Press. © Oxford University Press 2024. DOI: 10.1093/oso/9780197767832.003.0005

with significant if not exclusive influence from party leaders, was explored in depth by Barbara Sinclair (1997) in series of editions of a book by the same name.[2] In large part, Sinclair's notion of unorthodox lawmaking is articulated in terms of what it is *not*: it does not involve bills being referred to single committees, being marked up by those panels in each chamber, being brought to the floor as standalone bills for open amendment, and having differences between the chambers worked out in a conference committee.

Given the ways that the legislative process has evolved, there is an argument to be made that "regular order," and "unorthodox lawmaking" as its opposite, are no longer especially helpful concepts; in the words of legendary Congressional Research Service expert Walter Oleszek (2020, 1), "The regular order can be an elusive and changeable concept. People may legitimately contend that there is no such thing as *the* regular order for enacting laws." A more helpful articulation for the current era, then, comes from James Curry and Frances Lee's 2020 book, *The Limits of Party*, where they helpfully decompose the overall concept of unorthodox lawmaking into two separate elements: unorthodox bill development and unorthodox management of the floor consideration process. Here, again, "unorthodoxy" is measured largely by the absence of the sign posts associated with a more "regular" legislative process, especially in the case of the first element. Unorthodox bill development is measured by the absence of committee hearings and of committee reports. Unorthodox management, meanwhile, includes limitations on amendment opportunities in both chambers; ignoring the House's rules on how long a bill's text must be available before it is debated on the floor; last-minute edits made to a bill's text; the filing of cloture motions in the Senate; and the absence of a conference committee to resolve differences between the chambers.[3]

For examining the Senate in the Trump era, I will add a final Senate-specific component to Curry and Lee's conceptual framework: whether the legislation is considered under expedited procedures that shield it from a possible filibuster. Sinclair's examinations of unorthodox lawmaking included lengthy treatments of one such set of procedures—the budget reconciliation process, described at length in a later section—but in recent years, other sets of expedited procedures have also played an increasing role in the Senate. Mechanically, these protections flow from limits, written into

---

[2] Subsequent editions were published in 2000, 2007, 2011, and 2016.
[3] For a discussion of these definitions, see also Molly E. Reynolds and Peter C. Hanson, (2023). "Just How Unorthodox? Assessing Lawmaking on Omnibus Spending Bills," *The Forum* 21(2): 213–238.

particular statutes, on debate on specified future pieces of legislation. As a result, when the covered measure comes up for consideration on the Senate floor and the amount of time provided for debate has elapsed, debate ends—obviating the need to file cloture and obtain 60 votes to invoke it. In addition, under a combination of statutory language and Senate precedent, bills covered by expedited procedures are considered privileged for consideration in the Senate, eliminating the need to file and invoke cloture on the motion to proceed as well.

While much of the existing work in this area uses lawmaking as the outcome of interest, here, I focus somewhat more broadly on unorthodox *legislating.* Including legislative efforts that did not ultimately result in bills signed into law captures both situations where success appeared obtainable but where majorities ultimately failed, as well as instances where failure was expected (Gelman 2020). As I show, the Senate during the Trump years featured a number of high-profile cases in which the high likelihood of failure was known in advance, but legislators pursued a given course of action anyway.

Developing Major Legislation

Research suggests that committees engage in less lawmaking now than in previous eras, in part because the centralization of legislative power in the hands of party leaders has incentivized committees to focus more on oversight (Lewallen 2020). But that does not mean contemporary committees neglect lawmaking altogether, and examining several of the major legislative initiatives Congress pursued during the Trump administration provides a useful illustration of what "going through committee" means in the contemporary Congress. Let us consider three pieces of legislation included by David Mayhew on his list of landmark laws.[4]

Roughly every five years, Congress takes up a measure reauthorizing a range of agriculture and food policies—some of which lapse if a new bill is not signed into law, on a temporary or permanent basis, before the expiration of the previous one.[5] The major expiration dates for the previous farm bill,

[4] David R. Mayhew, "List of Important Enactments, 2017–2018," (2005), http://works.bepress.com/david-mayhew/297/; David R. Mayhew, "List of Important Enactments, 2019–2020," (2005), http://works.bepress.com/david-mayhew/410/.

[5] Jim Monke, Randy Alison Aussenberg, and Megan Stubbs, "Expiration of the 2014 Farm Bill," *Congressional Research Service*, October 11, 2018.

signed into law in 2014, were September 30 and December 31, 2018,[6] and House Agriculture Committee chair Michael Conaway (R-Tex.) "spent much of 2017 working on a draft five-year farm bill with subcommittee chairmen and [committee Ranking Member Collin] Peterson (D-Minn.)."[7] The panel and its subcommittees held 21 hearings in the 115th Congress and held an approximately five-hour long markup in April 2018—though it ended up being "an exercise in partisan sniping" and no Democrat supported the legislation in committee.[8] The Senate Agriculture Committee, meanwhile, also marked up a more bipartisan version of the legislation, sending it to the Senate floor by a vote of 20–1.[9] When two chambers had to work out the differences between the versions of their bill, a formal conference committee with 47 House members and nine senators was formed and negotiations were primarily led by the committees' chairs and ranking members.[10]

Major criminal justice legislation, known as the FIRST STEP Act, passed in December 2018 had a slightly different path. A narrower bill with the same name was marked up by the House Judiciary Committee in May 2018, with seven amendments considered—five from Democrats, two from Republicans. Of these, three passed by voice vote, two failed, and two were withdrawn.[11] The measure was the product, in part, of the committee's Criminal Justice Reform Initiative, launched on a bipartisan basis in 2015.[12] The Senate Judiciary Committee, meanwhile, marked up a bill that would address sentencing reform more broadly, the Sentencing Reform and Corrections Act, in February 2018. Given that, as Senate Judiciary Committee Chairman Chuck Grassley (R-Iowa) described it, "we had worked so darned hard and got such an overwhelming vote to get the bill out of committee," he and Judiciary ranking member Dick Durbin (D-Ill.) were reluctant to simply

[6] Monke, Aussenberg, and Stubbs, "Expiration of the 2014 Farm Bill."

[7] "2018 Legislative Preview: Agriculture," *CQ Magazine*, January 8, 2018.

[8] "Agriculture and Nutrition Act of 2018," Report of the Committee on Agriculture, H. Rpt. 115–661, 115th Congress, 2nd session, May 3, 2018; "GOP House Farm Bill Passes Out of Committee—Heads to House Floor," *Environmental and Energy Study Institute*, April 20, 2018 https://www.eesi.org/articles/view/gop-house-farm-bill-passes-out-of-committee-heads-to-house-floor; Catherine Boudreau and Liz Crampton, "Senate Passes Farm Bill, Setting Up Food Stamp Battle with the House," *Politico*, June 28, 2018.

[9] Jeff Daniels, "Senate Agriculture Panel Passes Farm Bill with Hemp Legalization," *CNBC*, June 13, 2018, https://www.cnbc.com/2018/06/13/senate-agriculture-panel-passes-farm-bill-with-hemp-legalization.html.

[10] "Fall Legislative Preview: Farm Bill," *CQ Magazine*, September 4, 2018.

[11] See "Markup of H.R. 5682, the 'FIRST STEP Act' and H.R. 5698, the 'Protect and Serve Act of 2018," https://docs.house.gov/Committee/Calendar/ByEvent.aspx?EventID=108291.

[12] "House Judiciary Committee Announces Criminal Justice Reform Initiative," June 10, 2015, https://judiciary.house.gov/media/press-releases/house-judiciary-committee-announces-criminal-justice-reform-initiative.

accept the House's measure.[13] The negotiations on the ultimate compromise legislation were led by Grassley, Durbin, and fellow Judiciary Committee member Mike Lee (R-Utah)—but in conjunction with Jared Kushner on behalf of the White House.[14] The fact that the final language did not, itself, go through committee was used by Senator Tom Cotton (R-Arkansas), an opponent of the bill, to criticize the legislation, but as Lee pointed out, both committees had worked on the legislation and "these are not new policies."[15]

A third measure—described as "the largest land conservation legislation in a decade"[16]—was signed into law in March 2019 and, like both the farm bill and the criminal justice legislation, illustrates how committee work can extend over multiple congresses. When the bill ultimately passed the Senate in February 2019, *The New York Times* described it as the result of "western lawmakers of both parties . . . working for four years."[17] The measure was—as is not uncommon for public lands legislation—an omnibus bill, incorporating a range of different proposals, some of which had been considered in committee on their own before being folded into the larger package.

Take, for example, the Every Kid Outdoors Act, a measure that would create a cross-agency program to provide every US fourth grader free access to a range of publicly accessible federal lands and waters, including national parks. The Committee on Natural Resources reported the bill as a standalone measure when it was first introduced in the House in 2017. When it reached the Senate after passing the House almost unanimously, it was reported out of committee there as well. The full Senate did not take up the bill before the end of the 115th Congress in December 2018. The proposal was available for inclusion in the larger public lands bill that Congress revisited at the start of the 116th Congress in 2019.[18]

---

[13] Carl Hulse, "How a Pact to Reform Sentencing Survived a Bitter Clash Over Kavanaugh," *New York Times*, November 16, 2018, A15.

[14] Nicholas Fandos and Maggie Haberman, "Senators Prepare Push for a Sentencing Overhaul," *New York Times*, November 13, 2018, A17.

[15] Louis Jacobson, "Were There No Hearings on Bipartisan Criminal Justice Bill?" *PolitiFact*, November 20, 2018, https://www.politifact.com/factchecks/2018/nov/20/tom-cotton/were-there-no-hearings-bipartisan-criminal-justice/.

[16] Charles Babington, "In Bipartisan Move, Congress Passes the Largest Conservation Bill in a Decade," *Trust Magazine*, October 11, 2019, https://www.pewtrusts.org/en/trust/archive/fall-2019/in-bipartisan-move-congress-passes-the-largest-conservation-bill-in-a-decade.

[17] Coral Davenport, "Senate Passes Bill Creating Huge Tracts of Protected Lands," *New York Times*, February 13, 2019, A14.

[18] "Summary of the Activities of the Committee on Transportation and Infrastructure for the 116th Congress," Committee on Transportation and Infrastructure, U.S. House of Representatives, H. Rpt. 116-717, 116th Congress, 2nd session, January 2, 2021.

The development of these bills illustrates an important dynamic of legislating in the contemporary Congress: committees, and/or key members thereof, may be deeply involved in the development of legislation, even if the later stages of the process—like in the case of the FIRST STEP Act—are less "orthodox." In addition, committee deliberation may or may not translate into a bipartisan product, as we saw with the development stage of the House farm bill in 2018. Finally, given the frequency with which issues end up gridlocked in the contemporary Congress (Binder 2021), meaningful committee involvement may extend over multiple congresses. Finally, the heavy use of omnibus legislating—explored in more detail in the next section—complicates our understanding of committee consideration and underscores the value in thinking about bill development and bill management separately.

The Role of Omnibus Legislating

To consider unorthodox legislating at the bill management stage, let us consider one common approach to bill passage in the contemporary Congress, especially in the appropriations context: the use of omnibus legislating. When members choose to package together a set of bills that they could consider separately, they do so under the logic that one bill may be easier to pass than several. Introducing more policy dimensions into a bill may garner it support from more different groups of members. In the Senate, building a single coalition rather than repeated, distinct ones may be a particularly attractive to deal with the 60-vote threshold implied by the filibuster (Black 1958; Krutz 2001; Hanson 2014; Riker 1982).

Indeed, when we examine the Trump administration, we see heavy use of omnibus legislating in both the appropriations process and the passage of the annual defense policy bill, the National Defense Authorization Act (NDAA). Importantly, the cores of these bills were generally worked on at length by their respective committees of jurisdiction. Of the individual appropriations bills for the first three fiscal years of the Trump administration (fiscal years 2018, 2019, and 2020), approximately 70 percent were reported out of subcommittees of the Appropriations Committees and more than 80 percent were reported out of the full committees. Fiscal year 2021, meanwhile, proceeded quite differently; individual bill markups in the Senate were delayed by a combination of COVID-19—both disruptions caused by reduced congressional activity overall and disagreements over including additional pandemic relief in the spending bills themselves—and the fact that, following the murder of George Floyd, Democrats were keen to include funding for racial justice initiatives generally opposed by Republicans.[19] Notably, no standalone appropriations bills were passed by the Senate before the October 1 deadline during the four years of the Trump administration. The closest the Senate came was in 2018, when it took up three separate "minibus" packages, covering nine of the 12 appropriations bills between them. The House also approved two of these measures, meaning that five bills were complete by October 1 and making the year the most productive one for appropriations in more than two decades.[20] Work on the other seven bills remained unfinished into December, when President Trump refused to sign a temporary spending measure that did not contain funding for a border wall, parts of the federal government were thrust into what became a record length lapse in operations that lasted into 2019.[21]

This experience illustrates both the promise and pitfalls of unorthodox legislating in the form of omnibus bills. Combining multiple bills together can give the package a "must pass" status, forcing members to accept individual provisions they might otherwise oppose because the consequences of not acting—a partial government shutdown—are so significant. But that strategy is not foolproof and if it fails, the results are painful.

Examining the defense policy bills passed during the Trump administration provides another angle on what omnibus legislating can accomplish in the contemporary Congress: the use of large bills as vehicles to carry other pieces of legislation—some small, some large—to passage. The defense legislation itself still tends to move through the House and Senate in an "orthodox way," with markups in subcommittee, full committee, floor consideration with amendment opportunities, and a conference committee to iron out differences between the chambers' bills (Heitshusen and McGarry 2021).

But what about the other components of the bill, outside its core authorizing mission, that get incorporated into it? The calendar year 2017 NDAA, for example, included legislation meant to prevent improper use of government purchase and travel cards; a standalone version of the bill had

---

[19] Niv Elis, "Fights Over Police Reform, COVID-19 Delay Senate Appropriations Markups," *The Hill*, June 17, 2020; Caitlin Emma, "Senate Spending Markups Paused Amid Disputes over Pandemic Aid, Police Reform," *POLITICO Pro*, June 17, 2020.

[20] Molly E. Reynolds and Peter Hanson, "There Might Not Be a Government Shutdown This Year," *Washington Post*, September 19, 2018.

[21] Andrew Restuccia, Burgess Everett, and Heather Caygle, "Longest Shutdown in History Ends After Trump Relents on Wall," *Politico*, January 25, 2019.

been introduced, marked up by the Committee on Homeland Security and Governmental Affairs, and passed by unanimous consent in the Senate.[22] The calendar 2018 defense policy bill, meanwhile, contained reforms to the government entity, known as the Committee on Foreign Investment in the United States, that reviews for national security concerns certain transactions made by foreign companies and persons. These changes were contained in the Foreign Investment Risk Review Modernization Act, which was marked up in both the House (by the House Financial Services Committee) and the Senate (by the Senate Banking, Housing, and Urban Affairs Committee). The House also debated and passed its standalone version of the bill.[23] A second measure contained in the calendar 2018 NDAA was the Export Control Reform Act, which had been marked up in the House and expanded executive authority to enforce export controls.[24]

The calendar 2019 NDAA, moreover, was especially ripe with additional provisions, on subjects including sanctions against North Korea, Syria, and foreign opioid traffickers and restrictions on the federal government's ability to examine job applicants' criminal histories. These measures had also, in various ways, been introduced and considered in committee in at least one chamber.[25] A major policy change providing up to twelve weeks of paid parental leave for federal employees also made into the final legislation; while it was not considered separately in either chamber, it was also not a new policy idea.[26]

The inclusion of these provisions in the NDAA and other large pieces of legislation complicates the notion of "unorthodox legislating" in the contemporary Congress. Many of the measures incorporated into, for example, the NDAA received some "orthodox" consideration during their individual development stage; it was only at the bill management or passage stage where the process became more unconventional. The question of whether following "regular order" is more important at some stages of the legislative process than others is a normative one, but the Trump era suggests that it is one that the Congress itself might appropriately consider. Examining

---

[22] S. 1099, 115th Congress, 1st session.

[23] H.R. 5841, 115th Congress, 2nd session; S. 2098, 115th Congress, 2nd session. See also Stephanie Zable, "The Foreign Investment Risk Review Modernization Act of 2018," *Lawfare*, August 2, 2018, https://www.lawfareblog.com/foreign-investment-risk-review-modernization-act-2018.

[24] H.R. 5040, 115th Congress, 2nd session.

[25] See H.R. 31, 116th Congress, 2nd session; S. 1591, 115th Congress, 2nd session; S. 1044, 116th Congress, 2nd session; H.R. 1076, 116th Congress, 1st session.

[26] Connor O'Brien, "Lawmakers Land 'Tentative Agreement' to Include Federal Worker Paid Leave in Final Defense Bill," *Politico,* December 7, 2019.

only conventional bill passage also, importantly, has implications for how observers of Congress assess which legislators are the most successful or effective. Empirical work on the inclusion of one piece of bill text into another suggests that examining only bill sponsorship undervalues the contributions of women and Black members of Congress to the legislative process (Eatough and Preece 2021).

Expedited Procedures in the Senate During the Trump Years

When the 115th Congress convened in January 2017, it marked the first period of unified Republican control in a decade, since Democrats had assumed control of the House and Senate in the 2006 midterms. The value of having majorities in both chambers and a same party president in the White House is limited, by the filibuster in the Senate; without a filibuster-proof majority of at least 60 votes—which Republicans did not have—the majority party is forced to work with the minority party on most legislation. A notable exception to this requirement are the bills that are eligible for consideration under expedited procedures in the Senate—procedures that were used heavily during the Trump administration.

The first type of expedited procedures that were consequential for the Senate during the Trump administration were the budget reconciliation rules. An optional component of the annual congressional budget process, reconciliation limits debate on certain legislation affecting revenue, mandatory spending (such as entitlement programs), and the debt limit to 20 hours, making it a powerful, filibuster-proof tool. Importantly, several key elements of congressional Republicans' agenda, including repealing the Affordable Care Act and cutting taxes, were potentially or definitively in bounds for using the reconciliation process.

By itself, using reconciliation should not necessarily be considered "unorthodox;" as Figure 4.1 illustrates, the procedures have been used regularly, to make major policy changes, since the 1980s (Reynolds 2017). But what *was* unorthodox about Republicans' deployment of the process in 2017 was the number of times they turned to the process (Reynolds 2021). Under current interpretations of the Senate's rules and precedents, the chamber is limited in the number of reconciliation bills that each iteration of the budget resolution can generate. More specifically, each iteration of the budget resolution

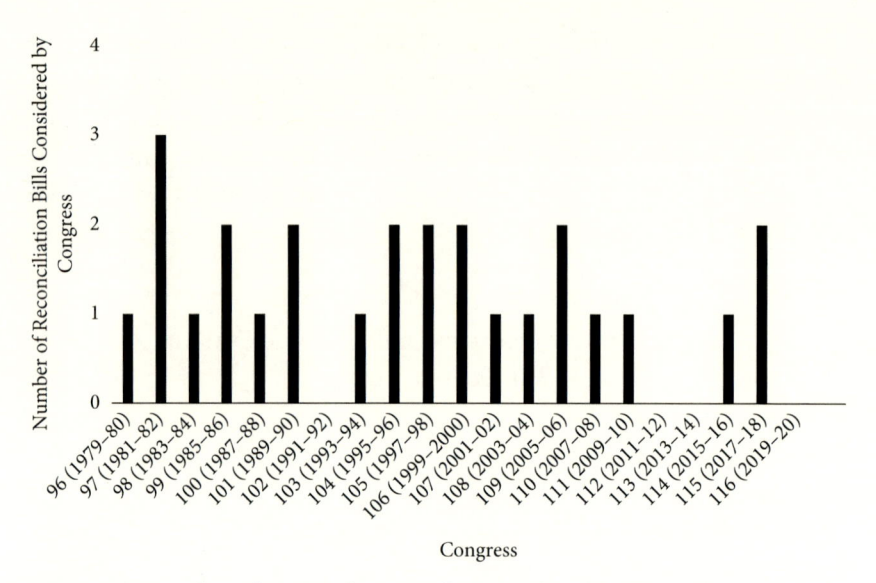

Figure 4.1 Number of Reconciliation Bills Considered by Congress, 1981–2020[a]

Note: Graph includes bills considered by Congress but vetoed by the president in the 104th, 106th (two bills), and 114th Congresses.

[a]Data from table 2 in Heniff (2022).

may spawn up to three reconciliation measures: one addressing revenue, one addressing spending, and one addressing the debt limit. If a given reconciliation bill touches two, or all three, of these elements, that "counts" as the permissible use of reconciliation for that purpose for that budget resolution.[27]

Notably, the federal fiscal year—which begins on October 1 of each calendar year—does not align perfectly with the timing of congressional sessions. The beginning of a new Congress in January of an odd-numbered year, then, falls in the middle of a fiscal year already in progress. Under the terms of

---

[27] When Republicans were deploying reconciliation in 2017, this limit was often described publicly as three bills per *fiscal year,* but some budget experts argued that the limit actually applied to each *budget resolution*; as a result, the argument went, if Congress chose to revise the budget resolution for a given fiscal year, that revision could *also* generate up to three reconciliation bills. (See Bill Dauster and Laura Dove, interview with Dean Hingson, *14th and G,* podcast audio, January 6, 2021, https://mehlmancastagnetti.com/podcast/14th-g-everything-you-ever-wanted-to-know-about-budget-reconciliation-but-were-too-afraid-to-ask/). In June 2021, the Senate Parliamentarian issued guidance confirming this interpretation. (See Paul M. Krawzak, "Parliamentarian Guidance Deals Blow to Reconciliation Strategy," *Roll Call,* June 2, 2021). While this revision-based strategy has yet to be used as of this writing, the Parliamentarian's guidance more formally opens the door for even more unorthodox uses of the procedures in the future.

the Congressional Budget Act, the previous Congress should have completed work on the budget resolution for the extant fiscal year—but if it did not, there is nothing preventing the *new* Congress from taking up that measure and, if it chooses to do so, including reconciliation instructions therein.

Republicans had originally entertained this idea of using reconciliation twice in one calendar year at the start of a new administration in 2013, but they did not find themselves in a position to actually do so until 2017. Shortly after the start of the new Congress in January, House Republicans took the first procedural steps necessary to use reconciliation for a repeal and replace bill.[28] The effort ultimately failed in the Senate—in dramatic fashion—in July,[29] but because of the unorthodox use of the extant fiscal year's budget resolution for their first attempt, Republicans were able to adopt a second resolution during calendar 2017. That measure included a set of reconciliation instructions that generated the Tax Cuts and Jobs Act, enacted in December and considered to be the most significant legislative achievement of Trump's first year in office.[30]

Reconciliation was not the only expedited procedure of which the Senate made heavy use during the Trump administration. Also occupying a sizable share of the Senate's agenda in 2017 were resolutions under the Congressional Review Act (CRA). Of the 22 legislative votes on which *Congressional Quarterly* coded President Trump as having taken a position in 2017, more than half involved CRA resolutions.[31] Initially enacted in 1996, the CRA allows Congress to overturn regulations promulgated by the executive within a specific window immediately following their completion; to ease this process, the law provides for resolutions of disapproval to be considered under expedited procedures, preventing their filibuster in the Senate (Carey and Davis 2021). Because a measure overturning a newly finalized rule must be either signed by the president or garner veto-proof majorities in the House and Senate, the CRA is most powerful as a tool to actually overturn regulations when three conditions are satisfied: it is the start of a new administration; there has been partisan change at the White House;

[28] Lindsey McPherson, "Mixed Bag of Republicans Vote Against Obamacare Repeal Vehicle," *Roll Call*, January 13, 2017.

[29] Robert Pear and Thomas Kaplan, "G.O.P. in Senate Trims Ambitions to Start Voting," *New York Times*, July 28, 2017, A1.

[30] Thomas Kaplan and Alan Rappeport, "Senate Overcomes Hiccups to Advance Tax Overhaul in 51–48 Vote," *New York Times*, December 20, 2017, A15.

[31] "He Divided, But Conquered," in *CQ Almanac 2017* (Thousand Oaks, CA: CQ Press, 2018), B2–B-6.

and there is unified party control of the White House, House, and Senate. Indeed, prior to 2017, the only successful use of the CRA was in 2001, at the start of the first period of unified party control since the law's enactment (Carey and Davis 2021).

Republicans, then, found themselves in 2017 with the ideal conditions for consequential use of the CRA in place; given the party's general support for less government regulation, they were also largely unconcerned with a provision of the CRA that limits additional regulatory activity that is "substantially the same" as the overturned rule (Carey and Davis 2021). Regulations successfully overturned in 2017 addressed topics such as stream protection, background checks for gun purchases, teacher preparation standards, state K–12 accountability standards, federal acquisition policies, requirements related to drug testing as a condition of unemployment benefits, Alaska wildlife protections, workplace injury reporting, Federal Communications Commission privacy standards, funding for family planning services, and pension requirements (Carey and Davis 2021). Figure 4.2, which includes CRA resolutions introduced in both the House and Senate, illustrates the

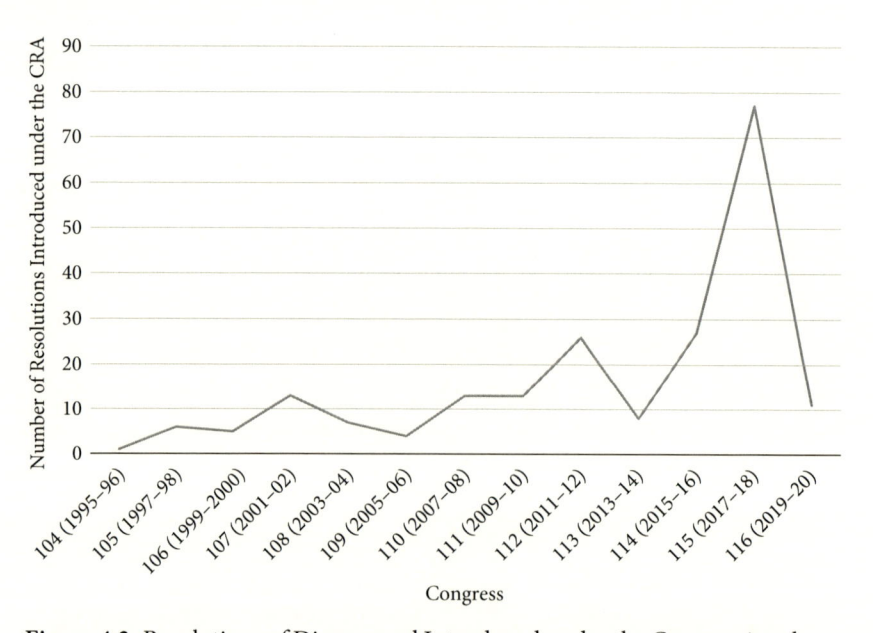

Congress

Figure 4.2 Resolutions of Disapproval Introduced under the Congressional Review Act in the House and Senate, 104th to 116th Congresses, 1995–2020[a]

[a]Data drawn from figure 2 in Bridget C. E. Dooling, Daniel Pérez, and Steven J. Balla, "Where Are the Congressional Review Act Disapprovals?" *The Brookings Institution*, March 2021 https://www.brookings.edu/research/where-are-the-congressional-review-act-disapprovals/>.

spike in the use of this tool during especially the first two years of the Trump administration.

It wasn't just the frequency of successful CRA resolutions that represented a further evolution of this unorthodox tactic. The Trump era also saw the first use of the CRA to overturn "guidance" issued by an agency. What is considered a "rule" under the scope of the CRA includes some material developed by agencies outside of the notice-and-comment rulemaking process. Even though some of these actions are subject to the CRA, agencies do not always submit them to Congress as the CRA requires. As a result, it can be unclear exactly when the "clock starts"—that is, when the period under which expedited procedures to overturn the rule are available begins. Congress has developed an ad hoc workaround for this that relies on opinions from the Government Accountability Office, with the date that GAO issues its ruling as the start of the period in which expedited procedures are available (Cross 2021). The first use of this alternative approach to designating the start of the disapproval period happened in 2018 when a resolution overturning guidance issued by the Consumer Financial Protection Bureau originally issued five years earlier, in 2013, was signed into law.[32] While this resolution was the only one addressed during the Trump administration after such an unusually long period, it serves as a proof of concept for potential expansive use in the future.[33]

Expedited procedures also played a significant role in messaging efforts in the Senate—that is, legislative measures that were expected to fail to be signed into law—during the Trump administration. Introductions of CRA resolutions targeting agency actions at odds with a party's priorities was not novel (Balla, Dooling, and Perez 2023). But Senate Democrats did make regular use of the procedures for that purpose, especially in the run-up to the 2018 midterms, when they used the CRA to force votes on issues they thought would be politically popular with voters.[34] In May, for example, they brought a CRA resolution to the floor related to internet regulation that passed the Senate before languishing in the House.[35] In October, meanwhile,

---

[32] S. J. Res. 57, 115th Congress.

[33] Susan E. Dudley, "We Haven't Seen the Last of the CRA Yet," *Forbes Policy*, October 13, 2017, https://www.forbes.com/sites/susandudley/2017/10/31/we-havent-seen-the-last-of-the-cra-yet/?sh=434923d82680.

[34] In addition to protecting the resolution from a filibuster, the CRA's expedited procedures and related Senate precedents make it easier for members of the minority party to force at least a procedural vote related to a measure than when the Senate is operating under its regular rules.

[35] S. J. Res. 52, 115th Congress.

they engineered ultimately unsuccessful vote to overturn a rule expanding access to short-term health insurance policies that would not comply with consumer protections required by the Affordable Care Act.[36] A few months before the 2020 presidential election, they deployed this strategy again, successfully forcing a successful vote on a resolution to overturn a rule making it difficult for defrauded borrowers from accessing student loan forgiveness.[37]

The CRA is not only the only statute that provides for expedited procedures designed to ease Congress's ability to push back against the president, and, indeed, unconventional legislating using expedited procedures was also an important way for groups of senators—in both parties—to signal their disapproval with certain exercises of executive power by President Trump. A provision of the Arms Export Control Act, for example, allows for a joint resolution of disapproval in response to executive branch proposals to sell weapons and other military equipment to other countries. Three separate times in 2019, the Senate—and House—approved resolutions that would prevent the Trump administration from selling arms, twice to Saudi Arabia and once to the United Arab Emirates. All three resolutions were vetoed by Trump without sufficient support in the Senate to override the veto.[38] Several other attempts to use the procedures, including against Bahrain and Qatar in 2019, failed in the Senate.[39]

The War Powers Resolution, first passed in 1973 and amended in 1983, similarly provides for expedited procedures that the Senate can use to consider a joint resolution directing the president to terminate the use of American forces in a specific conflict (Weed 2019). In 2018 and 2019, a bipartisan group of senators led by Senators Bernie Sanders (I-Vermont), Chris Murphy (D-Connecticut), and Mike Lee (R-Utah) forced a series of votes on ending US involvement in the Saudi-led war in Yemen; one of these, in 2019, was approved by both the Senate and the House before being vetoed by the president.[40] In 2020, a coalition of Republican and Democratic senators— Senators Lee, Tim Kaine (D-Virginia), Richard Durbin (D-Illinois), and Rand Paul (R-Kentucky)—led a similar effort regarding hostilities in Iran,

---

[36] Katie Keith, "Senate Democrats to Force Vote on Short-Term Plan Rule, Scheduled HealthCare. gov Maintenance," *Health Affairs*, October 10, 2018.

[37] H. J. Res. 76, 116th Congress.

[38] "Vetoes by President Donald J. Trump," https://www.senate.gov/legislative/vetoes/Trum pDJ.htm.

[39] Marianne Levine, "Senate Fails to Block Arms Sales to Bahrain and Qatar," *Politico,* June 13, 2019.

[40] Vote #58, 115th Congress, 2nd session; vote #250, 115th Congress, 2nd session; vote #48, 116th Congress, 1st session.

which also ended with a presidential veto.[41] While none of these votes ultimately prevented the Trump administration from continuing US involvement in the covered conflicts, the availability of unconventional procedures allowed senators from both parties to use the Senate floor to force their colleagues to go on record on administration policies.

A final notable use of expedited procedures to signal, via the Senate floor, opposition to a presidential initiative involved two votes in 2019 to overturn Trump's declaration of a national emergency related to immigration. The emergency declaration, which the president believed made it possible for him to redirect existing resources for the construction of a border wall in the southwestern United States, was a response to a deal to reopen parts of the federal government after a record-length shutdown in 2018 and 2019; Trump had refused to sign a temporary spending measure preventing the shutdown because it did not include funding for barrier.[42] The National Emergencies Act does provide for both the president's authority to declare emergencies and expedited procedures for considering joint resolutions to terminate them (Greene 2020). The Senate voted twice, once in March and once in October, with both resolutions garnering notable levels support from Republicans, especially for measures that were explicitly aimed at overturning a signature policy priority of a same party president, receiving 12 and 11 GOP votes, respectively.[43]

Disruption?

The use of expedited procedures as a position-taking device—especially on the votes to overturn the declaration of a national emergency related to the policy objective most important to president personally—by some members of Trump's own party is perhaps the most prominent example of how the president himself drove an evolution on unorthodox legislating during his time in office. Prior to the Trump administration, many recent occasions

[41] S. J. Res. 68, 116th Congress, 2nd session.

[42] Nicholas Fandos, Sheryl Gay Stolberg, and Peter Baker, "Shutdown Ends With No Funding for Wall," *New York Times*, January 26, 2019, A1; Kelsey Snell and Jessica Taylor, "Trump to Declare National Emergency As Well As Sign Spending Bill, White House Says," *NPR*, February 14, 2019 https://www.npr.org/2019/02/14/694647564/congress-sprints-to-pass-border-security-package-with-trumps-support-unclear; Charlie Savage, "How Trump Might Claim Emergency To Get Wall," *New York Times*, January 8, 2019, A16.

[43] Vote #49, 116th Congress, 1st session, March 14, 2019; Vote #302, 116th Congress, 1st session, September 25, 2019.

on which expedited procedures were used for similar position-taking purposes involved members of the out party using the Senate floor to take stands against presidential initiatives (Reynolds 2017). At other points, the disruption was less the result of the unorthodox legislating itself and more the consequence of Trump's reaction to an increasingly ordinary congressional process. Perhaps the most consequential example of this occurred in late 2018 when his unwillingness to sign a spending bill that did not contain funding for a border wall, ushering in a record-length partial government shutdown. But, at other points, Trump's periodic conflict with his own party's congressional leadership created unexpected roadblocks in the kind of high-stakes legislative negotiations that have become commonplace. In September 2017, for example, during deliberations over a proposal to raise the debt limit and, separately, to avoid an earlier government shutdown, Trump agreed to the plan favored by Democratic congressional leaders after Speaker of the House Paul Ryan (R-Wisconsin) had called it "ridiculous and disgraceful" (Baker and Glasser 2022, 131).

Indeed, most of the other trends discussed here were not new during the Trump years. Reconciliation, for example, has been a major vehicle for achieving policy changes that benefit the Senate's majority party since the 1980s. The reliance on omnibus legislating, especially in the appropriations process, also stretches back several decades; the last fiscal year that did not feature an omnibus appropriations bill or full year continuing resolution was 2006, during the George W. Bush administration (Saturno and Tollestrup 2016). The changing use of committee deliberation is, similarly, a longstanding trend.

These unorthodox legislating tactics that continued apace should be thought of as adaptations to the realities of these contemporary legislative process; using budget reconciliation to accomplish major partisan policy goals, for example, is, in part, the product of highly polarized parties and reluctance on the part of the minority party to be seen as helping the majority party achieve legislative wins. But adapting can be a double-edged sword. Changes can help the institution fulfill its basic responsibilities, like keeping government activities funded. But they can also undermine various other features of the institution, like the quality of deliberation or the incentives of committees to invest in labor-intensive legislative work. While Trump may not have driven this evolution during his term, his presence likely exacerbated it, as a deeply unpopular president serving amidst high levels of polarization and narrow congressional majorities.

References

Baker, Peter, and Susan Glasser. 2022. *The Divider: Trump in the White House, 2017–2021*. New York: Doubleday.

Balla, Steven J., Bridget C. E. Dooling, and Daniel R. Perez. 2023. "Beyond Republicans and the Disapproval of Regulations: A New Empirical Approach to the Congressional Review Act." *Journal of Empirical Legal Studies*, 20(2): 472–484.

Binder, Sarah A. 2021. "The Struggle to Legislate in Polarized Times." In *Congress Reconsidered*, 12th ed., Lawrence C. Dodd and Bruce I. Oppenheimer, eds. Washington, DC: CQ Press, 251–287.

Black, Duncan. 1958. *The Theory of Commitees and Elections*. New York: Cambridge Unversity Press.

Carey, Maeve P., and Christopher M. Davis. 2021. "The Congressional Review Act (CRA): Frequently Asked Questions." Washington, DC: Congressional Research Service.

Cross, Jesse M. 2021. *Technical Reform of the Congressional Review Ac*t. Report to the Admin. Conf. of the U.S.

Curry, James M., and Frances E. Lee. 2020. *The Limits of Party: Congress and Lawmaking in a Polarized Era*. Chicago: University of Chicago Press.

Eatough, Mandi, and Jessica Preece. 2021. "Crediting Invisible Work (Horses): Congress and the Lawmaking Productivity Metric." Working Paper.

Gelman, Jeremy. 2020. *Losing to Win: Why Congressional Majorities Play Politics Instead of Make Laws*. Ann Arbor: University of Michigan Press.

Greene, Michael. 2020. *National Emergencies Act: Expedited Procedures in the House and Senate*. Washington, DC: Congressional Research Service.

Haberman, Maggie. 2022. *Confidence Man: The Making of Donald Trump and the Breaking of America*. New York: Penguin Press.

Hanson, Peter. 2014. *Too Weak to Govern: Majority Party Power and Appropriations in the U.S. Congress*. New York: Cambridge University Press.

Heitshusen, Valerie, and Brendan W. McGarry. 2021. *Defense Primer: The NDAA Process*. Washington, DC: Congressional Research Service.

Heniff, Bill Jr. 2022. *The Budget Reconciliation Process: The Senate's 'Byrd Rule'*. Washington, DC: Congressional Research Service.

Krutz, Glen. 2001. *Hitching a Ride: Omnibus Legislating in the U.S. Congress*. Columbus: Ohio State University Press.

Lewallen, Jonathan. 2020. *Committees and the Decline of Lawmaking in Congress*. Ann Arbor: University of Michigan Press.

Oleszek, Walter. 2020. *The 'Regular Order': A Perspective*. Washington, DC: Congressional Research Service.

Reynolds, Molly E. 2017. *Exceptions to the Rule: The Politics of Filibuster Limitations in the U.S. Senate*. Washington, DC: Brookings Institution Press.

Reynolds, Molly E. 2021. "The Politics of the Budget and Appropriations Process in a Polarized Congress." In *Congress Reconsidered*, 12th ed., Lawrence C. Dodd and Bruce I. Oppenheimer, eds. Washington, DC: CQ Press, 349–374.

Riker, William H. 1982. *Liberalism Against Populism: A Confrontation Between the Theory of Democracy and the Theory of Social Choice*. San Francisco: W. H. Freeman and Company.

Saturno, James, and Jessica Tollestrup. 2016. *Omnibus Appropriations Acts: Overview of Recent Practices*. Washington, DC: Congressional Research Service.

Sinclair, Barbara. 1997. *Unorthodox Lawmaking: New Legislative Processes in the U.S. Congress*, 1st ed. Washington, DC: CQ Press.

Weed, Matthew C. 2019. *The War Powers Resolution: Concepts and Practice*. Washington, DC: Congressional Research Service.

5

High Stakes Negotiation

Reaching Agreement on Pandemic Aid in 2020

Frances Lee, Bettina Poirier, and Christopher Bertram

> If I were writing your headline I'd say the Senate has pivoted from one of the most contentious, partisan periods in the nation's history to passing this rescue package (unanimously) all in one quarter of this year. . . . [It] says a lot about the United States Senate as an institution, our willingness to put aside our differences, to do something really significant for the country.[*]
>
> —Senate Republican Leader Mitch McConnell to reporters after the passage of the CARES Act, March 27, 2020[1]

> We have our differences, but we also know what is important to us. And America's families are important to us.
>
> —Speaker Nancy Pelosi at a photo opportunity marking the enrollment of the CARES Act, with Republican Leader Kevin McCarthy and other members[2]

Introduction

The 2020 coronavirus pandemic stands at the forefront of the many disruptions to American government and politics during the Trump

---

[*] For excellent research assistance, we are grateful to James A. Campbell III. For comments, we thank Sarah Binder, Alison Craig, Ben Cook, Jim Curry, Larry Evans, Matt Green, Brian Mandell, Jane Mansbridge, Eric Schickler, and Rob Oldham, as well as our anonymous reviewers and editor, Sean Theriault

[1] Ledyard King, Christal Hayes, and Courtney Subramanian, "Stimulus Deal Brings Congress Together," *USA Today*, March 27, 2020, A2.

[2] Press Release, "Pelosi Remarks at Bill Enrollment Photo Opportunity for the CARES Act," March 27, 2020, https://www.speaker.gov/newsroom/32720.

Frances Lee, Bettina Poirier, and Christopher Bertram, *High Stakes Negotiation* In: *Disruption?*
Edited by: Sean M. Theriault, Oxford University Press. © Oxford University Press 2024.
DOI: 10.1093/oso/9780197767832.003.0006

presidency. The COVID crisis transformed the national governing agenda as the global economy came to a near halt, and US unemployment spiked to levels not seen since the Great Depression. At the time the pandemic was declared, it was certainly an open question whether the United States would be able to marshal an effective response, given the country's intense partisan polarization. Prior to the pandemic, political commentators often remarked that the country had been fortunate not to have faced a major crisis during the Trump presidency. When the country's luck ran out in early 2020, no one could have been confident that Congress and the president would come together to enact legislation sufficient to the scale of the problem.[3] Nevertheless, over the course of 2020, Congress marshaled by far the largest response to any domestic policy crisis in American history. In fact, the only policy mobilizations comparable to the COVID response occurred in wartime. Expenditures for pandemic aid roughly match what the United States spent on war production in 1943 (Romer 2021).

These sweeping aid packages were enacted, although Congress and the president faced a political context remarkably unsuited to major policy action. Party control of national government was as fragmented as is institutionally possible. President Trump faced a House of Representatives controlled by Democrats. Different parties controlled the House and Senate. Party polarization exceeded levels not seen for a century (McCarty 2021), and Republicans and Democrats widely diverged in their preferred policy responses to the pandemic. Trust and good will among the players was in short supply. President Trump's first impeachment trial had just concluded on February 5, 2020. It was a presidential election year, with political leaders preoccupied with winning political advantage in what was expected to be a highly competitive contest. Party control of the House and Senate was in play looking toward the November elections. It is difficult to imagine political circumstances less hospitable to bold bipartisan policymaking than those prevailing throughout 2020. In the assessment of Gadarian, Goodman and Pepinsky (2022, 20), a whole host of "preexisting conditions . . . [had] primed the United States for a bad pandemic."

Despite the manifold challenges, Congress passed five major pandemic aid enactments in 2020, totaling more than $3.5 trillion. In inflation-adjusted

---

[3] See, for example, Brian Klaas, "Trump Has Been Incredibly Lucky. But His Luck—And Ours—Might Be Running Out," *Washington Post*, July 23, 2019, https://www.washingtonpost.com/opinions/2019/07/23/trump-has-been-incredibly-lucky-his-luck-ours-might-be-running-out/.

terms, Congress spent much more on COVID aid than in the 2009 stimulus and the New Deal combined.

The goal of this chapter is to better understand how Congress succeeded in enacting a series of sweeping pandemic assistance packages amid such a challenging political context. To that end, we examine the success of these enactments through a negotiation lens. We apply concepts and insights from the literature on negotiation (e.g., Fisher et al. 2011; Lax and Sebenius 2006; Mansbridge and Martin 2016) to examine how policymakers "got to yes" on 2020's two largest COVID aid packages, the Coronavirus Aid, Relief, and Economic Security (CARES) Act passed in March and the Consolidated Appropriations Act in December, often referred to as the "Coronabus." Doing so yields insights into congressional policymaking amidst crisis, as well as perspective on how the Senate—and Congress generally—maintained its relevance as a deliberative body amidst the disruptions of the Trump presidency and an increasingly nationalized and president-centered politics (Hopkins 2018; Jacobson 2021).

We begin by examining the scope of the pandemic aid legislation in 2020 and its societal and economic impact. We next turn to the specific challenges Congress faced in negotiating agreement on the legislation. Then we employ a series of concepts from the negotiation literature to shed light on the factors that enabled legislators to pass a set of unprecedentedly vast enactments. We conclude with reflections on the legislation's significance for Congress's role in national politics during and following the Trump presidency.

The Scope of the COVID Response

No country had a more forceful fiscal response to the pandemic than the United States. By the end of 2020, it had deployed extra public spending worth 18 percent of its gross domestic product as compared to 10 percent in Germany and less in France, Italy, and Spain.[4] The $3.5 trillion in pandemic aid in 2020 was more than four times the size of the historic 2009 stimulus package and exceeded three quarters of total federal expenditures in FY 2019.

Congress passed five major COVID aid packages in 2020; three passed in March, one in April, and one in December (see Table 5.1). None of these acts

---

[4] International Monetary Fund, "Fiscal Monitor: A Fair Shot," April 2021, https://www.imf.org/en/Publications/FM/Issues/2021/03/29/fiscal-monitor-april-2021#Full%20Report, Figure 1.710.

Table 5.1 Major COVID Aid Enactments of 2020.

Enactment	Enacted	Votes	Amount
Coronavirus Preparedness and Response Act (HR 6074) Provided funding for public health, the development of vaccines and treatments, and COVID testing.	March 6	House: 415–2 Senate: 96–1	$8.3 billion
Families First Coronavirus Response Supplemental Appropriations Act (HR 2601) Provided free COVID testing, paid sick and family medical leave for workers, unemployment benefits, and increased food stamps.	March 18	House: 363–40 Senate: 90–8	$100 billion
Coronavirus Aid, Relief, and Economic Security Act (HR 748) To individuals, it provided direct cash payments, unemployment benefits, student loan deferrals, child tax credits, and expanded subsidies for health insurance. To large and small corporations, it granted generous (often forgivable) loans. For state and local governments, it boosted funding for Medicaid, transit, child care, and education, among others. It also included grants to a diverse range of entities, including hospitals, higher education, farmers, housing, defense, and the postal service, among many others.	March 27	House: voice Senate: 96–0	$2.2 trillion
Paycheck Protection Program and Health Care Enhancement Act (HR 266) Replenished the small business lending program (PPP) and provided more funding for hospitals and testing	April 24	House: 388–5, 1 present Senate: voice	$484 billion
Consolidated Appropriations Act (HR 133) Provided a second round of direct payments for individuals, extended unemployment benefits, replenished PPP funds, and a host of grants for varied purposes, including education, food aid, child care, and more.	December 27	House: 359–53* Senate: 92–6	$900 billion

* The December omnibus package came to the House floor under a special rule (H. Rept. 116-679) that divided the question presented to the House of Representatives so that groups of members could register their stances on different parts of the bill separately. In the first vote (#250) the House approved (by a vote of 327 to 85) the Defense; Commerce, Justice, Science; Homeland Security; and Financial Services parts of the omnibus. In the second vote (#251), the House approved (by a vote of 359-53) the COVID relief package and eight other spending bills. The special rule deemed the omnibus bill to have passed once the two parts received a majority vote.

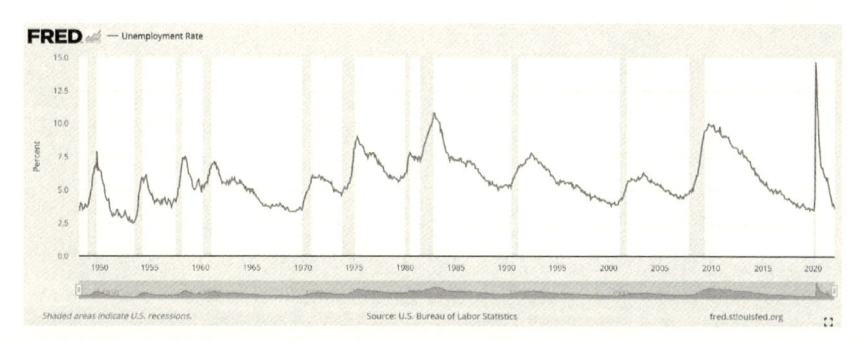

Figure 5.1 US Unemployment Rate, 1948–2022

Note: The unemployment rate represents the number of unemployed as a percentage of the labor force. Labor force data are restricted to people 16 years of age and older, who currently reside in 1 of the 50 states or the District of Columbia, who do not reside in institutions (e.g., penal and mental facilities, homes for the aged), and who are not on active duty in the Armed Forces. This rate is also defined as the U-3 measure of labor underutilization.

Source: U.S. Bureau of Labor Statistics, retrieved from FRED, Federal Reserve Bank of St. Louis; https://fred.stlouisfed.org/series/UNRATE.

had significant opposition on final passage, and several passed on voice vote or unanimous consent. The two largest enactments were, by far, the $2.2 trillion CARES Act approved in March, and the $900 billion in pandemic aid included in the December Coronabus.

All this spending made a big difference in the lives of Americans. During the height of the pandemic recession, more than 22 million Americans lost their jobs.[5] The national unemployment rate since 1948 displays the extraordinary spike in unemployment, which during the pandemic lacked precedent across the postwar period (see Figure 5.1). Despite this dire employment situation, the poverty rate did not rise (Han, Meyer, and Sullivan 2021). In fact, poverty during 2020 continued its post-2011 decline and fell lower than it had been in 2019 (see Figure 5.2). Reductions in hardship following each of the COVID-aid enactments were greatest among low-income households (Cooney and Shaefer 2021).

Rather than falling, personal disposable income surged during the pandemic. The CARES Act provided for direct payments of $1,200 per adult and $500 per qualifying child for individuals earning less than $75,000 per year, amounting to $3,400 for a family of four. The December Coronabus added another $600 per eligible adult and $600 for each qualifying child. Under

---

[5] Bureau of Labor Statistics, "COVID-19 Ends Longest Employment Recovery and Expansion in CES History, Causing Unprecedented Job Losses in 2020," *Monthly Labor Review*, June 2021, https://www.bls.gov/opub/mlr/2021/article/covid-19-ends-longest-employment-expansion-in-ces-history.htm.

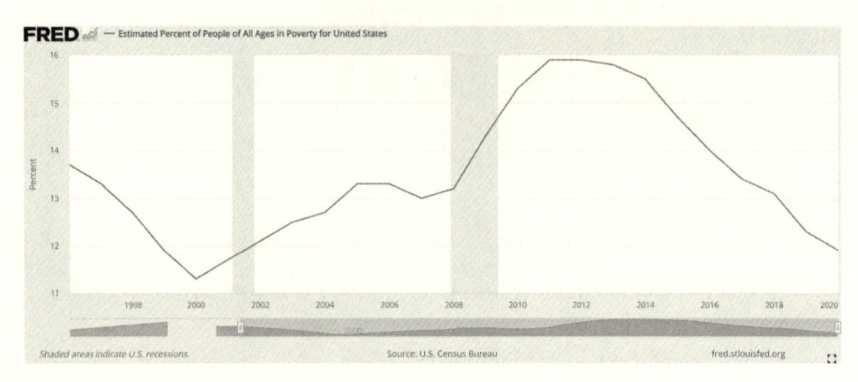

Figure 5.2 Estimated Percent of the US Population in Poverty.

Note: These estimates are derived from the Small Area Income and Poverty Estimates (SAIPE) program.

Source: U.S. Census Bureau, retrieved from FRED, Federal Reserve Bank of St. Louis, https://fred.stl ouisfed.org/series/PPAAUS00000A156NCEN.

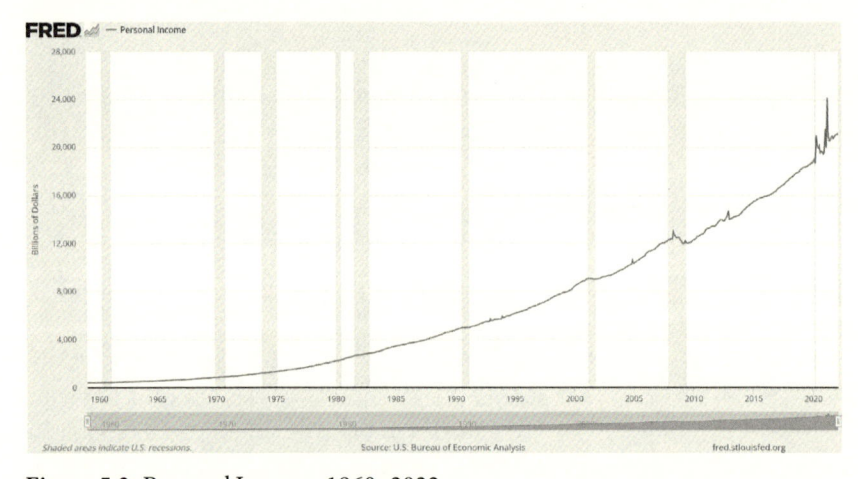

Figure 5.3 Personal Income, 1960–2022

Note: Personal income is the income that persons receive in return for their provision of labor, land, and capital used in current production and the net current transfer payments that they receive from business and from government.

Source: U.S. Bureau of Economic Analysis, Personal Income [PI], retrieved from FRED, Federal Reserve Bank of St. Louis; https://fred.stlouisfed.org/series/PI.

the pandemic unemployment program, the average unemployed American saw 146 percent of their lost wages replaced. The income growth associated with pandemic aid is immediately evident in personal income (see Figure 5.3). Pandemic aid fueled an unprecedented growth in disposable income (+10.6 percent from March 2020 to March 2021). Accordingly, the personal savings rate rose to two or three times its normal level during 2020 (Romer 2021). Meanwhile, in the absence of COVID relief, income would have instead fallen by about 5 percent.[6] Pandemic unemployment aid saved millions of Americans from economic hardship. No other country came close to this level of income replacement. By November 2021, the United States was the only G-7 country to have exceeded its prepandemic GDP.[7]

Over the course of 2020, Congress and the president came together with a series of forceful, efficacious policy enactments that blunted the economic impact of the pandemic. Encompassing direct and indirect aid to a vast array of entities, pandemic assistance preserved whole sectors of the economy (e.g., airlines, transit, child care, entertainment, hospitality, cultural institutions), funded hospitals, food aid, housing assistance, education, and state and local governments, as well as underwrote the fastest vaccine rollout in history. Rather than struggling with gridlock, Congress acted quickly and achieved near total consensus on these enactments. Subsequently, little policy debate about the sufficiency of the COVID response has occurred; instead, questions have centered on whether Congress overreacted.[8] Rarely has Congress moved in a bolder, more expeditious manner, and never facing such institutional fragmentation and polarization.

Viewing Pandemic Aid Through a Negotiation Lens

We analyze how Congress reached agreement on pandemic relief in 2020 through the lens of the negotiation literature (Fisher et al. 2011; Lax and Sebenius 2006; Mansbridge and Martin 2016). Use of a negotiation lens diverges from the analytical approaches more widely used in political science. Dominant approaches to the study of coalition building in Congress typically envision a zero-sum choice in which lawmakers must either "divide the dollars" to allocate a fixed sum (Baron and Ferejohn 1989) or adjust policy along a single continuum in which gains for the left are necessarily losses for the right and vice versa (Krehbiel 1998).

Research on negotiation, by contrast, emphasizes that successful deal-making does more than distribute a fixed pie or allocate value in a zero-sum game. Negotiation instead can expand the pie in which one or more parties to

---

[6] Committee for a Responsible Federal Budget, COVID Relief Lifted Personal Income to Record Levels, May 6, 2021, https://www.crfb.org/blogs/covid-relief-lifted-personal-income-record-levels.

[7] OECD, "OECD GDP Slows in Third Quarter but Regains Pre-Pandemic Level," November 18, 2021, https://www.oecd.org/sdd/na/GDP-Growth-Q321.pdf.

[8] Romer 2021; Jeanna Smialek and Ben Casselman, "Rapid Inflation, Lower Employment: How the U.S. Pandemic Response Measures Up," *New York Times*, April 25, 2022, B1.

the negotiation succeed in *creating value*, meaning that the players broaden the negotiation to identify "positive sum" or mutually beneficial outcomes, rather than "splitting the difference" on a compromise that just divides a fixed pie among themselves (Bazerman and Neale 1992; Fisher et al. 2011; Lax and Sebenius 2006). Dating back to Follett (1925), negotiation scholars emphasize the quest for *integrative* solutions that satisfy the needs and preferences of different players simultaneously. By logrolling, vote trading, or crafting multidimensional agreements, negotiators capitalize on differences across the players' priorities, thereby moving beyond narrow solutions that merely distribute or allocate a fixed sum (Mansbridge and Martin 2016).

A negotiation lens also differs from the work on congressional coalition building (Arnold 1990; Evans 2004) in that it considers dealmaking from multiple perspectives. Scholarship on coalition building focuses on the leader or policy entrepreneur who cultivates support for their proposal through strategic adjustments to its costs and benefits. Negotiation scholars, on the other hand, consider proposals from the perspective of multiple players. They focus on the give-and-take among negotiators with different, often conflicting interests, each seeking to maximize value, usually across multiple dimensions. Negotiations often yield outcomes not initially envisioned by any single actor.

Our visibility into the 2020 COVID negotiations is, of course, limited. Only the players themselves were in the "room where it happens." We rely on news reporting and the public record, along with some informal conversations with relevant Capitol Hill contacts on background. Nevertheless, as we show below, concepts from the negotiation literature offer some useful insights into how these packages came together amidst the party polarization and power fragmentation of 2020.

Challenges Facing the COVID Negotiators

The COVID negotiators had to resolve an astonishing array of questions under the pressure of a rapidly mushrooming public health and economic crisis. They faced significant challenges in doing so. The two parties—each in control of governing institutions and able to mutually block one another—brought different policy priorities to the negotiation. They routinely disagreed on the size of the aid packages needed, with Democrats favoring larger appropriations. Republicans and Democrats diverged on the need for aid to state and local governments, on the size and length of unemployment insurance benefits, on shielding businesses, schools and universities from COVID-related lawsuits, and on direct assistance to corporations, among many other matters. To put the situation in terms of Kingdon's (1984) famous framework, the COVID pandemic had clearly transformed the "problem stream" of American government, meaning the issue agenda on which national policymakers were focused. But the pandemic did not alone create a favorable "policy stream," in which key players agreed on all the appropriate policy responses, and it certainly did not give rise to a favorable "political stream," in which politically aligned elected officials were predisposed to act in concert.

Further complicating matters, the leaders in charge of assembling the COVID-aid packages—principally House Speaker Nancy Pelosi, Senate Republican Leader Mitch McConnell, Senate Democratic Leader Chuck Schumer, and Treasury Secretary Steven Mnuchin—were at all times engaged in two-level negotiations (Putnam 1988). In a two-level game, any deal the negotiators struck would need to be defended to other players who were not themselves privy to the negotiation. Party leaders had to be able to bring along their respective party caucuses. Mnuchin needed to maintain the support of a skeptical President Trump who had strong reelection-oriented motives to reach a deal, but who also suspected that Mnuchin was "giving away the store" in negotiations with Democrats given his eagerness to reach a deal.[9] Both leaders and rank-and-file Republicans repeatedly worried that they would support a deal only to have the unpredictable Trump later denounce the result, as occurred after Congress passed the December Coronabus.[10] Meanwhile, Democrats—looking back to the negative political fallout following the 2008 Wall Street Rescue—feared being tarred with having supported another set of corporate "bailouts."[11] The complexities of selling any deal to all these external actors compounded the negotiation challenges.

Increasing the difficulties, relationships among the various players were strained, with the crisis beginning mere weeks after Trump's first

---

[9] Jeff Stein, Josh Dawsey, and Robert Costa, "Mnuchin Emerges as Able Dealmaker in Stimulus Talks," *Washington Post*, March 29, 2020, A1.

[10] Rachel Siegel, Josh Dawsey, and Mike DeBonis, "Trump Threatens Relief Bill, Urging Bigger Checks," *Washington Post*, December 23, 2020, A1.

[11] David Lynch and Jeffrey Stein, "Stimulus Plan Plunges Trump into the Toxic Politics of Industry Bailouts," *Washington Post*, March 19, 2020, A21.

impeachment trial. Relations between Trump and Pelosi were downright hostile, and the two had not spoken to one another since October.[12] Democrats suspected that Trump himself might personally benefit from COVID aid by routing corporate assistance to his family businesses.[13]

A final challenge to dealmaking was the looming elections. With party control of the Senate and presidency hanging in the balance, party leaders were exquisitely sensitive to political risks. Both parties wanted to avoid being blamed for policy inaction. But neither party wanted to agree to a deal that might politically benefit their opponents. Even when the CARES Act passed 96–0, floor debate was surprisingly acrimonious. "The accusations and tone were ugly," recounted longtime *New York Times* correspondent Carl Hulse. "Democrats accused Republicans of being callous and trying to jam through legislation that would have enabled corporate corruption while giving short shrift to American workers. Republicans stepped it up a notch and essentially accused Democrats of killing their fellow citizens."[14]

In short, the circumstances in 2020 were poorly suited to major policymaking. The parties had divergent policy preferences. Negotiators had to navigate a complex two-level bargaining environment, including a president with a well-earned reputation as a "wild card."[15] The players had many reasons to mistrust one another. Nevertheless, Congress managed to come together repeatedly, boldly, and (nearly) unanimously. Concepts from the negotiation literature can offer some insight into these surprising dynamics.

The BATNA

Lax and Sebenius (2006, 27) describe the fundamental choice negotiators face: "On one side of the balance, you have the proposed deal; on the other, you have your 'walk-away' option—sometimes called your best alternative to a negotiated agreement, or BATNA." An extremely unfavorable

---

[12] Ledyard King, Christal Hayes, and Courtney Subramanian, "Stimulus Deal Brings Congress Together," *USA Today*, March 27, 2020, A2.

[13] Victor Reklaitis, "Schumer Says Coronavirus Stimulus Package Won't Provide Aid to Trump Family's Businesses," Marketwatch.com, March 26, https://www.marketwatch.com/story/schumer-emphasizes-that-coronavirus-stimulus-package-wont-provide-aid-to-trump-familys-businesses-2020-03-25.

[14] Carl Hulse, "A Unanimous Senate Vote That Nobody Seemed to Agree On," *New York Times*, March 29, 2020, A22.

[15] Alan Rappeport, "This Time, It's Mnuchin Joining Pelosi in Coming to the Rescue," *New York Times*, March 14, 2020, B3.

BATNA was the most important factor driving the enactment of the 2020 COVID aid packages. None of the major players had an acceptable alternative to a negotiated agreement of some kind. As much as they might have preferred otherwise, they simply had to deal with one another. "We are facing the abyss," remarked Sen. Marco Rubio (R-FL), during the CARES Act negotiations.[16] "We have to have a bill," Pelosi told reporters during the December negotiations, "and we cannot go home without it."[17]

At various points during 2020, the alternative to a negotiated agreement was so dire that it might be described as a "penalty default" (Ayres and Gertner 1989), meaning an outcome that none of the negotiating parties would want. Furthermore, the BATNA was not fixed during negotiations. Conditions were often deteriorating in real time. In the first month of the crisis, markets were in free fall. Between February 12 and March 23, the Dow lost 37 percent of its value. By March 21, a third of the United States was already under some form of stay-at-home order, and employers were shedding jobs. In just one week while Congress was debating CARES, more than 2.25 million people filed for unemployment, the largest weekly number ever recorded.[18] Meanwhile, members themselves were falling sick with the virus. On March 22, McConnell announced that Senator Rand Paul (R-KY) had tested positive, leading both Senator Mitt Romney (R-UT) and Senator Mike Lee (R-UT) to self-isolate as close contacts. It wasn't clear how much longer members would be able to stay in the Capitol before the virus had spread widely among them, a particular danger given many members' advanced age.[19] Once the Senate adjourned, it was not clear when it would be able to return or if it would have a full roster of senators when it did. The pressure to reach agreement under such circumstances was extraordinary.

Following the passage of CARES, negotiations for another major package stalled out for months. Pressure on Congress was never again as intense as before the passage of the CARES Act in March. But conditions steadily worsened during the fall, increasing pressure on Congress as assistance

[16] Jeff Stein, Mike DeBonis, Erica Werner, and Paul Kane, "Senate Republicans Release Massive Economic Stimulus Bill For Coronavirus Response," *Washington Post*, March 19, 2020, A17.

[17] Emily Cochrane, "Stimulus Deal Falters as McConnell Signals Republican Resistance," *New York Times*, December 11, 2020, B3.

[18] Erica Werner, Jeff Stein, Paul Kane, and Mike DeBonis, "Senate Struggles to Finalize Trillion-Dollar Stimulus Bill As Economic Calamity Grows," *Washington Post*, March 20, 2020, https://www.washingtonpost.com/us-policy/2020/03/20/trump-coronavirus-senate-economic-plan/.

[19] Nicholas Fandos and Catie Edmondson, "Rand Paul Tests Positive for Covid-19, Fueling Anxiety in the Capitol," *New York Times*, March 22, 2020, https://www.nytimes.com/2020/03/22/us/politics/coronavirus-rand-paul.html.

petered out. News reports projected an imminent rise in evictions as soon as moratoriums were lifted. People lined up at food banks in record numbers through the Christmas holidays.[20] A US Chamber of Congress Vice President said that replenishing PPP funds "was not something that can wait for a new president."[21] As Congress faced down the expiration of unemployment benefits in December 2020, a failure to strike a deal had become increasingly unpalatable.

Each party's BATNA during the December 2020 negotiations was shaped by the unresolved status of Senate party control. Leadership of the Senate hinged on the outcome of two run-off elections in Georgia, scheduled for January 2021. In this context, Republicans feared that intransigence on COVID relief would harm their electoral chances. Democratic challengers Jon Ossoff and Raphael Warnock hammered away at Republicans for opposing relief checks. Republicans worried that their incumbents might lose, costing them Senate control, if a deal was not reached. At the same time, the uncertainty involved with the Georgia runoffs also enhanced Democrats' incentive to reach a deal. Democrats could not know in advance what the Georgia outcomes would be. In the event that Democrats lost one or both of those run-offs, Republicans would control the Senate in the next Congress. Under those circumstances, Democrats feared that Republicans would be unwilling to strike a deal with President Biden. As such, Democrats thought that December 2020 might be their last chance for another major COVID relief package.[22] In short, the BATNA on COVID aid became less favorable for each party after the November elections, pushing negotiators to break through the deadlock.

In this context, congressional leaders of both parties also attempted to deliberately engineer a penalty default to increase their likelihood of reaching an agreement. By rolling pandemic relief into the regular appropriations necessary to keep the government open, they heightened the political pain involved with a failure to reach agreement. Failure entailed not just a continued

[20] Sharon Cohen, "Millions of Hungry Americans Turn to Food Banks for 1st Time," *AP News*, December 7, 2020, https://apnews.com/article/race-and-ethnicity-hunger-coronavirus-pandemic-4c7f1705c6d8ef5bac241e6cc8e331bb.

[21] Naomi Jagoda, "Bipartisan Support for New PPP Loans Gains Momentum in Congress," *The Hill*, December 8, 2020, https://thehill.com/policy/finance/529092-bipartisan-support-for-new-ppp-loans-gains-momentum-in-congress/.

[22] Burgess Everett, Andrew Desiderio, and Marianne Levine, "How Georgia is Driving Congress Toward a Stimulus Deal," *Politico*, December 17, 2020, https://www.politico.com/news/2020/12/17/coronavirus-stimulus-deal-georgia-447762.

impasse on COVID relief but also risked a government shutdown. Taken together, Congress's success in reaching agreement on COVID aid repeatedly in 2020 must be understood against a backdrop of unfavorable BATNAs for both parties.

Anchoring

The question was not so much whether Congress would enact pandemic relief in 2020 but what the legislation would contain. The negotiation literature's concept of *anchoring* sheds some light on leaders' strategic behavior as they sought to define the parameters of the COVID-aid negotiations. The first offer in a negotiation can anchor "perceptions of the bargaining range, [such that] more aggressive offers tend to be more influential than less aggressive ones" (Lax and Sebenius 2006, 189). Research also suggests that anchors exert more influence under conditions of uncertainty, such as those which prevailed amidst the COVID-aid negotiations.

McConnell sought to take advantage of anchoring by proposing the first "Phase 3" aid bill, which the players knew would be the largest aid package to that point. He began negotiations only among Republicans, seeking to reach agreement within the party before looking to win bipartisan buy-in.[23] Although Lax and Sebenius (2006, 101) do not recommend such an approach in every circumstance, McConnell adhered to a common negotiating rule of thumb to " 'get your allies on board first' or 'negotiate internally first then externally.' " McConnell unveiled his initial $1 trillion proposal on March 19, organized around what he called four "pillars": aid to small business, direct cash payments to individuals, loans for hard-hit industries, and funds for the health-care sector.[24] McConnell said he hoped this "bold new proposal" would receive "bipartisan respect and mutual urgency."[25]

With respect to the total cost of CARES, McConnell's $1 trillion bill only anchored the floor. Democrats harshly criticized McConnell's draft. In a joint

---

[23] Erica Werner, Jeff Stein, and Mike DeBonis, "White House Seeks $1 Trillion Stimulus," *Washington Post*, March 19, 2020, A1.

[24] Jeffrey Stein, Mike DeBonis, Erica Werner, and Paul Kane, "Senate GOP Releases Massive Stimulus Bill, But Some Oppose Cash Payouts," *Washington Post*, March 20, 2020, A17.

[25] Grace Segers and Stefan Becket, "Senate GOP 'Phase 3' Coronavirus Bill Includes Checks Up To $1,200 for Most Americans," *CBS News*, March 20, 2022, https://www.cbsnews.com/news/coronavirus-stimulus-bill-phase-3-senate-mcconnell-trump/.

statement, Schumer and Pelosi wrote: "We are beginning to review Senator McConnell's proposal, and on first reading, it is not at all pro-worker and instead puts corporations way ahead of workers."[26] Democrats had a range of costly demands before they would agree to support the bill, including a special pandemic unemployment bonus of $600 per week, a pause in student loan payments, expanded aid to hospitals, health systems, and state and local governments, and more. By the time the CARES Act was complete, it had snowballed to more than double its initial size, with the final legislation authorizing $2.2 trillion in expenditures.

Nevertheless, McConnell's bill had a significant anchoring effect in terms of which policies would eventually pass as part of CARES. Any skilled legislative negotiator would have expected the package to grow given the escalating crisis and the necessity of accommodating demands from other legislators before passage. But by crafting the bill among Republicans first and including all their major priorities in the original introduced bill, McConnell largely succeeded in centering negotiations on what Democrats wanted to add to the package.

Three of the "four pillars" in McConnell's draft proved uncontroversial in principle. The two parties would spend a fair bit of time haggling over the terms of the direct payments for taxpayers and the provisions of the Paycheck Protection Program for small businesses, but after McConnell's bill was released there was never any real question that the final bill would include programs along those lines.

Democrats did object to one of McConnell's pillars—the loans for hard-hit industries (see Table 5.2). The most controversial item in McConnell's draft involved the Federal Reserve's 13(3) Program, which would grant the Federal Reserve access to $425 billion in funding to lend to nonfinancial institutions, including corporations in sectors hard-hit by the pandemic. Democrats "expressed dismay at the prospect of doling out money without a clear road map for how the funds might be used," calling it a "slush fund" and fearing corruption and political favoritism.[27] This thorny issue consumed many hours. In the end, an agreement was worked out to address both parties' concerns. Republicans got the Federal Reserve authority they wanted; at the same time, Democrats secured an inspector general and an oversight

---

[26] Emily Cochrane, Jim Tankersley, and Alan Rappeport, "Senate Rescue Bill Includes Corporate Tax Cuts and $1,200 Checks," *New York Times*, March 20, 2020, A10.

[27] Jeanna Smialek and Alan Rappeport, "Republicans Push Dispersal of $425 Billion Through Fed," *New York Times*, March 23, 2020, B2.

Table 5.2 Major Party Priorities Subject to Negotiation in the 2020 CARES Act.

Republican	Democratic	Both Parties
Federal Reserve 13(3) Program Provides funding to the Secretary of the Treasury for direct loans to companies and local governments through both the Treasury and the Federal Reserve	Unemployment Insurance—expands eligibility for unemployment compensation benefits, increases the weekly benefit amount by $600, and extends the number of weeks of benefit eligibility	Direct Cash Payments— provides a recovery rebate of $1,200 per adult and $500 per child
	Oversight Provisions—inspector general; congressionally appointed oversight board, disclosure requirements for businesses receiving funds; prohibition on funds going to companies controlled by public officials (often seen as directed at Trump)	PPP—Payroll Protection Program—provides guaranteed loans, which may be forgiven, to small businesses
	State and Local Aid—provides grants to states, local, tribal, and territorial governments for spending related to the pandemic	
	Vaccines Cost—eliminates Medicare cost-sharing requirements for COVID-19 vaccines	
	Health Care System Funding: Funds HHS to reimburse hospitals and other health care providers	
	Student Loans—suspends payments on outstanding federal student loans	

panel appointed by Congress, as well as a prohibition on stock buybacks for companies that accepted money through the fund.[28]

Democrats had a heavier lift in negotiating to get their priorities included in the final bill (as evident in Table 5.2). They had a lengthy and expensive list of provisions and programs that had been left out of McConnell's initial proposal. Hard bargaining would prove necessary to get them included. Schumer, for example, raised last minute objections and delayed the passage of the legislation amidst the crisis in order to get Republicans to agree

[28] Emily Cochrane and Nicholas Fandos, "Senate Approves a $2 Trillion Virus Response," *New York Times*, March 26, 2020, A1.

to include the special $600 weekly pandemic unemployment benefit.[29] Then, even after the $600 bonus unemployment benefit was included, Democrats had to fend off a last-ditch effort to strip it out of the bill.[30]

In hindsight it is clear that McConnell's initial bill succeeded in establishing what Lax and Sebenius (2006, 186) would term the "Ambitious Target Price." McConnell's move ensured that negotiations largely focused on which of the Democrats' priorities would make it into the final bill. In this sense, rather than anchoring the total cost of the legislation, McConnell's initial bill offers a case of "meta-anchoring" (Lax and Sebenius 2006, 199) in which an early offer shapes the other side's perception of the problem and their expectations for the ultimate outcome of the negotiations.

Aggressive efforts at anchoring can also entail risks: "When the other party sees your offer as unrealistic, the offer is not effective as an anchor" (Lax and Sebenius 2006, 190). Along these lines, House Democrats may have overplayed their hand in seeking to anchor the post-CARES round of negotiations with their HEROES Act (HR 6800), a $3 trillion coronavirus relief bill that passed the House on May 15. Republicans dismissed the effort out of hand. McConnell deemed it "unserious."[31] Senate Appropriations Chair Richard Shelby (R-Alabama) said, "Democrats would have to come a long way back to reality with us to get a bill."[32] HEROES was simply far outside the roughly $500 billion package Republicans were prepared to consider at that juncture.[33] It may not have been in Democrats' political interest to strike another huge relief agreement—and send out another round of relief checks bearing President Trump's signature—so close to the elections. In the near term, the HEROES Act functioned more as a partisan messaging effort framing issues for the elections rather than a starting point for a bipartisan negotiation. In the longer term, the HEROES Act package went on to influence the construction of President Biden's American Rescue Plan, which

---

[29] Erica Werner, Paul Kane, Rachael Bade, and Mike DeBonis, "Senate Close to Deal on Stimulus Bill," *Washington Post*, March 24, 2020, A1.

[30] Joshua Jamerson, Andrew Duehren, and Natalie Andrews, "Senate Passes Stimulus Package," *Wall Street Journal,* March 26, 2020, A1.

[31] LeaderMcConnell [@LeaderMcConnell], *Twitter,* November 17, 2020, 12:47PM, https://twitter.com/LeaderMcConnell/status/1328756703899344907?ref_src=twsrc%5Etfw.

[32] Jordain Carney, "Coronavirus Relief at a Standstill With No Leadership-Level Talks," *The Hill,* November 18, 2020, https://thehill.com/homenews/senate/526509-coronavirus-relief-at-a-standst ill-with-no-leadership-level-talks/.

[33] Susan Cornwell, "McConnell Sets Senate Vote on Coronavirus Aid," *Reuters,* October 14, 2020, https://www.reuters.com/article/health-coronavirus-usa-congress-idINKBN26Z0JO.

passed on a party-line vote in March 2021.[34] Regardless of Pelosi's ultimate intentions, the episode illustrates the balance that effective negotiators need to strike in order to successfully establish an anchor with an aggressive—but credible—initial offer.

Defining the ZOPA for CARES

The central task for negotiators is to discover whether a zone of possible agreement (ZOPA) exists and, if so, to achieve the most favorable outcome acceptable to the other side. "The ZOPA simply means the set of possible agreements that is better for each side, given its interests, than its best no-deal option" (Lax and Sebenius 2006, 88). Clearly, a ZOPA for a COVID-package existed in March 2020—but its available range was initially unclear.

Discovering the ZOPA can require a lot of discussion. Effective negotiators need to draw out their partners to understand the underlying reasons for their positions. A classic maxim for negotiators is to "focus on interests, not positions" (Fisher et al. 2011, 42). If negotiators can find out *why* a partner is taking a particular position, they may be able to devise solutions to the underlying problem rather than "splitting the difference" between divergent positions or capitulating to another player's preference. But this kind of effort requires trust and self-disclosure, as well as time for engagement.

Interestingly, the Capitol Hill environment during COVID may have been favorable to negotiation in one respect. Scholars have noted that "allowing negotiations to take place in *private settings* encourages pondering rather than posturing" (Mansbridge and Martin 2016, 9). With the Capitol closed, there were no lobbyists roaming the halls. Journalists and the majority of staff were working from home. The key principals could thus engage with one another with less concern about how they might be perceived by external audiences. Obviously, we cannot observe a counterfactual, but the greater availability of private space for negotiation during COVID may have facilitated discussions.

The process of ascertaining the ZOPA happens at what Lax and Sebenius (2006, 199) call the "drawing board," where one or more parties look for ways

---

[34] Alice Miranda Ollstein, Megan Cassella, and Caitlin Emma, "Biden, Democrats, Plot 'Aggressive' Pandemic Response—Without the GOP," *Politico*, January 12, 2021, https://www.politico.com/news/2021/01/12/biden-coronavirus-stimulus-package-458445.

to "*create value*, not only for themselves but for the other parties as well." When McConnell released his first draft of CARES, Schumer indicated that it was time to go to the drawing board: "I would say to my Republican colleagues: we want to work with you, you will have different ideas, but our ideas must be contained in a package."[35] Both Senate and House Democrats had lengthy lists of priorities that they expected to include.

At this stage, negotiation leaders needed to identify the "all party map" (Lax and Sebenius 2006, 68), meaning that they had to take stock of all those who would matter for the eventual success of any deal. To be successful, they needed to look beyond the usual suspects to anticipate who would serve as possible influencers, allies, or opponents in deal making. In addition, they had to take into consideration all those needed to eventually approve and implement the deal.

To identify possible agreements across the many parts of a vast, multi-issue package, McConnell assembled working groups. He tasked Senate GOP Chairmen and senior Republicans to engage informally with their Democratic counterparts. McConnell created a division of labor to resolve major issues in the CARES Act negotiations (see Table 5.3). One can clearly see "party mapping" in the composition of these groups. The groups typically include the chairs and ranking members with jurisdiction over the policy issues involved. McConnell would surely have recognized that committee chairs and ranking members would resent dilution of their authority and would likely object to any effort to cut them out of the negotiation.

McConnell's groups, however, do not rigidly follow the lines of committee authority. McConnell created groups with an eye to including influential members likely to take a strong interest in the issues. Small Business Committee Chair Marco Rubio (R-Florida), for example, was asked to work with Sen. Susan Collins (R-Maine) on the small business aid piece of the package, even though Collins was neither a member of the Small Business Committee nor the subcommittee of Senate Appropriations with jurisdiction over the Small Business Administration. Banking Committee Chair Mike Crapo (R-Idaho) was asked to work with Sen. Pat Toomey (R-Pennsylvania) on issues involving oversight of the Treasury Department. Involving a small-government conservative like Toomey was likely an example of McConnell anticipating a potential "blocker" (Lax and Sebenius 2006, 65), meaning a

---

[35] Andrew Restuccia, Andrew Duehren, and Lindsay Wise, "Trump Urges $1 Trillion Aid Deal," *Wall Street Journal*, March 18, 2020, A1.

Table 5.3 Senate Division of Labor: Lead Negotiators on Issues, 2020 CARES Act.

Issue	Republicans	Democrats
Direct payments to individuals and taxes	Chuck Grassley—Chairman, Finance Committee	Ron Wyden—Ranking Member Finance Committee
Paycheck Protection Program	Marco Rubio—Chairman, Small Business Committee Susan Collins—Appropriations Committee	Ben Cardin—Ranking Member, Small Business Committee Jeanne Shaheen—2nd in seniority, Small Business Committee
Unemployment Insurance	Rob Portman—Chair, Subcommittee on Taxation and IRS Oversight, Finance Committee	Ron Wyden—Ranking Member, Finance Committee
Federal Reserve 13(3) Program	Mike Crapo—Chair, Banking Committee; Pat Toomey—Chair, Subcommittee on Securities, Insurance, and Investment, Banking Committee	Sherrod Brown—Ranking Member, Banking Committee
Airline Assistance	Mike Crapo—Chair, Banking Committee; Pat Toomey—Chair, Subcommittee on Securities, Insurance, and Investment, Banking Committee; Roger Wicker—Chair, Commerce Committee	Maria Cantwell—Ranking Member, Commerce Committee
Aid to Hospitals and Vaccine Funding (became Operation Warp Speed)	Lamar Alexander—Chair, Health, Education, Labor, and Pensions Committee; Roy Blunt—Chair, Republican Policy Committee	Patty Murray—Ranking Member, Health, Education, Labor, and Pensions Committee

player "who must approve the deal and . . . might block it." Including Toomey in the negotiations early could help to defuse potential opposition later. The Senate working groups McConnell established then engaged with House counterparts, both committee chairs and ranking members.

McConnell's informal working groups accepted input from House chairs and ranking members, thereby resolving disagreements across the parties and chambers. In her speech just before the House passage of the CARES Act, Pelosi praised "our distinguished chairmen on our side

[who] transformed a Republican, corporate focused bill into a Democratic, workers-first bill."[36]

One of the most important players establishing the ZOPA on CARES was President Trump, who as best as we can ascertain, did not have much direct influence over the details of the legislation. Although his idea for a payroll tax holiday failed to gain any traction, even among Republicans, he clearly indicated at the outset that he wanted to "go big."[37] Then, after the package was negotiated, Trump defended its size and contents against any challenge from congressional conservatives. When Rep. Thomas Massie (R-Kentucky) attempted to throw up roadblocks at House passage, Trump tweeted:

> Workers & small businesses need money now in order to survive. Virus wasn't their fault. It is 'HELL' dealing with the Dems, had to give up some stupid things in order to get the 'big picture' done. 90% GREAT! WIN BACK HOUSE, but throw Massie out of Republican Party.[38]

Trump's forceful advocacy and denunciation of Massie may have deterred other Republicans contemplating creating problems for the legislation. In any case, he provided political cover for any Republicans who may have had qualms about deficit spending. The biggest win in the package for Trump was the $1,200 checks mailed out to millions of Americans in an election year, which he insisted on personally signing.[39]

Clearly, the ZOPA on CARES was wide. McConnell and the administration established the floor with an initial $1 trillion package. Leaders, including the president, never clearly established any upper bound on cost. With deficits and total price tag no obstacle, negotiators were free to assemble a huge logroll in which the parties traded off items that were of high value to one side and low value to the other. The fact that the parties valued different parts of the package became the basis of the agreement (Fisher et al.

---

[36] Press Release, "Pelosi Floor Speech in Support of H.R. 748, the Coronavirus Aid, Relief, and Economic Security (CARES) Act," March 27, 2020, https://www.speaker.gov/newsroom/32720-1.

[37] Erica Werner, Jeff Stein, and Mike DeBonis, "White House Seeks $1 Trillion Stimulus," *Washington Post*, March 19, 2020, A1.

[38] Quint Forgey, "Both Parties Pile on Massie After Effort to Force Recorded Vote Flops," *Politico*, March 27, 2020, https://www.politico.com/news/2020/03/27/trump-congressman-thomas-massie-coronavirus-vote-151523.

[39] Lisa Rein, "In Unprecedented Move, Treasury Orders Trump's Name Printed on Stimulus Checks," *Washington Post*, April 14, 2020, https://www.washingtonpost.com/politics/coming-to-your-1200-relief-check-donald-j-trumps-name/2020/04/14/071016c2-7e82-11ea-8013-1b6da0e4a2b7_story.html.

2011, 75–77). At more than 800 pages and $2 trillion, the package contained something for almost everyone in Congress.

Defining the ZOPA for the December 2020 Omnibus

In contrast to the relatively swift negotiations surrounding the March CARES act, it took several months for negotiators to establish the boundaries of the ZOPA for the December 2020 Consolidated Appropriations Act. The parties started out trillions of dollars apart, with McConnell preferring a $500 billion aid package and Pelosi's House passing the $3 trillion HEROES Act. The parties continued to wrangle over the issue through the summer and fall.

Only after the elections did negotiations begin in earnest. In this case, the ZOPA was identified not by leadership but by a small group of senators—including Bill Cassidy (R-Louisiana), Susan Collins (R-Maine), Angus King (I-Maine), Joe Manchin (R-West Virginia), Mitt Romney (R-Utah), and Mark Warner (D-Virginia)—in conjunction with members of the bipartisan House Problem Solvers Caucus.[40] These informal bipartisan negotiators had arrived at a $908 billion package and a set of consensus funding priorities. The White House agreed to engage and put a $916 billion proposal on the table. The first genuine momentum toward a new agreement had been built.

Despite agreement on a top line figure, the negotiation bogged down over a set of priorities, one for Democrats, one for Republicans, neither of which could win bipartisan support. Democrats were demanding a new infusion of aid to state and local governments, which Republicans regarded as a "blue state bailout." McConnell's "red line" was legal protections against pandemic-related lawsuits for businesses and other entities, which Democrats viewed as a nonstarter. Despite lengthy talks, the parties never managed to bridge their differences on either of these issues. "We've had an eight-months impasse around liability issues, and it is proving to be extremely difficult to close that distance," said Senator Christopher A. Coons (D-Delaware), who had worked on resolving the disagreement.[41]

In the end, the December package came together by narrowing the scope of their negotiations. In an "anti-logroll," the parties agreed to McConnell's

---

[40] Mike DeBonis, Jeff Stein, and Seung-Min Kim, "Democrats Get Behind $908 Billion Relief Plan to Prod GOP Into Action," *Washington Post*, December 3, 2020, A18.

[41] Mike DeBonis, Jeff Stein, and Seung-Min Kim, "Trump Signs Stopgap Bill to Avert a Shutdown," *Washington Post*, December 13, 2020, A2.

proposal to set aside each party's most controversial priorities. "We were successful in getting $908 billion, getting people together to that number," said Romney. "We've solved a whole series of elements—maybe on state and local, the liability, we wait, given the time frame, until next year."[42]

Repeated Interactions

The players involved in the 2020 COVID negotiations had divergent policy goals, opposed political interests, and many reasons to mistrust one another. But the fact that they were enmeshed in an indefinite series of repeated negotiations helped to facilitate their ability to cooperate. As Mansbridge and Martin (2016, 9) write, "repeated interactions among participants establish informal punishments for deception and bloated claims at the same time that those interactions nurture norms of trustworthy behavior." All through the COVID-aid negotiations of 2020, the players knew that they would continue to have to deal with one another in the future, both on pandemic relief and other issues. The iterated nature of the game gave the players a long-term interest in maintaining trust and good working relationships. As Pelosi observed, "One of the motivations to have a good rapport [with other negotiators] is that there's always another bill down the road."[43] Even as the December 2020 package came together, McConnell acknowledged that members were still dissatisfied, but that everyone should know "full well we'll be back at this after the first of the year."[44]

Using a Negotiation Lens to Understand Congress

It has become conventional for scholars and journalists to characterize Congress as a dysfunctional institution, mired in polarization and gridlock, and unable to address pressing national problems. No doubt, the institution fails to live up to Americans' expectations in many ways. Nevertheless, Congress's response to the COVID crisis of 2020 shows that it is able to leap

---

[42] Cochrane, "Stimulus Deal Falters."

[43] Alan Rappeport, "This Time, It's Mnuchin Joining Pelosi in Coming to the Rescue," *New York Times*, March 14, 2020, B3.

[44] Emily Cochrane, "White House Offers $916 Billion Stimulus Proposal as Talks Intensify," *New York Times*, December 9, 2020, A11.

into life and negotiate beyond partisan stalemate when faced with a major problem on which all sides agree action is needed and where the alternative to action is unacceptable.

With inflation at 40-year highs in 2022, Congress may have overshot the mark with its COVID response. There were undoubtedly policy missteps. As Senator Rubio observed at the time, "We are facing circumstances for which there is no playbook."[45] But when the need was pressing, Congress was able to come together to act in what members saw as the national interest. As is clearly evident in the data shown here, Congress's actions helped to alleviate hardship and suffering imposed by the pandemic.

As we hope is evident here, congressional scholars can draw some insights from the literature on negotiation. Most work on negotiation focuses on the private sector or international diplomacy, but the concepts developed in this literature travel relatively well to a legislative setting. They offer some useful tools for understanding strategic behavior and negotiation processes in Congress. The concept of the BATNA affords a systematic way to think through the fundamental choice each side must weigh in negotiations. "All party mapping" is a critical skill for coalition leaders, as they anticipate the players who need to be included in a legislative negotiation. Congressional negotiations are shaped by anchoring, sequencing, and repeated interaction, just as negotiations in other settings are.

The negotiation literature also helps to advance congressional studies beyond simple theoretical models that assume a fixed bargaining space and a single dimension. Rather than dividing a fixed sum, negotiators accommodated one another's priorities, with the CARES Act dramatically expanding in cost as the parties worked out their differences. The upper bound of spending was as much a subject of negotiation as any other aspect of the policy, a reality that often characterizes congressional policymaking. The COVID-aid packages analyzed here were also highly multi-dimensional, involving numerous policies along multiple dimensions. Log-rolling and other "win-win" arrangements increased the value of the negotiation to both sides, rather than merely adjusting an outcome along a single dimension. In a Congress where legislating on the basis of broad, bipartisan agreement is more the norm than the exception (Curry and Lee 2020), these kinds of complex negotiations are hardly unusual, albeit rarely on the giant scale of the pandemic-aid packages of 2020.

---

[45] Stein, DeBonis, Werner, and Kane, "Senate Republicans Release Massive Stimulus."

The Art of the Deal?

This volume centers on the effects of the Trump presidency. To what extent did Trump disrupt congressional processes during the COVID-aid negotiations? Trump's public image might have led one to brace for major impact. After all, long before he launched any bid for public office, Trump presented himself as a master negotiator. In the opening paragraph of *Trump: The Art of the Deal*, Trump declares, "Deals are my art form" (Trump with Schwartz 1987, 1).

When it came to pandemic aid, however, Trump did not take a hands-on role. His influence over the specifics was limited. It is difficult to identify examples of Trump weighing in on provisions. During the CARES Act negotiations, he initially pushed for a payroll tax holiday. That idea never gained any traction, either in Congress overall or among Republican lawmakers, and was eventually dropped. Trump intervened on a relatively minor matter during the Coronabus negotiations. A 100 percent tax deduction for business meals—the "three martini lunch" deduction—was a Trump priority to help revive the restaurant industry.[46] A two-year 100 percent deduction for business meals was inserted into the Coronabus, reportedly at the cost of agreeing to some increases in tax credits for low-income workers demanded by Democrats.[47] Generally speaking, though, one has to look carefully to find Trump personally playing any active part in these negotiations. There was uncertainty throughout both sets of negotiations whether Trump would support the package in the end, uncertainty that was warranted in the case of the Coronabus.[48] But Trump did not attempt to micromanage the negotiations or even to wield much influence over the policy substance.

Looking back on these COVID-aid enactments, then, Trump was not a "disruptor" of congressional negotiations. Instead, Trump's actions (and inactions) facilitated congressional action in a few ways. First, he empowered a delegate who was able to negotiate on his behalf and to work effectively with

---

[46] Jeff Stein, "White House Secures 'Three Martini Lunch' Tax Deduction in Relief Package," *Washington Post,* December 22, 2020, https://www.washingtonpost.com/us-policy/2020/12/20/meal-tax-deduction/.

[47] Ibid.

[48] Seung Min Kim, Josh Dawsey, and Mike DeBonis, "Trump's Last-Minute Outburst Throws Pandemic Relief Effort into Chaos," *Washington Post*, December 23, 2020, https://www.washingtonpost.com/politics/trumps-last-minute-tantrum-throws-pandemic-relief-effort-into-chaos/2020/12/23/afb8626a-4534-11eb-a277-49a6d1f9dff1_story.html.

both Democrats and Republicans, Treasury Secretary Steven Mnuchin.[49] Second, his hands-off approach and relative lack of specific policy demands reduced the complexity of the negotiations, permitting Congress more freedom of maneuver.

Most importantly, Trump's willingness to "go big" and support huge expenditures gave Congress additional fiscal space within which to logroll Republican and Democratic priorities. Trump's strong support among the party's base voters created a permission structure for conservative Republicans to vote for these unprecedentedly large emergency packages. Clearly, Trump was hardly alone among Republicans in wanting a robust federal response. Many other Republicans were prepared to spend big, as well. Just after the CARES Act negotiations concluded, even McConnell was taking credit for having enacted a "wartime level of investment into our nation."[50] Still, it seems likely that there would have been more controversy on the party's right flank had Trump not intervened so forcefully in support. Notably, the Republican Party reverted to form in opposing deficit spending after Democrats won unified control of government in the 2020 elections and moved forward on another large-scale COVID aid package, the American Rescue Plan. If Trump can be said to have played a "disruptive" role with respect to the COVID negotiations, it was in preempting opposition among any fiscal conservative holdouts. In other respects, he neither disrupted the actual negotiations nor orchestrated them as a maestro dealmaker.

After close study of these enactments, we can only conclude that the bicameral Congress remains very much a separate and largely independent power center, despite America's nationalized and president-centered politics. In this sense, Congress's sweeping response to the COVID crisis reveals the institution's formidable institutional power in the American political system. Polsby (1975) famously termed Congress a "transformational" legislature, in contrast to so many other legislatures around the world that function largely as "arenas," meaning that they debate, approve, or (on rare occasion) reject executive branch proposals but exercise limited influence on the content of laws. Congress, in contrast, writes legislation in general terms as well as specific detail. Congress's capacities in this regard were very much on display

---

[49] Stein, Dawsey, and Costa, "Mnuchin Emerges as Able Dealmaker."
[50] James Politi and Lauren Fedor, "What's In the Historic $2Tn US Stimulus Deal?" *Financial Times*, March 25, 2020, https://www.ft.com/content/0925d61e-6eaa-11ea-89df-41bea055720b.

during the 2020 COVID crisis. In no sense was Congress merely reacting to proposals from the executive branch.

Even in a crisis context where leaders took a dominant role, congressional policymaking remained a co-production of many players. The 2020 COVID-aid negotiations featured coequal bargaining across parties, chambers, and branches of government, with Congress in the lead on many features of the policies eventually adopted. Notwithstanding the fierce polarization of the Trump era, Congress retained the capacity to engage in tough, constructive negotiation to address national challenges.

References

Arnold, Douglas. 1990. *Logic of Congressional Action*. New Haven, CT: Yale University Press.

Ayres, Ian, and Robert Gertner. 1989. "Filling Gaps in Incomplete Contracts: An Economic Theory of Default Rules." *Yale Law Journal* 99(1): 87–130.

Baron, David, and John Ferejohn. 1989. "Bargaining in Legislatures." *American Political Science Review* 83(4): 1181–1206.

Bazerman, Max H., and Margaret A. Neale. 1992. *Negotiating Rationally*. New York: The Free Press.

Cooney, Patrick, and H. Luke Shaefer. 2021. *Material Hardship and Mental Health Following the COVID-19 relief bill and American Rescue Plan Act*. Poverty Solutions, University of Michigan. May.

Curry, James M., and Frances E. Lee. 2020. *The Limits of Party: Congress and Lawmaking in a Polarized Era*. Chicago: University of Chicago Press.

Evans, Diana. 2004. *Greasing the Wheels: Using Pork Barrel Projects to Build Majority Coalitions in Congress*. New York: Cambridge University Press.

Fisher, Roger, William Ury, and Bruce Patton. 2011. *Getting to Yes: Negotiating Agreement Without Giving In*. New York: Houghton Mifflin.

Follett, Mary Parker. [1925] 1942. *Constructive Conflict. In Dynamic Administration: The Collected Papers of Mary Parker Follett*, ed. H. C. Metcalf and L. Urwick. New York: Harper.

Han, Jeehoon, Bruce D. Meyer, and James X. Sullivan. 2021. "Real-Time Poverty Estimates During the COVID-19 Pandemic Through June 2021." *Wilson Sheehan Lab for Economic Opportunities at Notre Dame and the Harris School of Public Policy*, 15 July.

Hopkins, Daniel J. 2018. *The Increasingly United States: How and Why American Political Behavior Nationalized*. Chicago: University of Chicago Press.

Gadarian, Shana Kushner, Sara Wallace Goodman, and Thomas B. Pepinsky. 2022. *Pandemic Politics: The Deadly Toll of Partisanship in the Age of COVID*. Princeton, NJ: Princeton University Press.

Jacobson, Gary C. 2021. "Driven to Extremes: Donald Trump's Extraordinary Impact on the 2020 Elections." *Presidential Studies Quarterly* 51 (3): 492–521.

Kingdon, John W. 1984. *Agendas, Alternatives and Public Policies*. Boston: Little, Brown.

Krehbiel, Keith. 1998. *Pivotal Politics: A Theory of U.S. Lawmaking*. Chicago: University of Chicago Press.

Lax, David A., and James K. Sebenius. 2006. *3D Negotiation: Powerful Tools to Change the Game in Your Most Important Deals*. Boston: Harvard Business School Press.

Mansbridge, Jane, and Cathie Jo Martin, eds. 2016. *Political Negotiation: A Handbook*. Washington, DC: Brookings Institution Press.

McCarty, Nolan. 2021. "How Congressional Polarization Is Transforming the Separation of Powers." In *Congress Reconsidered*, 12th ed. Lawrence C. Dodd and Bruce Oppenheimer, eds. Thousand Oaks, CA: Sage/ CQ Press, 431–461.

Polsby, Nelson W. 1975. "Legislatures." In *Handbook of Political Science*, Fred I. Greenstein and Nelson W. Polsby, eds. New York: Addison-Wesley, 257–319.

Putnam, Robert D. 1988. "Diplomacy and Domestic Politics: the Logic of Two-Level Games." *International Organization* 42(3): 427–460.

Romer, Christina. 2001. "The Fiscal Policy Response to the Pandemic," *Brookings Papers on Economic Activity*. 24 March.

Trump, Donald J., with Tony Schwartz. 1987. *Trump: The Art of the Deal*. New York: Ballantine Books.

6

The Surprisingly Effective Lawmaking of Minority-Party Democrats in the Senate during the Trump Era

Craig Volden and Alan E. Wiseman[*]

Introduction

With the inauguration of President Donald J. Trump on January 20, 2017, the Republican Party obtained unified control of the legislative and executive branches of government for the first time in a decade. Much had changed since the days when President George W. Bush, the self-defined "compassionate conservative," occupied the White House and sought initial bipartisan legislative successes on education, and (soon) on antiterrorism initiatives. Donald Trump had been elected to the presidency following a blistering campaign against the Democratic nominee, Hillary Clinton. He had constantly railed against Democrats and "the swamp" of the broader DC establishment, portraying America in crisis. Trump "offered himself to the American people as their sole hope for renewal and redemption" (Rucker and Leonnig 2020, 1) and boldly declared at the Republican Convention that "I alone can fix it!"

With an ambitious policy agenda on matters including immigration, prescription drug prices, income tax reform, international trade, and (most notably) repealing and replacing President Obama's Affordable Care Act (ACA), the Trump administration would seem to have found enthusiastic partners among Republican Party leaders in the House and the Senate. In the

[*] The authors thank Colin Achilles, Mike Xu, Nick Zeppos, and Chris Piper for their assistance with interview scheduling and data gathering; participants at the Spring 2022 Disruption conference for helpful feedback; and the Democracy Fund and the US Democracy Program of the Hewlett Foundations for their financial support of the Center for Effective Lawmaking (www.thelawmakers.org).

Craig Volden and Alan E. Wiseman, *The Surprisingly Effective Lawmaking of Minority-Party Democrats in the Senate during the Trump Era* In: *Disruption?* Edited by: Sean M. Theriault, Oxford University Press.

Senate especially, President Trump might have expected to benefit from the support of Senate Majority Leader Mitch McConnell (R-Kentucky). A seasoned veteran of the chamber, McConnell had a profound appreciation for the ways in which Senate procedure and policymaking could interact with presidential agendas to help presidents achieve (or, alternatively, to derail) their policy goals. After all, it was Senator McConnell who boldly stated in the early days of the Obama presidency that his party's primary goal was to do whatever it could to ensure that President Obama would only serve one term.[1] He then leveraged his party's positions (while in the minority and majority) to undermine the Obama Administration's many initiatives. Now McConnell was in a position to use his influence and experience to advance Republican policy interests, and those of President Trump, at the expense of Democrats.

In spite of these fundamentals, the Trump presidency did not go as many Republican politicians and congressional observers might have predicted. With the notable exception of the Tax Cuts and Jobs Act of 2017, Trump's long list of legislative-based campaign promises fizzled in Congress. The president seemed largely disinterested in engaging in the art of the deal, as needed in Congress; and the administration on the whole was plagued by mismanagement, often from the very top (e.g., Leonnig and Rucker 2021). As but one example of legislative troubles, his (arguably) most important campaign promise—to repeal and replace the ACA—failed memorably on July 27, 2017. Senator John McCain (R-Arizona), who had been repeatedly criticized and mocked by the president, cast a pivotal "no" vote on the "skinny repeal" measure advanced by Republicans, with a dramatic thumbs down. Lacking legislative successes, President Trump was left to rely on executive orders and judicial appointments to influence policy.

We argue that this high-level portrayal, while accurate, misses some of the important under-currents of lawmaking in the US Senate during the Trump years. Specifically, we examine the proposals put forth by Democratic and Republican senators and trace their fates, in comparison to prior periods of Republican control of the Senate. In so doing, we uncover four main patterns. First, we find that, similar to prior periods of Republican control, majority-party influence did not favor conservative Republicans over others. This result stands in contrast to liberal Democrats, who have historically

---

[1] https://www.nationaljournal.com/member/magazine/top-gop-priority-make-obama-a-one-term-president-20101023/ Accessed July 20, 2022.

thrived at lawmaking during periods of Democratic control. Second, we find that the gap in lawmaking activity and effectiveness between majority-party members and minority-party members was much narrower in the Senate during the Trump presidency than during previous congresses. In part this finding is due to less exertion of majority-party influence through committee structures, as evidenced by a relative low activity and effectiveness of committee chairs during these years. Third, we find that Democrats, despite being the minority party, stepped in to fill this lawmaking vacuum with numerous legislative proposals of their own. Their average levels of bill sponsorship—especially in the 116th Congress—exceeded the averages of either minority-party senators, or (even) majority-party senators in any congress since the early 1970s. We link this activity to responses to the global pandemic emerging in 2020, and to Democrats responding to President Trump's executive orders (and to his other activities that they felt demanded congressional responses). Finally, we show that this heightened activity, not matched by Republican senators, was followed by sufficient success in their bills surviving the Republican-majority Senate, as to place Democrats as the most effective group of minority-party lawmakers the Senate has seen in at least half a century.

These findings collectively suggest that, despite the widely observed hyperpartisan rhetoric during the Trump administration, the Republican majority (and Senator McConnell, in particular) did not actively seek to centralize lawmaking power in the hands of a select few committee leaders while simultaneously squelching any attempts by Democrats to engage in legislating. As a result, those Democrats who sought to advance their policy agendas found a path forward to effective lawmaking; and they ultimately positioned themselves well for taking control of the chamber in the 117th Congress.

Majority Party Control and Lawmaking Effectiveness Prior to Trump

The Senate has been widely perceived to be less partisan than the US House, owing to several factors, including that its members stand for reelection every six years (with staggered two-year terms across cohorts), that senators have larger and more diverse constituencies than representatives, and that the supermajority requirement to overcome filibusters yields a more bipartisan and consensus-based approach to lawmaking. Indeed, a wide body of

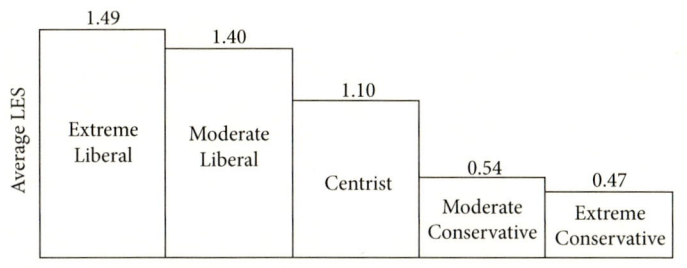

Ideological Quintiles, When Democrats Are the Majority Party

Figure 6.1 Lawmaking Effectiveness in the Senate during Democratic Majorities

Note: This figure plots the average Legislative Effectiveness Score by ideological quintile for every Senate in which the Democrats were the majority party between 1973 and 2017 (93rd-114th Congress). When Democrats control the Senate, the most effective lawmakers are those who are the most liberal members of the chamber; and the average lawmaking effectiveness of senators decreases as they become more ideologically conservative.

scholarly literature (e.g., MacNeil and Baker 2013; Pearson 2008; Sinclair 2017; Strahan 2011) has pointed to the relative absence of party politics and influence in the Senate (especially in comparison to the House) across much of its history.

Another line of research, however (e.g., Bradbury, Davidson, and Evans 2008; Evans 2018; Hershberger, Minozzi, and Volden 2018; Lee 2009; Patty 2008; Theriault and Rohde 2011; Volden and Bergman 2006), paints a more nuanced picture of the roles of the majority and minority parties in Senate policymaking. In a recent contribution to this debate, Volden and Wiseman (2021) explore the impacts of party control and members' ideologies in advancing senators' legislative initiatives through the chamber and into law. One main finding is that the impacts of ideology and party affiliation on lawmaking success vary significantly, depending on which party (Republican or Democratic) controls the Senate.

More specifically, in analyzing senators' Legislative Effectiveness Scores since the 1970s, we find that when the Democratic Party controlled the chamber, the most successful senators were those who were drawn from the most liberal wing of the chamber (i.e., the most liberal Democrats), and that the scope of senators' legislative success decreased as they became more ideologically conservative (see Figure 6.1).[2] In contrast, when the Republican

---

[2] Legislative Effectiveness Scores have been developed for the House (Volden and Wiseman 2014) and the Senate (Volden and Wiseman 2018) for all Congresses between 1973–2023. They parsimoniously capture how successful an individual Representative (or Senator) is at advancing her

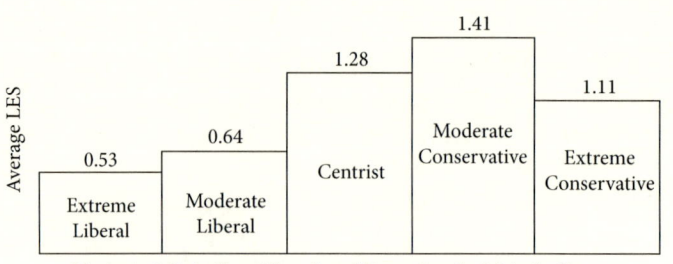

Ideological Quintiles, When Republicans Are the Majority Party

Figure 6.2 Lawmaking Effectiveness in the Senate during Republican Majorities

Note: This figure plots the average Legislative Effectiveness Score by ideological quintile for the Senate in which the Republicans were the majority party between 1973 and 2017 (93rd–114th Congress). When Republicans control the Senate, the most effective lawmakers are those who are closest to the median member of the Republican Party, with the most conservative Republicans obtaining less success than more ideologically moderate Republicans.

Party controlled the Senate, the most successful senators were *not* the most conservative. Instead, those near the ideological center of the majority party thrived, with lawmaking success decreasing for those with ideologies deviating from the center of the Republican Party (see Figure 6.2).

These patterns are illustrated in Figures 6.1 and 6.2 for those Congresses that were controlled by Democrats and Republicans, respectively, from 1973–2017 (i.e., prior to the Trump's presidency).

When we arrange all senators into ideological quintiles from most liberal to most conservative when Democrats control the Senate, the "extreme liberal" quintile of senators had the highest average Legislative Effectiveness Scores (LES). The average LES of each quintile decreased consistently for more and more conservative senators. Moreover, we see an especially large drop in lawmaking effectiveness between "centrist" and "moderate conservative" senators, with the average LES decreasing approximately 50 percent across these two quintiles.

When Republicans control the Senate, similarities appear, in that the least effective lawmakers are those who are most ideologically opposed to Republican policy interests: "extreme liberal," followed by "moderate liberal" senators. We also see that the greatest drop in lawmaking effectiveness

sponsored bills through the lawmaking process from introduction until (possibly) becoming law, in comparison to all other legislators in her chamber during a two-year Congress, where each bill is weighted for relative substantive significance.

occurs between "centrist" senators and "moderate liberal" senators: a decrease in the average LES across quintiles of 50 percent. One notable difference that emerges between when Republicans and Democrats control the Senate, however, is which majority-party senators (ideologically speaking) are the most effective lawmakers. Specifically, when Republicans control the Senate, we see that the most successful lawmakers are not the most ideologically extreme Republicans (i.e., those senators in the "extreme conservative" quintile), but rather those senators who are ideologically "moderate conservative." Indeed, ideologically extreme Republican senators are, on average, less effective at advancing their legislative agendas than are "centrist" senators when Republicans control the Senate.

Comparing across these figures, it appears that when Democrats control the Senate, they leverage their control of the chamber in an ideological manner, in that they seek to promote those policies that are proposed by the most liberal wing of the Democratic Party, followed by those of moderate and centrist Democrats, followed by those of moderate Republicans. The Republicans, on the other hand, appear to adopt more of the team-based approach, in that they promote the bills of Republicans over those of Democrats when they control the chamber, and the Republicans who are most successful at advancing their initiatives are those who are most ideologically aligned with the median members of their party's conference. Nevertheless, it's still worth emphasizing that all quintiles of Republicans in our data—including the most ideologically extreme conservatives—experience greater levels of lawmaking success than do Democrats during Republican-controlled Senates. Indeed, one might be quite surprised if that were not the case.

Lawmaking Effectiveness in the Senate during the Trump Era

Having illustrated the historical relationships between senator ideology and lawmaking effectiveness under Republican and Democratic majorities, a natural question emerges: "What, if anything, was different during the Trump presidency?" The answer to this question is: "Quite a lot!"

First, we determine the relationship between lawmaking effectiveness and ideology in the Senate for the 115th and 116th Congresses (2017–2021), which is analogous to Figure 6.2 (see Figure 6.3). In contrast to what we saw during the Republican majorities between 1973 and 2017, the differences in

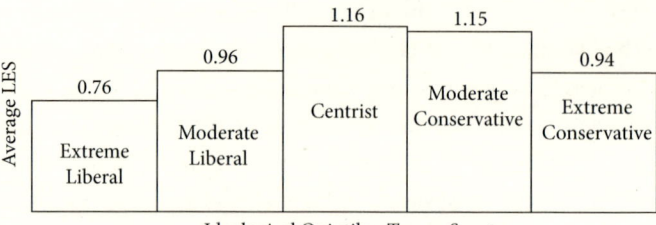

Figure 6.3 Lawmaking Effectiveness in the Senate during the Trump Era (2017–2021)

Note: This figure plots the average Legislative Effectiveness Score in the Senate by ideological quintile for the Trump years, when the Republicans were the majority party between 2017–2021 (115th–116th Congresses). The most effective lawmakers were those who were closest to the median senator in the chamber, but little difference exists between the average lawmaking effectiveness of most members of the Republican Party and those senators who were "moderate liberal."

the average LES across ideological quintiles during the Trump years were somewhat muted.

Although it's still the case that large portions of the Republican Party were more successful at advancing their agendas than most Democratic senators, the difference between the average LES of "moderate conservative" and "centrist" senators was de minimis (with the centrist senators actually having a higher average LES than any other quintile). We likewise see that the most extreme members of the Republican Party score no higher, on average, in lawmaking effectiveness than the "moderate liberal" quintile of the Senate (all of whom are Democrats). Even the most "extreme liberal" members of the Senate—all of whom are likewise Democrats—have notably higher average Legislative Effectiveness Scores than in previous periods under Republican majorities. Taken together, the Trump years definitely featured different patterns of lawmaking success in the Senate.

This coin though has two sides. Republican senators were, on average, less effective, and Democratic senators were, on average, more effective than during any previous period of Republican control that we've studied. The Senate during the Trump years had a relatively low level of lawmaking coming through majority-party dominance of committees, as indicated by the percentage of public laws originating as bills sponsored by Senate committee chairs (see Figure 6.4).

More specifically, for the 115th (2017–2019) and 116th (2019–2021) Congresses, 34 percent and 33 percent of Senate-originated public laws,

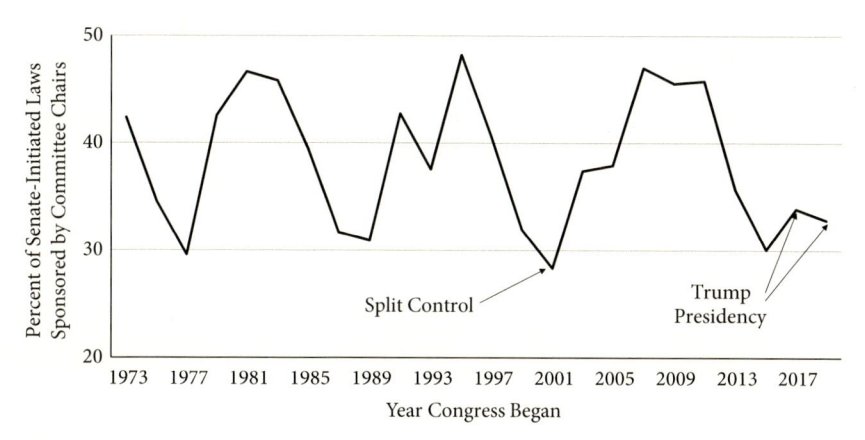

Figure 6.4 Percentage of Senate-Initiated Laws Sponsored by Committee Chairs, 1973–2021

Note: This figure plots the percent of Senate-initiated laws that were sponsored by Senate committee chairs between 1973 and 2021 (93rd–116th Congress). The figure demonstrates that chair-sponsored bills make up a relatively smaller portion of laws during the Trump years than in most earlier congresses.

respectively, arose from bills sponsored by Senate committee chairs. While these figures are slight upticks from what was obtained in the 114th Congress (30 percent), they were lower than the corresponding percentage in nearly every other recent congress; the one stark exception being the 107th Congress (2001–2003), when control of the Senate was split between the two parties, due to the post-election party switch of Senator Jim Jeffords of Vermont.

These findings suggest that lawmaking power was not concentrated in the hands of the Senate committee chairs during the Trump years—at least in comparison to other recent periods of congressional history. Did the decrease in the scope of Senate committee chair lawmaking success reflect a democratization of the lawmaking process across the Republican Party (and the Senate, more broadly considered)? Put another way, if committee chairs weren't carrying most of the legislative water, who was?

The data (see Figure 6.5) show that the answer to this question appears to be: "Not the majority Republican Party!"

Drawing on all public bills that were introduced into the US Senate between 1973 and 2021 (93rd–116th Congresses), we plot the percentage of bills passing the Senate that were sponsored by members of the majority party.

Figure 6.5 Percentage of Senate-Passed Bills Sponsored by Majority Party, 1973–2021

Note: This figure plots the percent of Senate bills that passed the chamber and were sponsored by the majority party between 1973 and 2021 (93rd–116th Congress). The figure demonstrates that majority-party sponsored bills made up a smaller share of passages during the Trump years than in prior congresses.

Consistent with our earlier findings (i.e., Volden and Wiseman 2018) that senators in the majority party are, *ceteris paribus*, more effective lawmakers than minority-party senators, we see that for nearly every congress (barring the split 107th Congress), majority-party sponsored bills make up a sizable portion of the bills that pass the Senate. Indeed, for much of the past half century, the percentage of bills passing the Senate that were sponsored by members of the majority party was well over 70 percent. During the Trump years, however, we see that the percentage of passed Senate bills that were sponsored by majority-party members hit low-water marks of approximately 63 percent and 61 percent, for the 115th and 116th Congresses, respectively. With the exception of the split-control 107th Senate, no other congress exists for which majority-party sponsored bills made up a smaller portion of bills that passed the Senate.

With neither committee chairs nor rank-and-file Republicans carrying forth the lawmaking agenda at previously common levels, Democrats appeared to have seen an opening for their own agenda items; and that agenda size was growing rapidly. When plotting the average number of public bills sponsored by Democratic and Republican senators across time, the Senate during the Trump years appears to be something of an anomaly (see Figure 6.6). Specifically, across the 114th–116th Congresses the majority

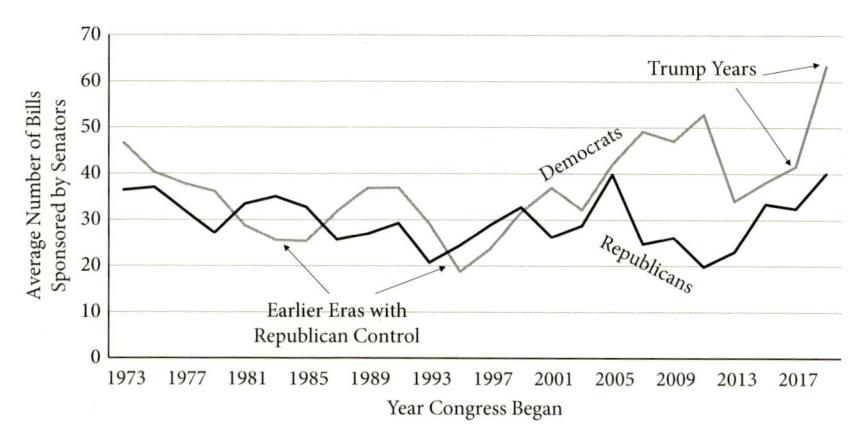

Figure 6.6 Average Number of Bills Sponsored by Senate Democrats and Republicans, 1973–2021

Note: This figure plots the average number of bills sponsored by Senate Democrats and Republicans between 1973–2021 (93rd–116th Congresses). Senate Democrats introduced more bills during the 116th Congress (2019–2021) than any previous Congress between 1973 and 2017, whereas the scope of Republican introductions was largely consistent with previous periods of Republican Party control.

(Republican) party introduced fewer bills, on average, than the minority party. Typically, minority-party legislators introduce fewer pieces of legislation than do majority-party lawmakers, including during earlier periods of Republican control of the Senate. The 115th and 116th Congresses, in particular, saw a notable uptick in the average number of bills sponsored by Democratic senators, in comparison to the 114th Congress (2015–2017), which was the most proximate one where Republicans were a majority. Indeed, across the entire time series, the 116th Congress corresponded to the highest average number of bills (63.3) being introduced by either party's members over the past fifty years. That such introductions came from the minority party is truly remarkable.

At the individual level, it is easy to identify Democratic senators who introduced a substantial number of bills in the 116th Congress, especially in comparison to the scope of their legislative agendas in the 115th Congress. Senator Gary Peters (D-Michigan), for example, introduced 86 bills into the 116th Congress, more than doubling the number that he introduced into the 115th Senate. Senator Jeff Merkley (D-Oregon) also more than doubled his portfolio, introducing 112 bills into the 116th Senate. And Senator Catherine Cortez Masto (D-Nevada) nearly quadrupled her proposed agenda between

Table 6.1 Top 10 Increased Bill Introductions across the 115th and the 116th Congresses (Democrats)

Name	115th	116th	Increase	% Increase
Edward Markey (MA)	69	134	65	94
Jeff Merkley (OR)	49	112	63	129
Catherine Cortez Masto (NV)	22	84	62	282
Gary Peters (MI)	37	86	49	132
Tina Smith (MN)	25	71	46	184
Richard Durbin (IL)	50	95	45	90
Robert Menendez (NJ)	56	100	44	79
Ron Wyden (OR)	59	100	41	69
Robert Casey (PA)	68	107	39	57
Chris Van Hollen (MD)	18	55	37	206

the 115th and 116th Congress. Senators Peters, Merkley, and Cortez Masto were clearly not lonely outliers in their party, as many Democratic senators introduced substantially more legislation, in both the absolute and relative sense, into the 116th Congress than they had introduced in the previous congress (see Table 6.1).

Of the top 10, increases in the raw number of bills across congresses range from a low of 37 (Senator Chris Van Hollen of Maryland) to a high of 65 (Senator Edward Markey of Massachusetts), with percentage increases across congresses ranging from 57 percent (Senator Robert Casey of Pennsylvania) to 282 percent (Senator Cortez Masto). These bills were nearly all substantive rather than commemorative measures. In the past, minority-party bill sponsorships tended to be low because senators did not want to waste time on activities with no chance of success; but many of these Democratic senators were quite successful at navigating several of their bills into law. Senator Peters, for example, saw 10 of his 86 bills ultimately become law, including the Safeguarding Tomorrow through Ongoing Risk Mitigation Act (STORM Act), the Support for Veterans in Effective Apprenticeship Act of 2019, and Protecting America's Food and Agriculture Act of 2019. Senator Merkley saw five of his 112 bills become law, including S. 2710, a "bill to prohibit the commercial export of covered munitions items to the Hong Kong Police Force." And Senator Cortez Masto saw three of her 84 bills become law, including S. 982, the Not Invisible Act of 2019, which sought to facilitate intergovernmental coordination to help to identify and diminish crimes against Native Americans.

On the Republican side, we see several high-profile pieces of legislation failing to make headway in the lawmaking process, despite seemingly being priorities of the Trump administration and the Republican Party. The Educational Opportunities Act (S. 5), introduced by Senator Marco Rubio (R-Florida), for example, was referred to the Committee on Finance, where it sat for the duration of the Congress. The Safe and Affordable Drugs from Canada Act of 2019 (S. 61), sponsored by Senator Chuck Grassley (R-Iowa), was referred to the Committee on Health, Education, Labor and Pensions following introduction where it, too, failed to advance further. Senator Lindsey Graham's (R-South Carolina) Defending American Security from Kremlin Aggression Act of 2019 (S. 482) was reported from the Foreign Relations Committee; but it failed to advance after being placed on the Senate's legislative calendar. For each of these high-profile Republican policy goals (as well as many others), Senate Republicans were unable to secure sufficient support for their initiatives to advance them all of the way through the lawmaking process.

The Sizable Democratic Agenda

What might explain the difference between the size of the legislative portfolios of Democratic and Republican senators during the Trump years, and especially in the 116th Congress? One possibility is that Democratic senators were simply introducing a substantial number of messaging bills, consistent with previous research (e.g., Lee 2016) suggesting that minority-party members introduce more messaging bills for campaigning purposes when majority control of the chamber is tenuous (e.g., Gelman 2020). That said, the unprecedented magnitude of the increase in minority-party introductions across congresses, combined with the fact that many Democratic senators obtained notable lawmaking successes in the 116th Congress, makes it unlikely that the increase was entirely (or even largely) due to messaging strategies.

To gain further clarity, we conducted open-ended interviews with senior legislative staff in the offices of Democratic (and some Republican) senators whose portfolios increased during the Trump presidency.[3] We asked about the nature of their increasing agenda sizes and their perceived prospects for success; especially for those in the minority party. Two primary themes emerged regarding the heightened portfolios sizes of Democratic senators. First, the onset of the COVID-19 pandemic required the Congress to react quickly, which led to a sizable body of legislation being introduced. Beyond the 2020 Coronavirus Aid, Relief, and Economic Security (CARES) Act and health-related matters, the pandemic affected constituents in myriad ways. As one staffer articulated, "We received many ideas and pressure from constituents to help in areas from assisting nonprofits, to tax policy needs, to small business issues."

The second explanation, offered by several Democratic staff members, is that Democratic senators—in the 116th Congress in particular—aggressively sought to pass legislative measures in response to numerous executive actions being advanced by the Trump administration. As one Democratic staffer said, the Trump administration was "breaking the government," and the Senate (often with Democrats in the lead) needed to respond.

We explore the plausibility of either (or both) of these explanations, by plotting the average number of health policy bills and government operations policy bills, respectively, that were introduced by Senate Democrats and Republicans between 1973 and 2021.[4] To the extent that the increase in Senate Democrat-sponsored bills in the 116th Congress was being driven by COVID-19 related considerations, we would expect to see a notable increase in the number of health policy bills sponsored by Senate Democrats, in comparison to previous congresses, which is precisely the picture that emerges (see Figure 6.7). More specifically, the average number of Democratic-sponsored bills rose from approximately five bills apiece in the 115th Congress to 8.5 bills in the 116th Congress: nearly a 65 percent increase, yielding the greatest emphasis on health issues over the past fifty years. We observe an increase on the Republican side as well, but the scope of the increase, with respect to raw number (2.7 bills) and percentage (53 percent) is smaller than among Senate Democrats.

Of course, the pandemic presented more than just a health care crisis. Democratic senators also increased their bill sponsorship significantly

---

[3] We relied on UVA IRB Protocol #5148.

[4] Bills are labeled as engaging with health policy or government operations based on how the bill is coded by the Congressional Research Service, as reported in Congress.gov.

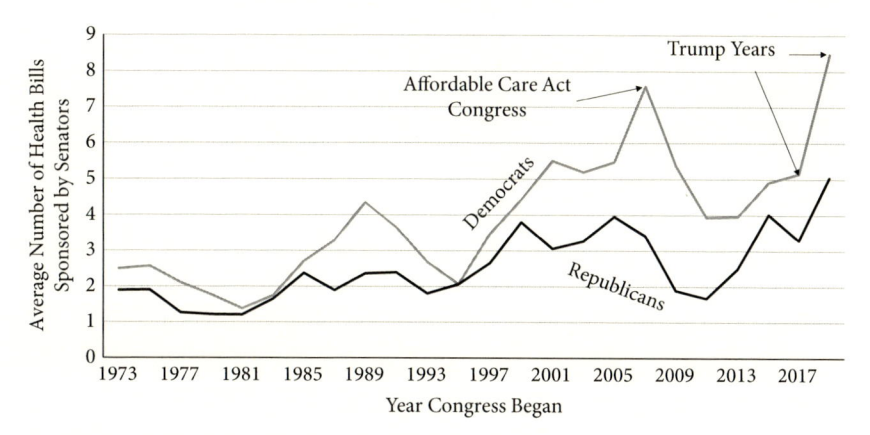

Figure 6.7   Average Number of Health Policy Bills Sponsored by Senate Democrats and Republicans, 1973–2021

Note: This figure plots the average number of health policy bills sponsored by Senate Democrats and Republicans between 1973–2021 (93rd–116th Congress). The figure demonstrates that Senate Democrats introduced more health policy bills during the 116th Congress (2019–2021) than any previous Senate since 1973, as well as more health policy bills (with respect to average number and percentage) than Republican Senators relative to the preceding (115th) Congress.

between the 115th and 116th Congresses in such related policy areas as commerce (87 percent increase), housing (188 percent), labor (103 percent), and welfare (123 percent). While Republican senators increased their bill sponsorship in these four areas as well, that increase was much more modest, averaging 37 percent. We also explore the extent to which the increase in Senate Democrat-sponsored bills in the 116th Congress was being driven by Democrats reacting to executive actions by the Trump administration (see Figure 6.8). Doing so might result in the introduction of a wide range of legislation that would generally fall under the "government operations" issue categorization. Similar to Figure 6.7, we see that the average Democratic senator did, indeed, introduce notably more government operations-related bills in the 116th Congress (approximately 5.7 bills, up from 3.8 bills); which was likewise an increase over the average number of Democratic-sponsored bills in this issue area in the 114th Congress (2.95), prior to the election of President Trump. Similar to Figure 6.7, we also observe an increase on the Republican side between the 115th and 116th Congress, but the scope of the increase, with respect to raw number (a 1.0 bill rise) and percentage (35 percent increase) was smaller than what was occurring with Senate Democrats. While both parties were engaging more with Government Operations in the 116th Congress, it was the Senate Democrats, more so than Senate

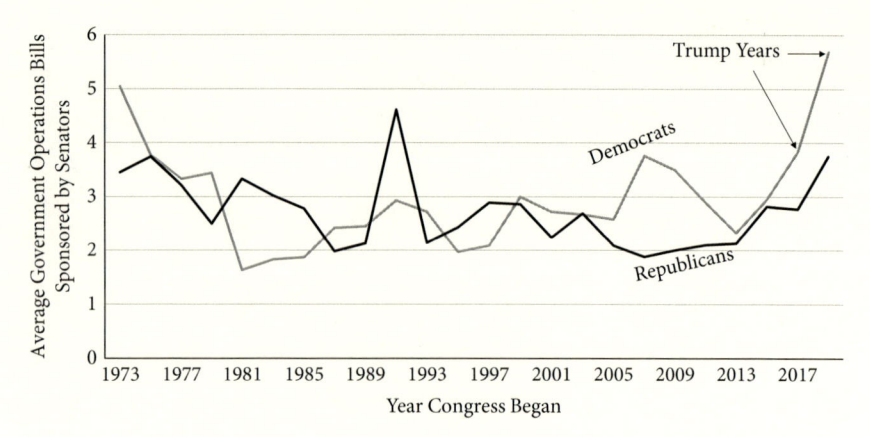

Figure 6.8 Average Number of Government Operations Policy Bills Sponsored by Senate Democrats and Republicans, 1973–2021

Note: This figure plots the average number of government operations policy bills sponsored by Senate Democrats and Republicans between 1973–2021 (93rd–116th Congresses). The figure demonstrates that Senate Democrats introduced more bills that engaged with government operations during the 116th Congress (2019–2021) than any previous congress since 1973, as well as more government operations policy bills (with respect to average number and percentage) than Republican senators relative to the preceding Congress.

Republicans, driving the policy agenda in this area. Senate Democrats also responded with increased bill sponsorship in other areas of Trump executive branch initiatives, with a 62-percent increase in immigration proposals between the 115th and 116th Congresses, and a 127-percent increase in international affairs bills.

Hence, the data suggest that conjectures offered by Democratic staff are both plausible: Democratic senators' lawmaking priorities were being driven by pandemic considerations, and they were also being influenced by the desire to provide a counterweight to the executive activities of the Trump administration. Similar to the fate of the large majority of all bills introduced in Congress, most of these proposals fell by the wayside, often dying in committee. That said, the enhanced legislative activity of Democratic senators, coupled with the types of successes noted above, showed the minority party to be a highly active and involved lawmaking partner during the Trump years.

In comparison to the average Legislative Effectiveness Scores of members of the Senate majority and minority parties for all congresses since the 1970s, we see that the average LES for minority-party members in the 115th and 116th Congresses (0.80 and 0.93, respectively) were among the very highest for minority-party members across our entire time series (see Figure 6.9).

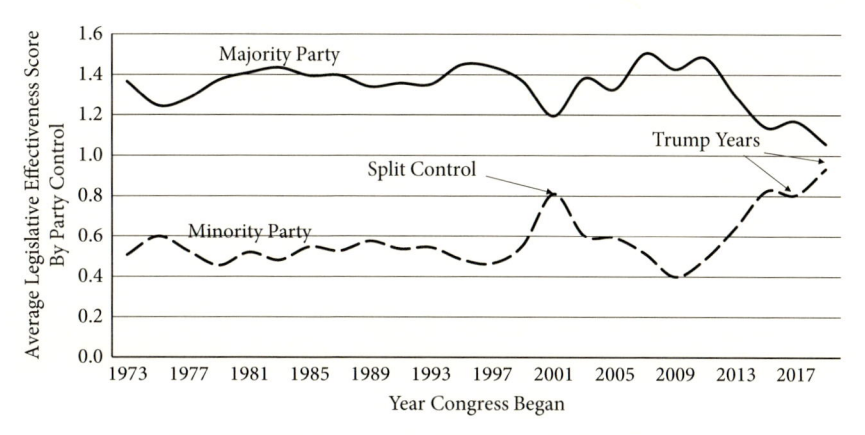

Figure 6.9 Average LES for Majority and Minority Party Senators, 1973–2021

Note: This figure plots the average Legislative Effectiveness Score for majority- and minority-party senators between 1973 and 2021 (93rd–116th Congress). The figure demonstrates minority-party LESs were higher for Democrats during the Trump years than almost all other congresses between 1973 and 2015; and majority party (Republican during the Trump years) LESs were among the lowest average scores for any congresses in our time series.

Indeed, the average LES for minority-party senators in the 116th Congress was *the* highest value for our dataset. In contrast, we see that the 116th Congress corresponded to the lowest average majority-party LES (1.06) for our entire time series.

As illustrated in Figure 6.6, one reason that the average Republican senator had such a low LES, despite being in the majority party, is that they simply were introducing less legislation (comparatively speaking). This pattern of behavior is consistent with the observations of a Republican staffer we interviewed who noted that Majority Leader McConnell often did not receive clear direction from the Trump administration on legislative priorities. As one Democratic staffer put it, the president was more focused on getting "tons of judicial nominees" and "Twitter fodder" than on actual legislative accomplishments. In terms of nominees, McConnell focused his attention on confirming federal judges, a task over which he had significant autonomy, and which yielded a clear political payoff.

In sum, despite having to engage with a highly partisan president who openly opposed Democratic initiatives, and a majority leader who recognized clear ties between legislative victories and political victories, Democratic senators navigated these choppy waters to achieve greater levels of success than any minority party had achieved in any prior congress that we have measured. To be sure, they needed to moderate their proposals and engage in bipartisan compromise along the way (Harbridge-Yong, Volden, and Wiseman 2023). But the data show Democratic senators during the Trump years serving as lawmaking partners to an unprecedented extent relative to what is typical of the minority party. In contrast, the (majority) Republican Party sought to advance a relatively limited legislative agenda; and it was historically less successful in advancing that agenda, in comparison to the minority party, than at any other point in time since our data began, in 1973.

Break with the Past, Or Business as Usual?

Political scientists, journalists, and more casual observers of politics have pointed to the Trump presidency as years marked by profound political change in the United States and its governing institutions. Had this vitriolic rhetoric and extreme polarization extended to lawmaking in the Senate, we might have expected all Democratic proposals to be dead on arrival, and an even starker difference than before, between majority-party lawmaking success and minority-party legislative failure. We might have expected majority-party lawmakers, and committee chairs in particular, to secure significant legislative achievements, putting in place a record of conservative accomplishments. In fact, the patterns were just the opposite.

Democratic senators engaged in putting forward legislative proposals at an unprecedented rate—on the pandemic, in counter to Trump actions, and beyond. And, despite being in the minority party, their proposals gained sufficient support to yield a greater number of substantive laws originating from minority-party senators than was found in any previous congress for at least the past half-century.

Do these patterns and outcomes represent a clear break from the past, a continuation of prior trends, or something simply unique to the Trump years? Our interviews with senior Senate staff suggested that they experienced and observed unique features over this time period. In particular, many commented on how disengaged the president was with lawmaking and deal-making in Congress. This is consistent with scholarly arguments about President Trump being largely devoid of policy interests (e.g., Lawless and Theriault 2021). Without his leadership, Republican initiatives did not have the natural support and thus the level of success enjoyed by most previous presidents sharing congressional majorities.

In terms of a continuation of trends, Majority Leader McConnell's continued efforts at judicial nominations, at the expense of legislative initiatives, continued with enthusiastic Trump support. Most notably, this effort forged a likely long-enduring conservative majority on the Supreme Court, and, perhaps, throughout the entire federal court system. Also continuing prior trends, the percentage of Senate-initiated laws that were sponsored by committee chairs had been declining since the mid-2000s (from Figure 6.4), as part of a pattern of "unorthodox lawmaking" (Sinclair 1997). The percentage of Senate bills passed that were sponsored by the majority party had likewise been declining since the late 2000s (as illustrated in Figure 6.5). While the Trump presidency represented notable accelerations in both of these trends, it would be inappropriate to say that the Senate displayed a clear break from its past.

The extent to which the minority party was able to overperform, with regards to their lawmaking effectiveness, is clearly worthy of further study. It should also be considered a good sign for American democracy. Despite partisan polarization, if ideas for policy improvements can come from both sides of the aisle and have a reasonable chance of consideration and passage, that bodes well for addressing policy needs that arise—whether due to pandemics, governing crises, or other major challenges. We are intrigued to see whether the lawmaking enthusiasm of Democrats continues in the years ahead with shifting control of Congress and the presidency, as well as whether minority-party involvement and lawmaking successes will be equally evident among Republicans. If so, a perhaps surprising result of the Trump years will be heightened bipartisan lawmaking in the US Senate.

References

Bradbury, Erin, Ryan Davidson, and C. Lawrence Evans. 2008. "The Senate Whip System: An Exploration." In *Why Not Parties? Party Effects in the United States Senate.* Nathan W. Monroe, Jason M. Roberts, and David W. Rohde, eds. Chicago: University of Chicago Press, 73–99.

Evans, C. Lawrence. 2018. *The Whips: Building Party Coalitions in Congress.* Ann Arbor: University of Michigan Press.

Gelman, Jeremy. 2020. *Losing to Win: Why Congressional Majorities Play Politics Instead of Make Laws.* Ann Arbor: University of Michigan Press.

Harbridge-Yong, Laurel, Craig Volden, and Alan E. Wiseman. 2023. "The Bipartisan Path to Effective Lawmaking." *Journal of Politics* 85(3): 1048–1063.

Hershberger, Ethan, William Minozzi, and Craig Volden. 2018. "Party Calls and Reelection in the U.S. Senate." *Journal of Politics* 80(4): 1394–1399.

Lawless, Jennifer L, and Sean M. Theriault. 2021. "The People, the President, and the Congress at a Crossroads: Can We Turn Back from Gridlock?" In *The Presidency: Constitutional Crossroads*. Michael Nelson and Barbara A. Perry, eds. Charlottesville: University of Virginia Press.

Lee, Frances E. 2009. *Beyond Ideology: Politics, Principles, and Partisanship in the U.S. Senate*. Chicago: University of Chicago Press.

Lee, Frances E. 2016. *Insecure Majorities: Congress and the Perpetual Campaign*. Chicago: University of Chicago Press.

Leonnig, Carol, and Philip Rucker. 2021. *I Alone Can Fix It: Donald J. Trump's Catastrophic Final Year*. New York: Penguin Press.

MacNeil, Neil, and Richard A. Baker. 2013. *The American Senate: An Insider's History*. New York: Oxford University Press.

Patty, John W. 2008. "Equilibrium Party Government." *American Journal of Political Science* 52(3): 636–655.

Pearson, Kathryn. 2008. "Party Loyalty and Discipline in the Individualistic Senate." In *Why Not Parties? Party Effects in the United States Senate*. Nathan W. Monroe, Jason M. Roberts, and David W. Rohde, eds. Chicago: University of Chicago Press, 100–120.

Rucker, Philip, and Carol Leonnig. 2020. *A Very Stable Genius: Donald J. Trump's Testing of America*. New York: Penguin Press.

Sinclair, Barbara. 1997. *Unorthodox Lawmaking: New Legislative Processes in the United States Congress*. Washington, DC: CQ Press.

Sinclair, Barbara. 2017. "Patterns and Dynamics of Congressional Change." In *Congress Reconsidered*, 11 ed. Lawrence C. Dodd and Bruce I. Oppenheimer, eds. Washington, DC: CQ Press.

Strahan, Randall W. 2011. "Party Leadership." In *Oxford Handbook of the American Congress*. Eric Schickler and Frances E. Lee, eds. New York: Oxford University Press, 371–395.

Theriault, Sean M., and David W. Rohde. 2011. "The Gingrich Senators and Party Polarization in the U.S. Senate." *Journal of Politics* 73(4): 1011–1024.

Volden, Craig, and Elizabeth Bergman. 2006. "How Strong Should Our Party Be? Party Member Preferences Over Party Cohesion." *Legislative Studies Quarterly* 31(1): 71–104.

Volden, Craig, and Alan E. Wiseman. 2014. *Legislative Effectiveness in the United States Congress: The Lawmakers*. New York: Cambridge University Press.

Volden, Craig, and Alan E. Wiseman. 2018. "Legislative Effectiveness in the United States Senate." *Journal of Politics* 80(2): 731–735.

Volden, Craig, and Alan E. Wiseman. 2021. "Party, Ideology, and Legislative Effectiveness in the U.S. Senate." In *Congress Reconsidered*, 12 ed. Lawrence C. Dodd, Bruce I. Oppenheimer, and C. Lawrence Evans, eds. Washington, DC: CQ Press, 375–402.

7

Leadership in the Modern Senate

Introduction

The claim that former president Donald J. Trump disrupted politics in the United States is reasonable. Trump is a polarizing figure.[1] His behavior as president and his postpresidency has divided Americans into rival camps that see the world differently.[2] In many respects, however, the people in each camp view politics through the same Trump-tinted lens.[3] For example, Trump's supporters and critics alike credit the former president with disrupting business-as-usual in the nation's capital. Trump's 2016 pledge to "drain the swamp" and his ongoing effort to transform the Republican Party since leaving office signal to his supporters that he disrupted Washington's out-of-touch political establishment. Trump's critics similarly believe that the former president disrupted the political status quo, albeit negatively. In their opinion, Trump's behavior in office and his continued influence over the Republican Party since leaving office have endangered American self-government.[4]

[1] According to *Gallup*, Trump has "the most polarized approval ratings of any president." See Frank Newport, "The Public Opinion Context for Trump's Reelection Bid," *Gallup*, February 21, 2020.
[2] There are relatively few Americans who do not have an opinion of Trump. See "4 in 10 Would Back a Trump Presidential Bid in 2024," *Monmouth University*, August 9, 2022.
[3] According to a recent poll conducted by the Pew Research Center, approximately nine self-identifying Republicans (89 percent) presently view their party favorably. The *PEW* poll also found that approximately six-in-ten Republicans (59 percent) who "identify strongly with the Republican Party say they like political leaders who assert that Trump won" the 2020 election. See "As Partisan Hostility Grows, Signs of Frustration With the Two-Party System," *Pew Research Center*, August 9, 2022.
[4] For example, see Alexander Burns and Jonathan Martin, "Trump's Takeover of the Republican Party Is Almost Complete," *New York Times*, April 3, 2019; Janet Hook, "'It Is the Era of Trump': How the President Is Remaking the Republican Party," *Wall Street Journal*, August 27, 2018; Steve Peoples, "In a Party Dominated by Trumpism, Growing Ranks of Forgotten Republicans Sound Warning," *Chicago Tribune*, August 18, 2018; Trump's critics also acknowledge the former president's continued influence on the Republican Party. For example, President Joe Biden asserted in a prime-time address that "Donald Trump and the MAGA Republicans represent an extremism that threatens the very foundations of our republic." See Joe Biden, "Remarks by President Biden on the Continued Battle for the Soul of the Nation," *The White House*, September 1, 2022.

James Wallner, *Leadership in the Modern Senate* In: *Disruption?* Edited by: Sean M. Theriault, Oxford University Press. © Oxford University Press 2024. DOI: 10.1093/oso/9780197767832.003.0008

Trump's supporters and critics cite Congress's recent dysfunction as evidence that the former president disrupted business-as-usual politics. In short, they believe Trump caused the House of Representatives and Senate to operate differently. Trump's critics, especially, believe that the former president used his popularity with Republican voters to change lawmakers' behavior.[5] Trump's popularity with Republican voters caused Republican lawmakers to become more extreme. Republican lawmakers in thrall to Trump pursued more extreme goals and were less willing to compromise with Democrats.[6] This Trump-fueled extremism made lawmakers more polarized and partisan than they were before Trump was president. And that made legislating harder. In other words, Trump caused Congress to gridlock. By gridlock, I mean instances when lawmakers do not act and, by extension, Congress does not legislate.

Yet the Trump-tinted lens through which millions of Americans view politics distorts what happens inside Congress on a regular basis, especially in the Senate. This is because the observed behavior of senators before, during, and immediately after Trump's presidency suggests that the former president did not cause the institution to operate differently, which is evident in the persistence of business-as-usual politics inside the Senate from 2009 to 2022. During that time, senators used the same cluster of procedural practices to regulate the legislative process, regardless of who was president of which party controlled the House and Senate. Those practices empowered the Senate's majority and minority leaders to regulate the legislative process. In doing so, Senate leaders made it harder for rank-and-file senators to participate in the legislative process. And that made it harder for the Senate to legislate. That is why the Senate struggled to pass legislation during this period dealing with salient issues like abortion, gun control, health care, immigration, and voting rights. In other words, the Senate and its leaders caused gridlock. Not Trump.

---

[5] For example, See: Jonathan Martin and Maggie Haberman, "Fear and Loyalty: How Donald Trump Took Over the Republican Party," *New York Times*, December 1, 2019; Perry Bacon Jr., "Trump completed his takeover of the GOP in 2019," *FiveThirtyEight*, December 23, 2019; Daniel J. Galvin, "Party Domination and Base Mobilization: Donald Trump and Republican Party Building in a Polarized Era," *The Forum* 18(2) 2020: 135–168. Galvin argues, "The source of Trump's power thus lies not in his mastery of political hardball, per se, but rather in the reliable support he receives from devoted Republican voters and the broader conservative organizational ecosystem, both of which back up Trump's threats wit real consequences" (152).

[6] "Trump has established a commanding influence over his party—some have even likened it to a 'cult of personality.'" Ibid., 149.

This chapter aims to bridge the gap between Trump-centric views of the Senate and the reality of everyday politics in the institution by first considering how the Senate operated before, during, and immediately after Trump's presidency. Reviewing the Senate's legislative record from 2009 to 2022 demonstrates that gridlock is not unique to the Trump-era Senate. The chapter next details the cluster of procedural practices that senators used throughout the thirteen years to structure the legislative process. It concludes by considering the implications of Trump-centric interpretations of gridlock for the Senate moving forward.

The Senate's Legislative Record

Comparing what happened inside the Senate when Trump was president to how it operated before and after his time in office indicates that he did not disrupt business-as-usual politics in the institution. The Senate's legislative record is instead remarkably consistent from 2009 to 2022. The institution was gridlocked throughout this period, and its decision-making process was centralized under the majority and minority leaders.

Upon first inspection, the Trump-era Senate does not appear gridlocked. Indeed, the Senate's overall performance in the 115th and 116th Congresses (2017–2021) suggests that Trump positively impacted the institution's legislative productivity. For example, the Senate passed more bills in both congresses than in any comparable two-year period during Obama's presidency or during the first two years of Biden's (see Figure 7.1). A top spokesman for Majority Leader Mitch McConnell (R-Kentucky) went so far as to describe the Senate's legislative record in the 115th Congress as "the most accomplished . . . in decades."[7]

A closer inspection of the bills that senators approved when Trump was president and how they passed them indicates that such an upbeat assessment of the Senate's record is unwarranted. Instead, the Trump-era Senate only appears productive juxtaposed to the institution's recent nadir in the 112th Congress when Obama was president. When assessed more broadly, the Trump-era Senate looks a lot like the Obama-era Senate and the early Biden-era Senate (see Figure 7.2).

---

[7] Derek Willis and Paul Kane, "How Congress Stopped Working," *Washington Post*, November 5, 2018.

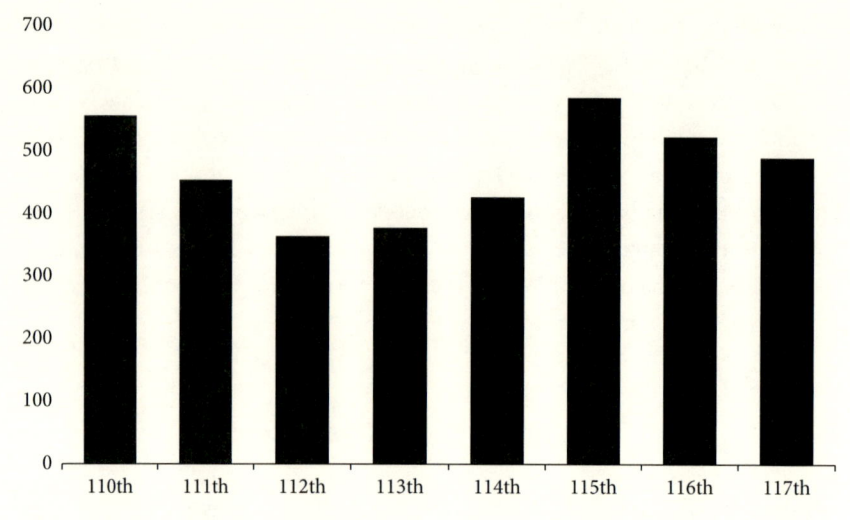

Figure 7.1 The Number of Bills the Senate Passed, 110th to 117th Congresses (2009–2023)

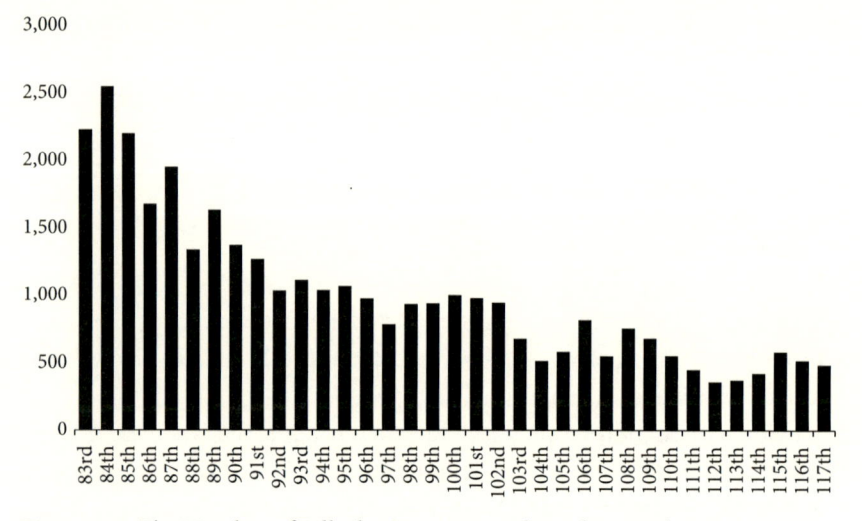

Figure 7.2 The Number of Bills the Senate Passed, 83rd to 117th Congresses (1953-2023)

The Senate also appeared productive when Trump was president because of the number of uncontroversial bills passed in the 115th and 116th Congresses. Of the 585 total bills that the Senate passed in the 115th Congress, 106 of them renamed post offices or other federal buildings. One bill (Public Law 115–277) renamed a piece of legislation enacted into law in 2012.[8] Twenty-five bills temporarily extended existing programs or delayed statutory deadlines. In addition, senators made routine technical corrections to legislation they had passed on six occasions. Furthermore, the Senate approved thirty-three bills that were commemorative.

In the 116th Congress, the Senate passed 523 bills, of which 96 renamed post offices or other federal buildings. One bill (Public Law 116–198) allowed the Scopio A. Jones Post Office in Little Rock, Arkansas, to hang a portrait of Scopio A. Jones on its walls. Another bill (Public Law 116–115) changed the address of a Post Office. Twenty-nine bills temporarily extended existing programs, maintained current funding levels, or delayed statutory deadlines. Senators made routine technical corrections to legislation they had passed previously on four occasions. The Senate approved thirty-four commemorative bills. Furthermore, senators passed six bills approving new citizen regents to the Smithsonian's Board of Regents.

How the Senate approved bills during Trump's presidency further suggests that they dealt with mostly uncontroversial issues. How the Senate passes a bill is a useful proxy for its controversy, given that senators typically clear uncontroversial legislation by voice vote or unanimous consent, whereas they typically approve controversial legislation with a roll call vote.[9] Senators almost always use roll-call votes to pass controversial bills because it is relatively easy for any senator to require it. Once recognized by the presiding officer, any senator may request the "Yeas" and "Nays" (i.e., a roll-call vote) provided they have a "sufficient second."[10] In contrast, senators usually pass uncontroversial bills through voice votes and unanimous consent because it is more efficient. Roll-call votes take longer than asking for a voice vote or propounding a unanimous consent request.[11]

Senators used a similar mix of these three methods to pass bills when Trump was president that they used when Obama was president and during the first two years of Biden's presidency. From 2009 to 2022, senators used

---

[8] HR 6870 (Public Law 115–277) renamed the Stop Trading on Congressional Knowledge Act of 2012 in honor of Representative Louise McIntosh Slaughter.

[9] Senators can pass a bill in four ways: voice vote, roll call vote; division vote; unanimous consent. The Senate rarely uses division votes. For a description of division votes, see Floyd M. Riddick and Alan S. Frumin, *Riddick's Senate Procedure* (Washington, DC: Government Printing Office, 1992), 1404–1409.

[10] Ibid., 1397. The number of senators constituting a "sufficient second" varies depending on the total number of senators present (i.e., the Senate's quorum size)

[11] Senators establish the 15-minute recorded vote time limit by unanimous consent at the beginning of each Congress.

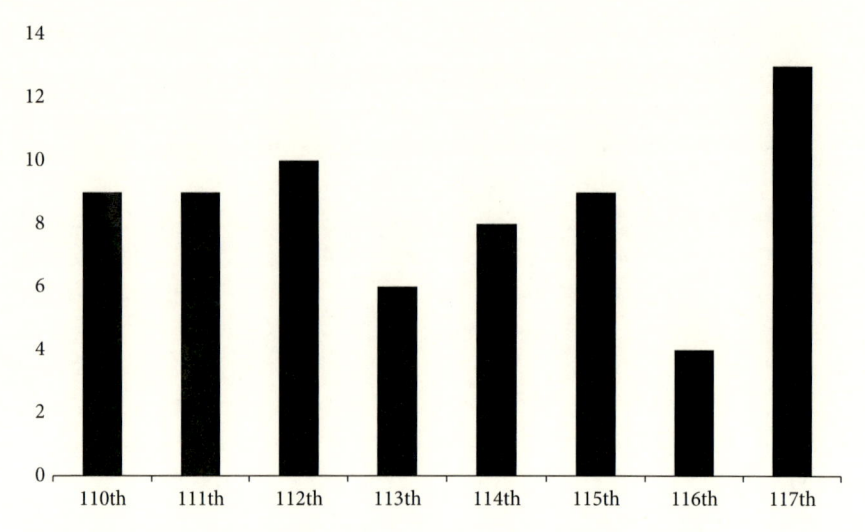

Figure 7.3 Percent of Bills Passed on a Roll-Call Vote in the Senate

roll-call votes to pass legislation less often than voice votes and unanimous consent (see Figure 7.3). For example, the Senate passed 52 bills (out of 585) using a roll-call vote in the 115th Congress. It passed 533 bills using a voice vote or by unanimous consent. In the 116th Congress, the Senate passed 22 bills (out of 523) by a roll call vote. It approved the remaining 501 bills by voice vote or by unanimous consent. In the 117th Congress, the Senate passed 38 bills (out of 490) using a recorded vote.

In contrast, senators struggled to debate, much less pass, controversial bills when Trump was president. The Republican-controlled Senate was especially gridlocked during Trump's first 100 days in office, a period when presidential initiatives are usually successful in Congress, especially when the same party controls Congress and the presidency.[12] One contemporaneous account notes that the Senate did not pass a significant bill for the first eleven months of 2017.[13]

---

[12] For example, see David R. Mayhew, *Divided We Govern: Party Control, Lawmaking, and Investigations, 1946–2002* (New Haven, CT: Yale University Press, 1991); Matthew N. Beckman and Joseph Godfrey, "The Policy Opportunities in Presidential Honeymoons," *Political Research Quarterly* 60(2): 250–62.

[13] Matt Fuller, "Republicans Leave Town With Nothing To Show: The GOP's failure to pass any major legislative priorities has imperiled the Trump administration's agenda." *Huffington Post,* August 3, 2017.

Divisions among Republicans when Trump was president encouraged Republican Leader McConnell to clamp down on the legislative process while developing a consensus bill that could unite the party. The Senate worked when McConnell succeeded. And it gridlocked when he failed. For example, Republicans failed to repeal and replace the Affordable Care Act (Public Law 111–148) in 2017.[14] And while their tax reform effort was successful, it was much harder than Republicans initially anticipated.[15] In both examples, Republican leaders planned to keep each bill's provisions a secret until the last minute to make it harder for its critics to pick it apart and, relatedly, for Democrats to defeat the proposal on the Senate floor.[16]

Managing the Senate

The limits of Trump's ability to disrupt business-as-usual politics in the Senate are also evident in the cluster of procedural practices senators used to structure the legislative process before, during, and after Trump's presidency. Under the so-called regular order, senators first consider bills in committee before debating them on the floor. And senators face few constraints on their ability to debate and amend legislation during floor debate. Under irregular order, which characterized Senate decision-making consistently from 2009 to 2022, senators often skip the committee stage when considering controversial bills. Instead, the majority and minority leaders determine policy outcomes by crafting must-pass bills with little or no input from rank-and-file senators. And the leaders structure floor debate so that senators have few opportunities to participate in it. As a result, the floor debate is truncated. And senators are barred from offering amendments.

Gridlock is more likely to happen in debates structured by irregular order because the cluster of procedural practices it embodies prevents a "legislative struggle" from happening (Gross 1953). In doing so, irregular order makes it harder for senators to compromise because struggle creates the conditions for compromise to emerge. Leaders, therefore, make compromise harder to

---

[14] Maggie Haberman and Robert Pear, "Trump Tells Congress to Repeal and Replace Health Care Law 'Very Quickly,'" *New York Times*, January 10, 2017).

[15] The Senate passed the Tax Cuts and Jobs Act of 2017 (Public Law 115–197) on December 2, 2017, by a vote of 51 to 49. Initially optimistic, McConnell observed early in the debate, "If there's anything that unifies Republicans, it's tax reform." Bess Levin, "Republicans Hope to Save Themselves With Tax Plan Nobody Wants," *Vanity Fair*, October 25, 2017.

[16] Scott Wong and Alexander Bolton, "GOP Plans Tax Blitzkrieg," *The Hill*, October 28.

achieve and gridlock more likely by preventing senators from debating and amending bills on the Senate floor.

Senate parties are more likely to embrace the cluster of procedural practices observed from 2009 to 2022 when they have significant internal divisions. In such circumstances, senators are more in need of delegating agenda power to their leaders to ensure that those divisions do not jeopardize their ability to act in other areas (Aldrich 2011). As more and more issues divide a given party's members, the need is a greater to exclude more issues from the agenda to prevent the preexisting party coalition from fracturing. In addition, the fear of a messy and potentially majority-costing break-up leads senators to empower their leaders further to keep divisive issues off the agenda.

Party leaders are skilled at using their ability to control the agenda to serve senators in another way. When potentially coalition-splitting decisions must be made, such as passing legislation government funding legislation, leaders engineer "must pass" bills that make passage more likely and effectively diminish senators' accountability. Leaders almost always wait until the last minute to unveil legislation to confront senators with a fait accompli. If they fail to assent, the story goes, voters will punish them for their abject failure by voting against them in the next election. Leaders can thus keep divisive issues from disrupting the appearance of partisan unity without jeopardizing a bill's passage.

Irregular order's centralized leader control of Senate decision-making is evident in the cluster of procedural practices that senators used to regulate the legislative process before, during, and immediately after Trump's presidency. Those practices empower leaders by allowing them to speed up the legislative process by bypassing committee consideration of controversial bills and putting them directly on the Senate's calendar of business.[17] And the majority and minority leaders effectively control when and how the Senate votes to begin debate on a bill.

The Senate routinely bypassed the committee stage of the legislative process from 2009 to 2022.[18] According to a 2018 study conducted jointly by

---

[17] The Senate's calendar of business is the list of measures eligible for floor consideration. It includes all bills reported by the Senate's committees and those placed directly on the calendar by senators. *Riddick's Senate Procedure*, 253–267.

[18] Senate Rule XIV stipulates that the Presiding Officer shall refer bills to the appropriate committee of jurisdiction after senators introduce them. Rule XIV also empowers senators to skip committee consideration and place bills directly on the Senate calendar, making them eligible for immediate floor consideration. "Rule XIV: Bills, Joint Resolutions, Resolutions, and Preambles Thereto," *Standing Rules of the Senate*, (Washington, DC: Government Printing Office, 2007), 9.

the *Washington Post* and *Pro Publica*, Senate committees met to consider legislation only 69 times in 2016, down from 252 times in 2006.[19] Democratic and Republican majorities increasingly bypassed committee consideration of controversial bills and put them directly on the calendar from 2009 to 2022. The Senate's increased reliance on Rule XIV indicates a broader shift in how the Senate operates.

Regardless of how a bill gets on the calendar, the majority leader typically works with the minority leader to schedule bills for floor debate during the period in the structured consent pattern. The two leaders cooperated because it was in both of their interests to prevent a free-flowing decision-making process from unfolding on the Senate floor during this period. In addition, the leaders limited amendment opportunities to prevent rank-and-file senators from forcing hot-button issues onto the institution's agenda unexpectedly and before deciding how best to deal with them.

When Obama was president, the Senate increasingly used cloture to end the motion to proceed debate. Those votes were not always partisan. For example, in the 110th Congress, 69 senators voted to invoke cloture on the Medicare Improvements for Patients and Providers Act (Public Law 110–275) and the Comprehensive Immigration Reform Act (S. 1348), and 64 senators voted to invoke cloture on another comprehensive immigration bill (S. 1639). In the 111th Congress, 72 senators voted to end the debate on the motion to proceed to the Lilly Ledbetter Fair Pay Act of 2009 (S. 181), bringing together 100 percent of the majority party and 43 percent of the minority party. During consideration of the Family Smoking Prevention and Tobacco Control Act (HR 1256), 84 senators voted to invoke cloture on the motion to proceed, including 98 percent of Democrats and 74 percent of Republicans. The Affordable Care Act was the exception.

The Amendment Process

The majority and minority leaders also worked together to control the amendment process when the Senate considered controversial bills on the floor before, during, and immediately after Trump's presidency. Their efforts are evident because the Senate considered few amendments from 2009 to 2022 (see Figure 7.4).

---

[19] Derek Willis and Paul Kane, "How Congress Stopped Working," *Washington Post*, November 5.

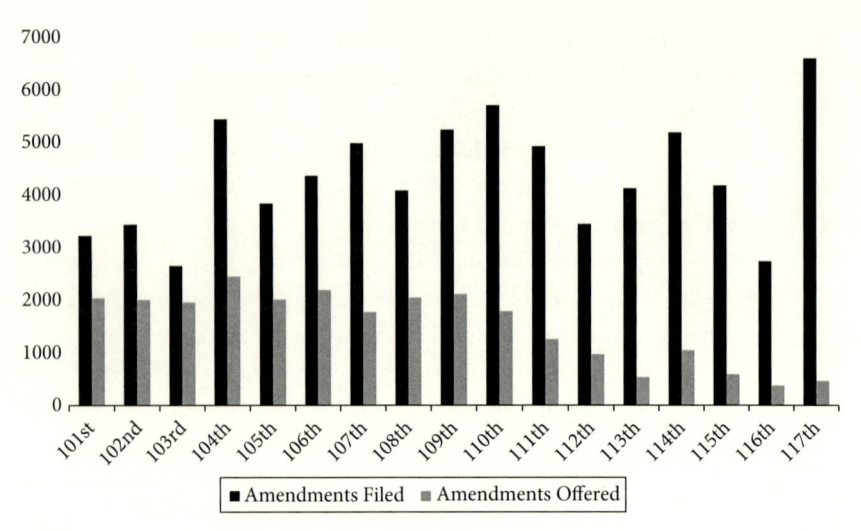

Figure 7.4 Amendments Filed and Offered

Senators offered, on average, 1,773 amendments in every congress from the 97th Congress to the 114th Congress. The 599 amendments that senators offered during the 115th Congress represent a 68 percent decline from that average. The Senate's amendment activity remained relatively consistent, fluctuating up and down every two years until the 111th Congress when senators began to offer fewer amendments consistently. The number of amendments senators offered in the 111th Congress fell by 30 percent, 23 percent in the 112th Congress, and 44 percent in the 113th Congress.

The Senate considered more amendments after Republicans won a majority in the 2014 elections, increasing 94 percent in the 114th Congress. These gains were temporary, and the Senate's amendment activity declined again when Trump was president. The number of amendments that the Senate considered fell by 43 percent in the 115th Congress and 37 percent in the 116th Congress. In doing so, the Senate was reverting to the trend of fewer amendments that began when Obama was president (see Figure 7.5). Of the amendments offered, those considered are disposed of primarily by voice vote and unanimous consent instead of by a roll-call vote (see Figure 7.6).

Using voice votes and unanimous consent to dispose of amendments makes it difficult for polarized parties to use them for messaging purposes or to differentiate their members from one another. In contrast, roll-call

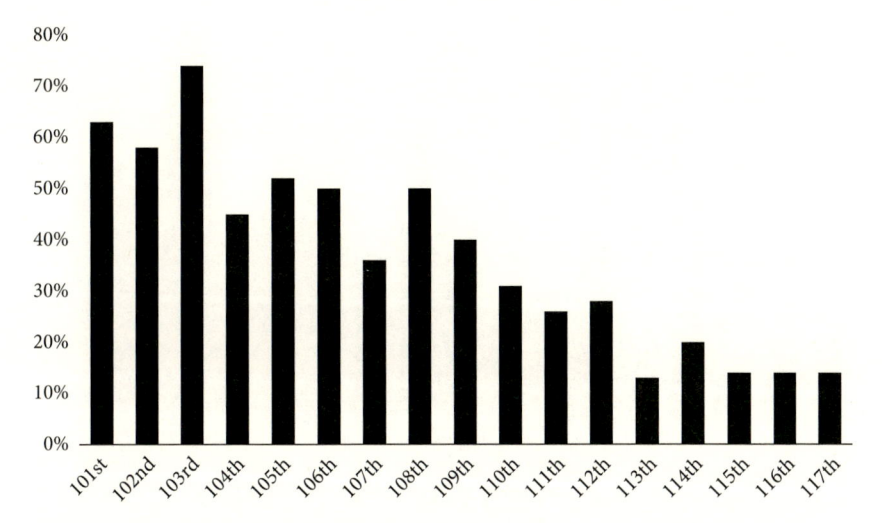

Figure 7.5 Percentage of Filed Amendments Offered

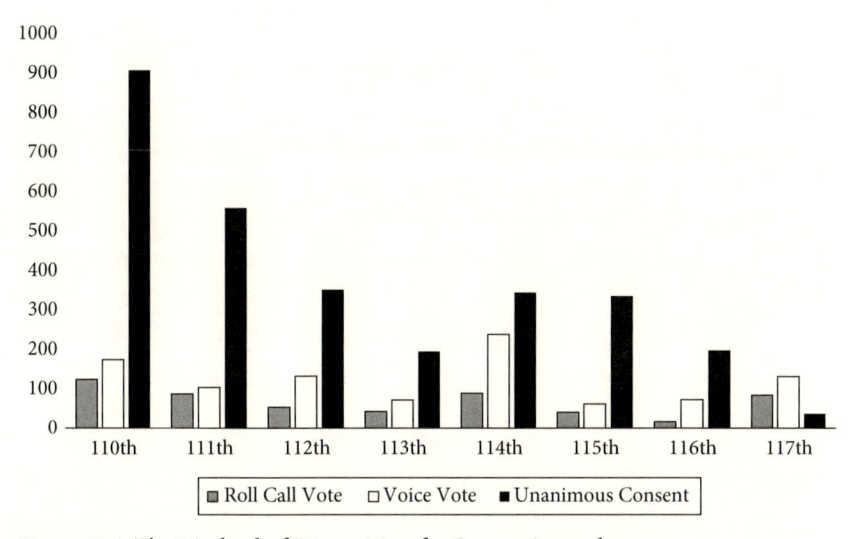

Figure 7.6 The Method of Disposition for Senate Amendments

votes clearly distinguish senators. The amendment data, because Senate rules include few limits on the amending process, should be nimble enough to measure Trump's influence on senators. Moreover, the ability to offer amendments on the floor is particularly useful for senators in the minority

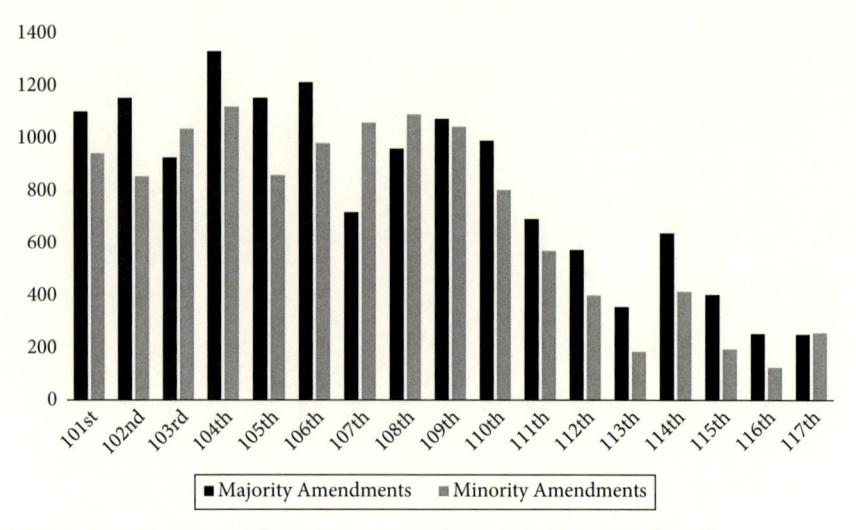

Figure 7.7 Majority and Minority Amendments (Filed and Offered)

party, especially if the majority-controlled committees resist reporting minority-sponsored measures. Minority party senators thus have a powerful way to achieve their policy and political goals through their ability to offer amendments. The data should therefore reflect Democrats offering more amendments when Trump was president and Republicans offering more amendments when Obama and Biden were president. What the data show is a declining trend in the number of minority amendments offered before, during, and after Trump's presidency (see Figure 7.7). These amendment data suggest that senators behaved the same when Trump was president as they did when Obama and Biden were president.

Conclusion

This analysis implies that Trump did not cause the Senate to gridlock. Senators and their leaders did. The observed behavior of senators from 2009 to 2022 suggests that they behaved similarly before, during, and immediately after Trump's presidency. They did not act inside the Senate to achieve their individual goals. Senators deferred to their leaders to structure the legislative process in ways that ensured nothing happened to advance controversial legislation on the Senate floor until they agreed. They believed that doing so was needed to achieve their goals. But the leaders managed the Senate in such a way that made it harder for senators to legislate. Consequently, senators spent their time in quorum calls and voting to confirm presidential nominees instead of debating controversial issues on the Senate floor, offering amendments, and voting on legislation.

The Senate was mired in gridlock before, during, and after Trump's presidency because its leaders managed the Senate in a way that made it harder for senators to compromise, which emerges from the legislative process when senators debate controversial issues on which they disagree in committee and on the floor. It happens when senators try to win. It happens when they act. And gridlock happens when senators do nothing instead.

The Trump-centric view and some Senate scholarship claim (explicitly or implicitly) that Trump caused gridlock instead. Trump exacerbated the forces that make legislating hard—ideological polarization and partisan competition—and, in the process, caused gridlock to occur by increasing the size of the gridlock region and, therefore, causing more issues to get stuck in it.

Underpinning this claim is the idea that gridlock happens when two sides in a legislative debate do not want to cooperate and instead act in ways that effectively prevent each other from achieving their goals inside the Senate: Democrats filibustered Trump's agenda, and Republicans filibustered Biden's agenda.

And therein lies the source of the disconnect between the Senate viewed through Trump-tinted lenses and the Senate in reality. The filibuster is not a veto. Consequently, it can never level the playing field between the majority and minority sides in a debate. Instead, it merely grants a senator (or senators) the opportunity to speak for as long as he or she can. Using it to obstruct the majority systematically requires senators in the minority to expend considerable effort to succeed. As such, the filibuster cannot cause gridlock in a debate of reasonable length because no two sides in a legislative debate can be evenly matched in terms of the efforts their members are willing to expend, especially in the age of Trump when people are emboldened to act. One group of senators must always prevail after a debate. Whichever side does is, by definition, the side with more members.

Gridlock, properly understood, only arises in those situations in which senators in both majority and minority parties are unwilling to expend the effort required for their side to prevail. In such cases, neither side acts to achieve its goals. Gridlock is thus caused by senators' inaction, not their actions. Amidst such inaction, it is misleading to suggest that Trump caused a minority to act in ways that prevented the majority from acting or that it caused the majority to run roughshod over the minority. The procedural data presented in this chapter does not support this claim. Instead, it demonstrates that both the minority and the majority refrained from acting before, during, and after Trump's presidency. Had senators not refrained from acting, their actions on one side or the other lead to definitive outcomes. When gridlock is understood in this way, it is apparent why Trump, ideological polarization, or partisan competition can be its cause. All of these forces induce senators to act inside the institution. For that reason, they are theoretically incompatible with the Senate's state of persistent inaction on most controversial legislation from 2009 to 2022.[20]

Trump disrupted our ability to recognize this dynamic. His polarizing nature blinded us to the underlying problems plaguing the Senate. Consequently, Trump-centric views of politics and the Senate hinder future efforts to reform the institution.

References

Aldrich, John H. 2011. *Why Parties? A Second Look*. Chicago: University of Chicago Press.

Beckman, Matthew N. And Joseph Godfrey. 2007. "The Policy Opportunities in Presidential Honeymoons." *Political Research Quarterly* 60 (2): 250–262

Binder, Sarah A. 2003. *Stalemate: Causes and Consequences of Legislative Gridlock*. Washington, DC: Brookings Institution Press.

Binder, Sarah A. 2015. "The Dysfunctional Congress." *Annual Review of Political Science* 18: 85–101.

Brady, David W., and Craig Volden. 2006. *Revolving Gridlock: Politics and Policy From Jimmy Carter to George W. Bush*, 2 ed. Boulder, CO: Westview Press.

Gross, Bertram M. 1953. *The Legislative Struggle: A Study in Social Conflict*. New York: McGraw-Hill.

Hetherington, Marc J., and Thomas J. Rudolph. 2015. *Why Washington Won't Work: Polarization, Political Trust, and the Governing Crisis*. Chicago: University of Chicago Press.

---

[20] Binder (2003) concedes, acknowledging that "polarized views are not necessarily counterproductive to legislative motion. On the contrary, the more cohesive and ideologically extreme a majority coalition, the harder it might fight to pass favored measures. Polarization might then be helpful for pushing important measures through to passage" (87). While Binder agrees that this appears to "ring true for the House," she nevertheless counters that the dynamic does not pertain to the Senate. Citing the filibuster, Binder claims that, as a consequence of the filibuster, "as partisanship on an issue grows in the Senate, we might expect chances of enacting a related bill to decline" (87).

Krehbiel, Keith. 1998. *Pivotal Politics: A Theory of U.S. Lawmaking*. Chicago: University of Chicago Press.

Lee, Frances E. 2016. *Insecure Majorities: Congress and the Perpetual Campaign*. Chicago: University of Chicago Press.

Mayhew, David R. 1991. *Divided We Govern: Party, Control, Lawmaking, and Investigations, 1946-2002*. New Haven, CT: Yale University Press.

Mayhew, David R. 2000. *America's Congress: Actions in the Public Sphere, James Madison Through Newt Gingrich*. New Haven, CT: Yale University Press.

McCarty, Nolan, Keith T. Poole, and Howard Rosenthal. 2006. *Polarized America: The Dance of Ideology and Unequal Riches*. Cambridge, MA: MIT Press.

Persily, Nathaniel. 2015. "Introduction." In *Solutions to Political Polarization in America*, Nathaniel Persily ed. New York: Cambridge University Press, 3–14.

8

McConnell's President

The Anti-institutionalist Partisan

Julian E. Zelizer

Introduction

On February 13, 2021, Senator Mitch McConnell delivered a blistering speech to his colleagues about the former president, Donald J. Trump. After the Senate, including McConnell, had voted to acquit President Trump in his second impeachment trial by a vote of 57 to 43—missing the two-thirds threshold for conviction—the new minority leader laid into his party colleague.[1] Speaking about the insurrection that rocked Capitol Hill on January 6, McConnell appeared to finally let loose: "There's no question, none, that President Trump is practically and morally responsible for provoking the events of the day . . . A mob was assaulting the Capitol in his name. These criminals were carrying his banners, hanging his flags, and screaming their loyalty to him."[2] Many media observers treated McConnell's speech as a watershed moment. Finally, they said, the Republican Party had broken from the divider-in-chief.

Several recent books about the Trump presidency report that McConnell expressed the same sentiment behind the scenes. McConnell, as well as House Minority Leader Kevin McCarthy who was exploring the possible use of the 25th Amendment given the dangers the nation faced, were livid about the president's actions. The senator promised colleagues that he was determined to drive Trump out of politics. The relationship between the two men had deteriorated by the end of the presidency. McConnell finally worried

[1] The best book-length examination of McConnell is Ira Shapiro, *The Betrayal: How Mitch McConnell and the Senate Republicans Abandoned America* (Lanham, MD: Rowman & Littlefield, 2022). See also, Alec McGillis, *The Cynic: The Political Education of Mitch McConnell* (New York: Simon & Schuster, 2014).

[2] Carl Hulse and Nicholas Fandos, "McConnell, Denouncing Trump After Voting to Acquit, Says His Hands were Tied," *New York Times,* February 13, 2021.

Julian E. Zelizer, *McConnell's President* In: *Disruption?* Edited by: Sean M. Theriault,
Oxford University Press. © Oxford University Press 2024. DOI: 10.1093/oso/9780197767832.003.0009

about the detrimental impact that Trump could have on Republican power. Trump had come to see the Senate Majority Leader as a threat to his future (he called him a "piece of shit" for failing to support his effort to overturn the election).[3] Before the House had voted on the articles of impeachment, McConnell told Republicans that "the Democrats are going to take care of the son of a bitch for us."

Yet, after McConnell seriously considered supporting the second impeachment, he backed away upon realizing that most members of his party were firmly opposed.[4] Without a signal from McConnell to convict, there was absolutely no chance that the Senate would move forward with the impeachment. Trump was not removed from office. McConnell delivered his condemnatory speech only *after* the impeachment failed. On February 25, McConnell stood by 45. When asked by a reporter what he would do if Trump won the Republican nomination for the 2024 presidential election, McConnell responded that he would "absolutely" support him.[5] "I didn't get to be leader by voting with five people in the conference," the senator explained to a friend. Just as important, the Kentucky Republican would remain silent about the matter from that point forward. When Democrats launched investigations into January 6, McConnell and the Republican Caucus obstructed.[6]

The apparent flip-flops took a few Washington's pundits by surprise, or at least it was the kind of material that lent itself toward inside-the-Beltway intrigue. The cadre of reporters who were perpetually looking for a turning point in the modern GOP thought they were finally on to something when McConnell blasted Trump. Now they couldn't understand how McConnell could blame Trump for a violent attack on Congress as it certified the 2020 election and then say with such certainty that supporting his nomination would be a sure thing.

Of course, they shouldn't have been surprised. McConnell's career in the GOP, which started when he was elected to the Senate in 1984 to represent

[3] Maggie Haberman, *Confidence Man: The Making of Donald Trump and the Breaking of America* (New York: Penguin, 2022), 495.

[4] Alexander Burns and Jonathan Martin, "'I've Had it With This Guy': G.O.P. Leaders Privately Blasted Trump After Jan. 6," *New York Times*, April 21, 2022; Rachel Bade and Karen Demirjian, *Unchecked: The Untold Story Behind Congress' Botched Impeachments of Donald Trump* (New York: William and Morrow, 2022).

[5] Paul LeBlanc, "McConnell Says He'll 'Absolutely' Support Trump in 2024 If He's the GOP Nominee," *CNN.Com*, February 25, 2021.

[6] Burns and Martin, "'I've Had it With This Guy.'" McConnell's strategy and actions are well captured in Bade and Demirjian, *Unchecked*.

Kentucky, with the help of campaign consultant and Republican media guru Roger Ailes and Larry McCarthy (who would make the infamous Willie Horton of the 1988 campaign), has been remarkably consistent. McConnell is part of a generation of Republicans who have put all their chips into maintaining partisan power above almost everything else. "You are only as good as the next election," he liked to say (MacGillis 2014). Refusing to relive the period when the GOP had been a "permanent minority" in Congress, the position the party found itself in from 1955 to 1995 other than the moment when Republicans held the Senate from 1981 to 1987, McConnell and his colleagues were determined to do whatever was necessary to maintain legislative power (see Figure 8.1). They have been willing to abandon core norms that had helped to hold some of the worst partisan excesses in check and been vital to the functioning of Congress. Republicans like McConnell believed that without a strong congressional base of support, a conservative president like Ronald Reagan or anyone who followed him would never achieve their transformative goals.

He would always be willing to engage in the roughest of campaign tactics. When McConnell faced a Democratic challenger in 1990, Harvey Sloane, the senator agreed to release campaign ads that depicted his opponent as a drug addict. When McConnell learned that the former Louisville mayor, whom he called a "wimp from the East" had renewed his script for sleeping pills that he was using for problems with his hip the senator used this to depict him as an addict. "If they throw a stone at you, you drop a boulder on them," McConnell

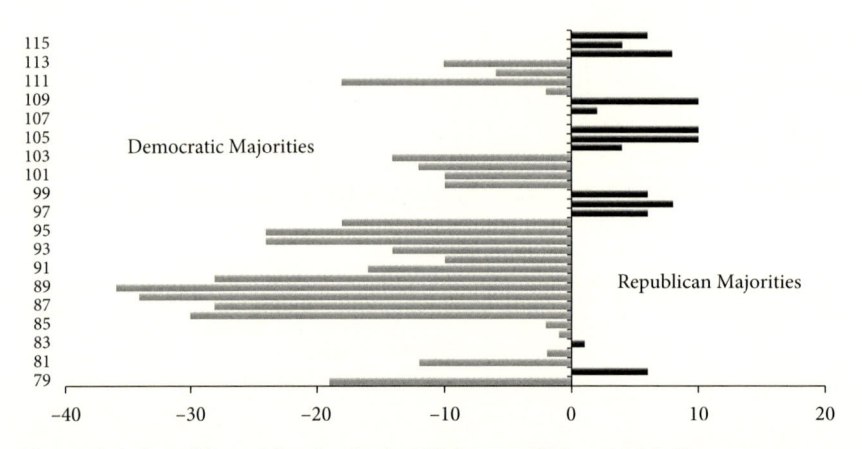

Figure 8.1 Republican Margins in the US Senate, 79th to 116th Congresses (1945–2021)

said.[7] The campaign aired blistering spots with a voice warning viewers that Sloan was reliant on "depressants" that had been illegally prescribed.

While some leaders, such as Georgia Congressman Newt Gingrich, deployed toxic rhetoric and explosive scandal warfare to bring down Democrats (Zelizer 2020), McConnell preferred a different approach. He mastered a legislative style whereby he would manipulate every possible process to his party's advantage and bring his opponents to their knees. While the previous generation of Republicans and Democratic leaders had balanced the goals of partisanship, governance, and the preserving democratic institutions, McConnell and his generation of Republicans went all in with the first objective.

The guiding spirit of Republicans like McConnell had been stated in clear terms during the resignation speech of former House Majority Leader Tom "The Hammer" DeLay on June 9, 2006. Upon leaving office, DeLay offered a staunch defense of partisanship. "You show me a nation without partisanship," he said, "and I'll show you a tyranny. For all its faults, it is partisanship, based on core principles, that clarifies our debates, that prevents one party from straying too far from the mainstream, and that constantly refreshes our politics with new ideas and new leaders. Indeed, whatever role partisanship may have played in my own retirement today or in the unfriendliness heaped upon other leaders in other times, Republican or Democrat, however unjust, all we can say is that partisanship is the worst means of settling fundamental political differences—except for all the others."[8]

The symbiotic relationship between the president and McConnell was possible only because Trump was much less of a disrupter than some believed when it came to policy and, to some extent, norms. Under the guidance of McConnell, Republican senators were willing to protect the president from being held accountable during the moments he dangerously abused executive power. During a historic two impeachments, most of the conference stood firm. Not only were many Republican senators comfortable with his smashmouth approach to partisan warfare, something they had become familiar with, and participated in, since Congressman Gingrich's rise to power in the 1980s, but Trump delivered on fiscal legislation and judicial appointments. Throughout his four years in the Oval Office, Trump generally

---

[7] Jane Mayer, "How Mitch McConnell Became Trump's Enabler in Chief," *New Yorker*, April 12, 2020.

[8] Quoted in Carl Hulse, "Defiant to the End, DeLay Pats Himself on the Back and Bids the House a Torrid Goodbye, *New York Times*, June 9, 2006.

stuck to the GOP playbook, proving to be effective at sending McConnell key items that the party demanded. Besides the occasional barbs that each man uttered about the other, generally McConnell found in Trump an effective leader for the party. Given the trajectory of the GOP since the era of Ronald Reagan, Trump made perfect sense.

The Making of a Senator

Four years before McConnell was elected to fill Kentucky's Senate seat, the basic environment of the upper chamber had changed in profound ways. During the elections, Republicans won control of the Senate for the first time since 1955. Indeed, Republicans had only controlled Congress for two short moments since FDR came to town in 1932: 1947–1949 and 1953–1955. Though it was not apparent at the time, the election of 1980 began a period that would see control of the House and Senate shift more frequently after decades of Democratic dominance. As Frances E. Lee (2016) has argued, this meant that partisan incentives would become stronger as senators calculated every move with an eye toward obtaining or maintaining majority control. Compromise became more difficult when either party might find itself in power come the next election. The fact that McConnell entered the Senate when Republicans held power meant that he would always be able to imagine the GOP keeping or regaining that position of authority. McConnell was not part of the generation when Republicans were the "permanent minority." He never felt the kind of resignation so many senior colleagues had felt about partisan dynamics.

Elected in 1984 by defeating Senator Walter "Dee" Huddleston, a World War II veteran, McConnell always looked at institutional and procedural questions through the lens of partisan power. Over the years, he had demonstrated a willingness to shift positions in dramatic fashion when it served his political interests. "He clearly doesn't care about being labeled a hypocrite," one colleague said, "It just doesn't bother him. He is brazen about it. That's one of the cynical sides of Mitch. He doesn't care. If it's expedient, he'll do it."[9] During his first decade in office, the senator emerged as one primary opponent of campaign finance reform in the 1990s. Even though he

[9] Michael Kranish, "Mitch McConnell Spent Decades Chasing Power. Now He Heeds Trump, Who Mocks Him and Wants Him Gone," *Washington Post*, November 8, 2021.

had been an earlier supporter of reform, including public financing at the height of the Watergate scandal (he penned at op-ed in 1973 calling money a "cancer" in the system) and later a legislative amendment that would protect regulations against big organization donations, he turned into a human battering ram against efforts to curtail the flow of private money into the system.[10] As a growing cohort of senators, including Republican colleague John McCain, were pushing to clean up the growing influence of soft money in the election system, McConnell stood firm in protecting the soft money loopholes in the campaign finance reform legislation that had passed in the wake of President Richard Nixon's scandal. He dismissed campaign finance reform as coming close to "static cling as an issue most Americans care about."[11] McConnell blitzed network television and talk radio shows to champion his cause, working with conservative think tanks and even courting the American Civil Liberties Union, which he knew was sympathetic to free speech issues (MacGillis 2014).

McConnell mounted numerous filibusters against major campaign finance reform bills. "On a more personal level," he said, "my first run for the Senate brought these issues to light in a concrete way. I never would have been able to win my race if there had been a limit on the amount of money I could raise and spend."[12] The senator emerged as one of the most unabashed supporters of the "mother's milk" of American campaign politics, attacking efforts to limit spending or contributions as restrictions on free speech. Believing that Republicans held a distinct advantage in the money race as big business and Wall Street established sophisticated political operations in Washington, and the Religious Right created a massive grassroots fundraising network for small donors, Senator McConnell didn't mind being on the side of a battle over good government (see Figure 8.2). The "cancer" he decried as a young lawyer was the basis for funding effective campaigns in an age of high-cost television. While arguments about free speech and individual rights rippled through his statements about why the status quo should

---

[10] Ella Nilsen, "Mitch McConnell's Dark Secret: He Used to Support Campaign Finance Reform," *Vox*, February 15, 2019; Fred Wertheimer, "Meet a Younger Mitch McConnell as Bold Campaign Finance Reformer," *Democracy 21*, February 13, 2019.

[11] Jane Mayer, "How Mitch McConnell Became Trump's Enabler in Chief," *New Yorker*, April 12, 2020.

[12] Ella Nilsen, "Mitch McConnell's Dark Secret: He Used to Support Campaign Finance Reform," *Vox*, February 15, 2019; Fred Wertheimer, "Meet a Younger Mitch McConnell as Bold Campaign Finance Reformer," *Democracy 21*, February 13, 2019.

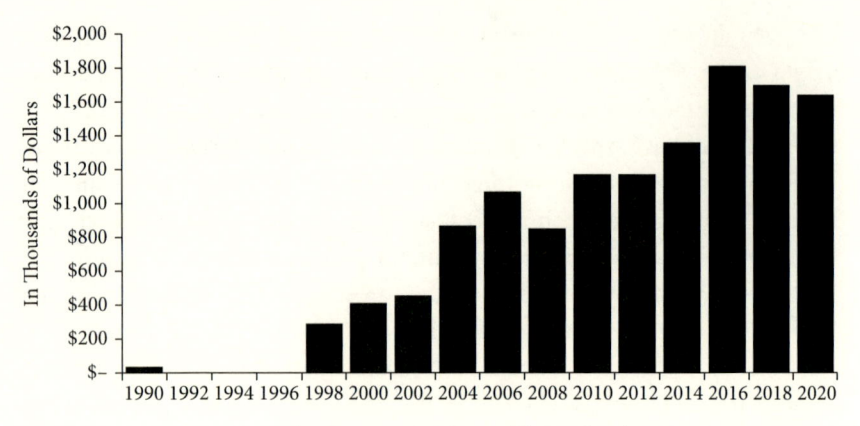

Figure 8.2 Amount Spent by Senator McConnell's Leadership PAC, 1990–2020

stand, his understanding of how the system would help the party were the central motivations.

Whereas many Republicans remained silent about the largesse of the Charles and David Koch to their party and conservative campaigns like the fight against climate change, McConnell courted and defended them. "Charles and David Koch have become household names," the senator said at a speech at the American Enterprise Institute in 2012, "not for the tens of thousands of people they employ, not for their generosity to charity, and not for building up one of the most successful private corporations on the planet, but because of their forceful and unapologetic promotion and defense of capitalism." McConnell had opposed the McCain-Feingold Act of 2002 that regulated "soft money" and defended the Supreme Court's controversial *Citizens United* decision that allowed corporations and other organizations to give unlimited donations. The ruling, he said, was a "strong validation of a fight I've aged for nearly three decades against those within the government who would micromanage political speech."[13]

The Shield and the Sword

The filibuster became McConnell's political weapon of choice on most issues. Both parties had accelerated the use of the filibuster since the 1970s

---

[13] Tarini Parti, "McConnell Defends Kochs," *Politico*, June 15, 2012.

as partisan polarization intensified. The procedure, once reserved for high profile issues like civil rights and a move that even concerned older senators like Georgia Democrat Richard Russell who deployed the tactic (as Joseph Crespino argues in this book), was becoming normalized as the number of moderates in each party diminished. McConnell was willing to keep pushing the boundaries as to what it was legitimate to do. He proved one of the leaders of his generation who abandoned norms altogether so that existing procedures could be weaponized in more aggressive fashion. When it came to filibustering, the senator had no problem using this as a tool of scorched earth obstruction. McConnell leaned in on any of the Republicans seeking to compromise with President Barack Obama on his signature legislation, including an economic stimulus bill to help the nation out of the worst recession and financial crisis since the Great Depression, determined to prevent the president from being able to claim a genuine bipartisan victory. As McConnell famously said in October 2010, just before Republicans had regained control of the House, "the single most important thing we want to achieve is for President Obama to be a one-term president."[14] The influx into the upper chamber of "Gingrich Senators," as Sean Theriault (2013) has called members who cut their teeth in the House under Gingrich's smashmouth principles in the 1980s and 1990s, offered McConnell an army of foot soldiers who were eager to support him.

By showing his willingness to use the filibuster on all matters, no matter how small or large, Senator McConnell played an important role in solidifying a 60-vote norm for passing legislation or confirming judicial and executive level appointments. Republicans could afford this sort of legislative landscape more easily than Democrats. Since Republicans were not eager to pass major, transformative pieces of legislation, other than tax cuts that could be folded into the budget reconciliation process and deregulations, which could be moved via executive action, a dysfunctional upper chamber didn't clash with the party's policy goals. The frustration became so great that in 2013 then Senate Majority Leader Harry Reid agreed to use the "nuclear option," which allowed federal judicial and executive nominations (other than SCOTUS nominations) to be confirmed by the Senate through a majority vote. "This isn't obstruction on substance, on qualifications," Reid said, "It's just to gum up the works." He defended his actions by saying that it was

---

[14] Quoted in Glenn Kessler, "When Did McConnell Say He Wanted to Make Obama a 'One-Term President,'" *Washington Post*, September 25, 2012.

essential "to change the Senate before this institution becomes obsolete."[15] Unfortunately for Democrats, Republicans regained control of the Senate in 2014. But McConnell found other ways to slow down nominations, including using methods like holds. When asked why there had been so many vacancies in the federal courts during Obama's final two years (only 28.6 percent of his judicial nominees were confirmed during those years), McConnell would look back by proudly saying, "I'll tell you why. I was in charge of what we did the last two years of Obama administration."[16]

Rampant filibustering was not the only place where McConnell showed his willingness to threaten the health of institutions for partisan gains. After Republicans had gained control of the House in the 2010 midterms, he joined Tea Party colleagues in rallying his caucus behind the threat to not raise the federal debt ceiling in 2011. Not a total surprise because McConnell had long been willing to tie the debt ceiling to policy demands even when a fellow Republican, George W. Bush, was president.[17]

Republicans shocked much of Washington by announcing that they would not authorize the routine debt ceiling increase, which allows Treasury to pay for what Congress has already appropriated. Although legislators had been threatening for decades, it had always been symbolic. Legislators only issued this warning when they knew that the votes were in place to pass the bill. When Barack Obama was president, Republicans changed the nature of the threat. It was real. Many members of the conference were willing to go through with an action that would send the nation into federal default. In the end, McConnell would help to resolve the crisis, fearing the economic and partisan implications of failing to do so, but only after he helped to legitimate this tactic. Threatening to send the nation into default, McConnell would explain, was "a hostage that's worth ransoming [because] it focuses the Congress on something that must be done."[18] In 2014, Republicans won back control of the Senate, electing McConnell as Majority Leader in 2015. The GOP was in power in the upper chamber, and he was at the top of their power pyramid. After hearing the State of the Union Address, all McConnell

---

[15] Quoted in Burgess Everett and Seung Min Kim, "Senate Goes for 'Nuclear Option,'" *Politico*, November 21, 2013.

[16] Quoted in Priyanka Boghani, "How McConnell's Bid to Reshape the Federal Judiciary Extends Beyond the Supreme Court," *Frontline*, 2020.

[17] Jonathan Weisman, "As the U.S. Hurtles Toward a Debt Crisis, What Does McConnell Want?" *New York Times*, October 5, 2021.

[18] Quoted in Jack M. Balkin, "The Not-So-Happy Anniversary of the Debt-Ceiling Crisis," *The Atlantic*, July 31, 2012.

could say was that Obama was "almost without exception indicated he's not for much of anything the American people voted for last November."[19]

McConnell's Nuclear Option

The length to which McConnell was willing to weaponize procedure became clear when, as Majority Leader in 2016, he prevented his colleagues from even considering President Obama's nomination for the Supreme Court. Following the death of Justice Antonin Scalia, a key voice for the judicial right, the president selected a nominee who seemed as if he would be acceptable to most colleagues—Merrick Garland. Judge Garland, a highly respected legal mind who served on the US Court of Appeals for the District of Columbia Court, was a graduate of Harvard and Harvard Law as well as a Department of Justice lawyer when he prosecuted the men who were guilty of bombing the Oklahoma City government building in 1995 as well as the Unabomber case. Senator McConnell said no. Soon after Obama announced the nomination, in a statement McConnell's spokesperson told reporters that he would not be holding a "perfunctory meeting," but he "wished Judge Garland well."[20] The senator would explain that an appointment by a sitting president so close to the end of his term was not legitimate and antidemocratic. Citing a tradition that historians and legal scholars were unable to confirm, he said the choice to fill the vacant seat had to be done by Obama's predecessor. "Of course, the American people should have a say in the court's direction. It is a president's constitutional right to nominate a Supreme Court justice, and it is the Senate's constitutional right to act as a check on the president and withhold its consent."[21] McConnell never had doubts about what he had done. "The most important decision I've made in my political career was the decision not to do something," he said in retrospect.[22]

One of his boldest moves yet, McConnell demonstrated how his concerns about the Republican Party would be stronger than any warning about the damage that could be incurred to basic institutional processes because of

---

[19] Quoted in Jeremy W. Peters and Emmarie Huetteman, "Republicans Have One Word for President's Proposals and Veto Threats: 'No.'" *New York Times*, January 21, 2015.

[20] Quoted in "McConnell Tells Garland the Senate Will Not Act," *New York Times*, March 16, 2016.

[21] Quoted in Katie Waddington, "Then and Now: What McConnell, Others Said About Merrick Garland in 2016 vs. After Ginsburg's Death," *USA Today*, September 19, 2020.

[22] Quoted in Jane Mayer, "How Mitch McConnell Became Trump's Enabler in Chief," *New Yorker*, April 12, 2020

his decisions. Transforming the courts had been central to the Republican agenda, something that right-wing activists insisted upon in exchange for their support. Since Ronald Reagan was in the White House, the GOP made great strides in confirming conservative justices. Most legal scholars were stunned by the decision. "You really cannot find any single comparable case," one expert said, "We really did not find any precedent for the idea, notwithstanding the Senate's very broad powers in this area, that a sitting president could be denied outright the authority to offer up a nominee who would receive evaluation through normal Senate processes."[23] In the name of partisan warfare, McConnell had shown, nothing was sacrosanct. Anything could be weaponized. He forced the seat to remain empty until the next election.

The Dynamic Duo

With Donald Trump, McConnell and other Republicans of his generation found a president who agreed with their political strategy and philosophy. Although critics liked to paint him as a television-addicted buffoon who acted according to his latest whim, Trump had absorbed the fact that America had become a deeply polarized nation after many decades where the center had disappeared. In some ways, he saw the political world more clearly than Washington's pundits who consistently yearned nostalgically for a period of civil bipartisanship where centrists ruled the roost. From the time that he started his campaign, the power of partisanship was the basis of Trump's victory. As a candidate, Trump dismissed the pundits who predicted that his full-throated appeals threatened a replay of the 1964 election when Senator Barry Goldwater's right-wing extremism pushed some Republicans to vote for Lyndon Johnson. When Trump secured the nomination over "establishment" types like Florida Governor Jeb Bush or even Texas Senator Ted Cruz, McConnell didn't sound especially concerned. "He's not going to change the platform of the Republican Party, the views of the Republican Party," McConnell said on CNBC, "I think we're much more likely to change him because if he is president, he's going to have to deal with sort of the right-of-center world, which is where most of us are."[24] When intelligence agencies were reporting that Russia was interfering in the campaign to help Trump

[23] "Study Calls Snub of Obama's Supreme Court Pick Unprecedented," *New York Times*, June 13, 2016.

[24] Tom DiChristopher, "Trump Won't Change the GOP," *CNBC*, June 1, 2016.

win, with evidence of contacts with the Republican presidential campaign, McConnell helped to provide the candidate with political cover. He refused to accept Obama's request in September for congressional leaders to sign a bipartisan letter condemning Russian interference (Shapiro 2022).

In the end, the 2016 election proved that Trump's strategy of partisan division could work. The electoral map moved little despite all the disruptive ways in which he ran (Lawless and Theriault 2021). Although a small number of Democrats voted for Trump in states such as Wisconsin, Pennsylvania, and Michigan, the real key to Trump's Electoral College victory was that in the final weeks of the campaign—using Hillary Clinton's email scandal as a perfect foil and capitalizing on Russian social-media hijinks to stir division—Trump whipped up Republican energy behind the ticket. In an important decision, Trump moved forward with the idea of legal counsel Don McGahn to draw up and release a list of judicial picks—put together based on the recommendations of the Federalist Society and Heritage Foundation—from which he would pick nominees.

The plan worked. Despite speculation of a 1964 style landslide, with Trump being the modern-day Barry Goldwater, the red states did not turn blue, which was essential, or his approximately 78,0000-vote margin in three swing states would not have mattered. Faced with the choice between Trump and Clinton on Election Day, Republicans came home. Although McConnell had not been excited about a Trump candidacy at the start, by the end of the campaign he fully embraced the nominee. He saw the way that most top Republicans had turned and he had no interest in standing in the way of a party victory. When briefed by CIA Director John Brennan about Russian interference that was taking place in the election, McConnell protected the party. He dismissed the reports and told officials "not to get involved" in these questions as "they were touching something very dangerous."[25]

At some level, whether it was instinctive or deliberative, President Trump also understood what political scientists would call asymmetric polarization (Mann and Ornstein 2012; Hacker and Pierson 2005; Theriault 2006; Zelizer 2020). No surprise that it was Steven Bannon who quipped that Democrats had pillow fights as Republicans went for the head wound (Zelizer 2020).

Today's politics can be partially explained by two distinct, though interrelated phenomenon that have been influential since the 1970s. The first

---

[25] Quoted in Jane Mayer, "How Mitch McConnell Became Trump's Enabler in Chief," *New Yorker*, April 20, 2020.

has been growing polarization. The distance between two political parties has grown and the number of voters and legislators who can identify—through their votes—as being in between has diminished.

The second is that the parties have polarized in different ways. The Republicans moved much further to the right than Democrats moved to the left. Moreover, starting with Congressman Gingrich's rise to power in the 1980s, the Republicans were more willing to engage in a style of partisan combat without guardrails than Democrats. As a party that had more at stake in the government functioning, Democrats still abided by certain norms that Republicans were happy to abandon. An entire generation of Senate Republicans, such as Phil Gramm of Texas, Rick Santorum of Pennsylvania, and Jim DeMint of South Carolina who were more conservative, more eager to obstruct Democratic presidents as their primary agenda, and went to extreme lengths to obstruct the legislative purpose for partisan gain (Theriault 2013). Though quieter than Gingrich—less willing to use the news media as a platform—McConnell has been part of this shift. As a result, McConnell could live with a president who broke almost every rule that he encountered, if he remained loyal to the party line.

Between 2017 and 2021, Trump governed the way that he campaigned, and this worked for Senator McConnell. The senator didn't like Trump personally. He acknowledged privately the danger he posed to the GOP—and even to the country more broadly.

But McConnell also believed that Trump could be politically valuable to the party and was open when Chief of Staff John Kelly brokered a truce between the two men. Robert Porter, who worked on the Hill and was on Trump's staff, had explained to the president early on: "What animates him, first and foremost, is being Senate majority leader. What he cares most about is making sure that Republicans continue in the majority, that they have at least fifty-one Republican senators" (Baker and Glasser 2022). This was the kind of crass and cold calculus that Trump could understand from his days in the real estate business. McConnell, according to Trump's biographer Maggie Haberman, was telling colleagues that the party didn't need a new version of Abraham Lincoln but rather a "right-of-center president who could help them achieve their goals" (Haberman 2022). One of the goals that excited him most, which McConnell (2016, 268–269) noted in his memoir was at the top of his mind on election night was the judiciary: "Before I went to bed on election night, I had resolved to make the federal judiciary my top personal priority in the next Congress."

Senate Republicans were able to push policy debate in certain directions when Trump didn't play ball. Although the president didn't have much interest in rolling back health care, McConnell mobilized his colleagues to support "repeal and replace" in the reconciliation process. He broke every element of the "regular order" to get the legislation to a vote despite deep Republican ambivalence about taking this controversial stand. After Senator McCain stopped this effort, the president then picked up on the campaign by using executive authority to weaken certain elements of ACA. In this case, McConnell's own political miscalculations about the politics of retrenching benefits was the reason for the failure (Shapiro 2022).

After tensions publicly flared early on between the men over Trump's failed effort to dismantle the Affordable Care Act—McConnell blamed the president for having "excessive expectations about how quickly things happen in the democratic process" to which Trump responded on Twitter, "Can you believe that Mitch McConnell, who has screamed Repeal & Replace for 7 years, couldn't get it done"—they came together a few months later in the Oval Office around a plan to transform the federal judiciary. The courts remained common ground. A few days after the social media blasts, Trump sang a different tune, telling reporters in the Rose Garden, with McConnell standing by his side, "We have been friends for a long time. We are probably now, I think, at least as far as I'm concerned, closer than ever before." For two men who craved power, partisan interests offered a path toward negotiating the peace.[26]

Despite all the turbulence and chaos that flowed out of the White House, on several key issues that McConnell believed to be essential for strengthening support of the Republican Party, Trump was quite traditional. He started his presidency by nominating Neil Gorsuch for the Supreme Court, a conservative jurist who believed in deregulation and a limited role for the state. McConnell helped make sure he was successful by going further than his predecessor Harry Reid in ending the filibuster for federal court *and* Supreme Court nominees. When another seat opened and the president nominated Brett Kavanaugh in July 2018, McConnell, again, did everything in his power to make sure the confirmation was successful. He allowed a lawyer chosen by the White House, William Burck, to collect and share documents that were relevant for the Senate Judiciary Committee rather than the nonpartisan

---

[26] Peter Baker and Susan Glasser, *The Divider: Trump in the White House, 2017–2021* (New York: Doubleday, 2022), 131–133.

National Archives. McConnell sat quietly when the administration invented the concept of "constitutional privilege" to stonewall on more than 100,000 pages of material. And when bombshell revelations emerged that Christine Blasey Ford accused the nominee of sexually assaulting her while he was drunk at a party, causing many in the White House to consider jettisoning the nomination, McConnell—along with McGahn stood firm. "I'm stronger than mule piss," he told the wavering president (Shapiro 2022). With the confirmation of Amy Coney Barrett in October 2020 McConnell and Trump had transformed the Court by solidifying a 6–3 conservative bloc—a rightward response to the Earl Warren Court of the 1960s—that would have long-term ramifications on policy. McConnell moved the confirmation in record time, with weeks left until the election, a stark contrast to how he kept Scalia's seat open until it could be filled by the right president. "McConnell," wrote the historian Leandra Zarnow (2022), "pushed through Barrett's nomination, for Republican leadership understood that overturning *Roe v. Wade,* continued to motivate their base." SCOTUS was not the only court that experienced massive change. During Trump's four years in office, the Senate would confirm 226 federal judges. His 54 federal appellate judges were the most striking achievement, just one less than President Obama had appointed during his two terms.[27] "I certainly didn't expect to have three Supreme Court justices," McConnell told one reporter, "At the risk of tooting my own horn, look at the majority leaders since L.B.J. and find another one who was able to do something as consequential as this."[28]

Trump pushed through Congress a major corporate tax cut, the sort of red meat that the GOP clamored for every time one of its own inhabited the White House. The president used power to gut environmental agreements and an executive order, enthusiastically articulating climate change denialism, in ways that surely thrilled Republican powerhouses such as the Koch brothers who had been working since the 1980s to roll back the green movement. Even some of the issues that were seen as coming from the far right— such as a stringent position on immigration—had become well ensconced in Republican politics since the 1990s. While there were some Republicans who cringed as Trump ramped up the verbal and tariff wars with China, a substantial part of the GOP and their allies in the business sector—as well

[27] https://www.pewresearch.org/short-reads/2021/01/13/how-trump-compares-with-other-recent-presidents-in-appointing-federal-judges/

[28] Carl Hulse, "How Mitch McConnell Delivered Justice Amy Coney Barrett's Rapid Confirmation," *New York Times*, October 27, 2020.

as many Democrats—agreed that the time had come to be tougher against the threats that the world's last remaining communist superpower posed to America. Trump was simply less wed to older positions, such as George W. Bush had been, and much more in tune with where the GOP had moved.

There were moments when Trump touched on a few genuine fault lines within the party. He insisted on conciliatory language and relations with Russian leader Vladimir Putin, going so far as to publicly challenge reports from US intelligence agencies about interference in the 2016 election and avoiding strong action as Russia prepared to assault Ukraine, despite the hardline anti-Russian views that most Republicans championed. Senator McConnell disagreed with Trump's push to withdraw US forces from Syria and Afghanistan.

On those occasions when interests didn't align, McConnell was willing and able to remind Trump of who was boss by standing his ground. When Trump decided to go rogue on nominations, such as nominating Herman Cain and Stephen Moore to the Federal Reserve, McConnell revealed the limits of his transactional relationship by refusing to rubber stamp them. During a government shutdown over funding a border wall in 2018–2019, a shutdown that McConnell didn't support with memories of the high political cost incurred to the GOP as a result of the shutdowns in 1995 and 1996 under Speaker Gingrich, the Senate Majority Leader pressured Trump into backing down, something the president loathed to do as he believed it to be a sign of weakness. In exchange for the concession McConnell allowed the president to declare a national emergency to secure the funds on his own, further evidence of how McConnell was willing to even trade away the powers of Congress in pursuit of partisan power; funding the wall, McConnell knew, also played well within a Republican electorate that had embraced a hardline anti-immigration stance since the mid-1990s.[29]

Overall, though, Trump did not detour that much from the party orthodoxy. Because the administration was supporting so much of the mainstream Republican agenda and having difficulty checking Senate Republicans when they moved in a different direction than him, McConnell's party served as a guardian of Trump as he used executive power in dangerous ways. When McConnell (2019, xiii–xv) released the second edition of his memoir in 2019, the book included a forward from Trump full of praise for their work

[29] Baker and Glasser, *The Divider*, 282–283; Sarah Coleman, *The Walls Within: The Politics of Immigration in Modern America* (Princeton, NJ: Princeton University Press, 2021), 104–141.

on the federal courts, saying, "I couldn't have asked for a better partner." (Trump, after he soured on McConnell in 2021, denied writing the forward, claiming the senator wrote it himself.[30]) During the two impeachment trials, the president was protected by the firewall in the Senate. In the first trial, no Republican senators except Mitt Romney defected though the president threatened using foreign assistance for personal political gain. Even most of the so-called moderates of the party, such as Maine's Susan Collins, refused to vote in favor of conviction while admitting the president's actions were egregious. McConnell was never subtle about where he stood on the matter. "I'm not an impartial juror," McConnell told reporters in December 2019, "This is a political process. There's not anything judicial about it. The House made a partisan political decision to impeach. I would anticipate we will have a largely partisan outcome in the Senate. I'm not impartial about this at all."[31] His success at preventing the Democrats from hearing witnesses, especially former National Security Advisors John Bolton, all but killed any chance of finding broader Republican support (Haberman 2022; Bade and Demirijan 2022). During the second impeachment, with members themselves the victims of the attack, only seven Republican senators voted for conviction. Despite the warnings and admonitions, McConnell could keep his coalition firm. President Trump could act with impunity because McConnell was unwilling to risk Republican power to contain the president. It wasn't much of a surprise that after leaving office he continued to fuel the flames of those who didn't believe the election was legitimate. And while doing so he remained a top contender for 2024.

To be sure, McConnell's success at deploying this strategy depended on the unwillingness of Democratic leaders on Capitol Hill to challenge the president on this front. Speaker Nancy Pelosi, as Rachael Bade and Karoun Demirjian (2022) have persuasively argued, attempted to prevent impeachment proceedings in 2019, worried about a political backlash and shifting the agenda away from popular programs. Congressmen Jerry Nadler, chair of the House Judiciary Committee, and Jamie Raskin only succeeded by continuing to push the leadership and eventually finding a way to back the speaker into a corner. But once they did, they only received support for a narrow focus and half-hearted process that rendered the chances of success almost

---

[30] On Trump's denial of writing it, see Jon Jackson, "Trump Denies Writing Forward in Mitch McConnell Memoir Praising Him as Ace in the Hole," *Newsweek*, November 8, 2021.

[31] Quoted in Katelyn Burns, "Murkowski 'Disturbed' by McConnell Pledge to Work with Trump White House on Impeachment," *Vox.Com*, December 26, 2019.

nil from the very start. After the insurrection on January 6, the speaker still refused to give support for a robust proceeding fearing it would derail President-elect Joe Biden's agenda. With such tepid feelings in the speaker's office, which were shared by Senate Majority Leader Chuck Schumer in the second impeachment, McConnell's firewall was a smashing success (Bade and Demirijan 2022).

McConnell's president, Donald Trump, was a useful vehicle for everything he hoped to achieve. As the conservative Bill Kristol argued, McConnell was a "pretty conventional Republican who just decided to go along and get what he could out of Trump."[32] An orthodox Republican who stuck to the key elements of the party's playbook, while also being someone who openly courted the most extremist elements in the party, only solidified and strengthened the Republican coalition that had been taking form since the 1980s. Although the 2020 election clearly did not end the way McConnell wanted, with Democrat Joe Biden in the White House and Democrats with the vice president's vote a Senate majority, and the outcome greatly exacerbated the tensions between these two Republican powerbrokers overall, the position was not as might be expected after an unpopular and destabilizing presidency. Large numbers of Republicans had turned out to vote for Trump in the election despite everything. The margins on Capitol Hill were so narrow that Senate Majority Leader Charles Schumer would not have much room to maneuver and Republicans would only need to flip one Democratic seat to regain control of the chamber. These circumstances gave McConnell solace in the face of defeat, sufficient to keep him quiet about the effort to overturn the election. When news leaked that the Supreme Court, with the 6-3 conservative majority that he and the former president had built, was prepared to overturn *Roe v. Wade*, it was difficult not to imagine that somewhere in Washington, DC, McConnell was sitting back smiling.

Too much commentary treated President Trump as some sort of outlier. But he was not. He in fact was very much in tune with where the GOP had moved. And Senator McConnell, one of the most ruthless partisans to lead the conference in decades, understood that. He was fine with the disruption; he was willing to live with the chaos. If Trump provided the party with deliverables, which he did, he would stick with him. The reason that McConnell kept his party lined up on the same page and protected the

---

[32] Quoted in Jane Mayer, "How Mitch McConnell Became Trump's Enabler in Chief," *New Yorker*, 2020.

president at every turn was because the two men, despite very different personal styles, were not at odds at all. They were on the same Republican page. Once that was no longer the case, as became apparent in February 2024, the senator would be gone.

References

Bade, Rachel, and Karen Demirjian. 2022. *Unchecked: The Untold Story Behind Congress' Botched Impeachments of Donald Trump.* New York: William and Morrow.

Baker, Peter, and Susan Glasser. 2022. *The Divider: Trump in the White House, 2017–2021.* New York: Doubleday.

Balkin, Jack M. 2012. "The Not-So-Happy Anniversary of the Debt-Ceiling Crisis." *The Atlantic.*

Haberman, Maggie. 2022. *Confidence Man: The Making of Donald Trump and the Breaking of America.* New York: Penguin.

Hacker, Jacob S., and Paul Pierson. 2005. *Off Center: The Republican Revolution and the Erosion of American Democracy.* New Haven: Yale University Press.

Lawless, Jennifer L., and Sean M. Theriault. 2021. "The People, the President, and the Congress at a Crossroads: Can We Turn Back from Gridlock?" In *The Presidency: Facing Constitutional Crossroads*, Michael Nelson and Barbara A. Perry, eds. Charlottesville: University of Virginia Press, 72–85.

Lee, Frances E. 2016. *Insecure Majorities: Congress and the Perpetual Campaign.* Chicago: University of Chicago Press.

Mann, Thomas E., and Norman J. Ornstein. 2012. *It's Even Worse Than It Looks: How the American Constitutional System Collided With the New Politics of Extremism.* New York: Basic Books.

McConnell, Mitch. 2016. *The Long Game.* New York: Sentinel.

McConnell, Mitch. 2019. *The Long Game.* Rev. ed. New York: Sentinel.

MacGillis, Alec. 2014. *The Cynic: The Political Education of Mitch McConnell.* New York: Simon & Schuster.

Shapiro, Ira. 2022. *The Betrayal: How Mitch McConnell and the Senate Republicans Abandoned America.* Lanham, MD: Rowman & Littlefield.

Theriault, Sean M. 2006. "Party Polarization in Congress: Member Replacement and Member Adaptation." *Party Politics* 12(3): 483–503.

Theriault, Sean M. 2013. *The Gingrich Senators: The Roots of Partisan Warfare in Congress.* New York: Oxford University Press.

Zarnow, Leandra. 2022. "'Send Her Back': Trump's Feud with Feminists and Conservative Women's Triumph." In *The Presidency of Donald J. Trump: A First Historical Assessment*, Julien E. Zelizer, ed. Princeton, NJ: Princeton University Press, 121–143.

Zelizer, Julian E. 2020. *Burning Down the House: Newt Gingrich, the Fall of a Speaker, and the Rise of the New Republican Party.* New York: Penguin.

9

Trump's Disregard for Senate Norms and Prerogatives

Niels Lesniewski

Introduction

This chapter demonstrates that, more often than not, Republican senators showed little enthusiasm for asserting their legislative and oversight powers to serve as a check on Trump, and perhaps partly as a result Trump showed a disregard for traditional norms and the separation of powers, testing the limits of executive authority. Senators were more likely to try to reign in Trump when they saw him encroaching on their powers, rather than trying to expand the reach of the executive more generally.

The cases include where expedited legislative remedies and softer powers, like the declining to confirm nominations, were available—and it of course culminated with the two impeachments. With some notable exceptions, the Senate often found itself either unequipped or uninterested in responding to Trump's pushing of the envelope, in some cases because the balance of power between the legislative and executive branch had already shifted.

On one very significant occasion when the Senate demonstrated the capacity to stand up to the former president's attempted incursions into the purview of the legislative branch, it was because the Senate would have needed to take an affirmative step in order for Trump's desired outcome to take place—and because the then-president was trying to coerce the Senate to change itself. Trump wanted McConnell, the majority leader, to cajole his conference into eliminating the legislative filibuster in order to enable swift passage of legislation backed by the Republican-led House that existed for the first two years of the president's term. And perhaps the most significant legislative rebuke of Trump came not until after he had lost reelection in 2020, with the House and Senate acting to override his veto of an annual defense authorization bill.

Niels Lesniewski, *Trump's Disregard for Senate Norms and Prerogatives* In: *Disruption?* Edited by: Sean M. Theriault, Oxford University Press. © Oxford University Press 2024. DOI: 10.1093/oso/9780197767832.003.0010

It wasn't that the former president's approaches were entirely novel, but on multiple occasions, the Trump administration seemed to take to the extreme powers that had been granted by Congress. And on some occasions, the administration went to exceptional lengths to shield the decision-making process and associated justifications not only from the public, or the media, but from the Senate as well.

The administration did not follow established protocols for the appointment of acting officials, in what was effectively an end-run around the will of the Senate in the advice and consent process, and the president took an arguably overly broad view of national emergency powers when it came to his efforts to control migration at the Southern border. A similarly broad-brush approach applied to the Trump White House's actions regarding the imposition of tariffs under the auspices of national security. But, in none of those cases, despite the bipartisan consternation about both the process and the substance of the president's decisions, could the Senate find a response that stopped the activity.

Of course, the ultimate remedy for Congress to respond to what it perceives as abuse of power is the impeachment power, with the House having the ability to send articles of impeachment to the Senate for consideration at a trial. The Democratic-controlled House ultimately took that action twice against the Republican Trump, with the former president being acquitted of all charges by the Senate during the two trials.

Acting Officials

Trump had a well-documented penchant, and in fact a stated preference, for having federal departments and agencies run by acting officials, as opposed to those confirmed by and with consent of the Senate. When Trump was asked during a February 2019 interview with the CBS News program "Face the Nation" about the number of cabinet roles, including the interior secretary and the attorney general—with the confirmation of William Barr not yet completed—he responded by saying it was actually easier for him. "It's OK. It's easier to make moves when they're acting," Trump said, adding that "it gives me more flexibility."[1] For a president who previously hosted a

---

[1] President Donald Trump, interviewed by Margaret Brennan, *Face the Nation*, CBS News, February 3, 2019, https://www.cbsnews.com/news/transcript-president-trump-on-face-the-nation-february-3-2019/.

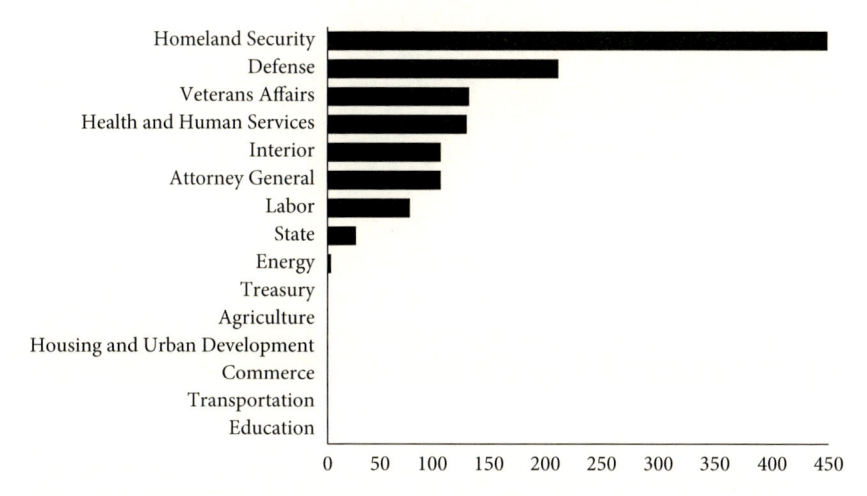

Figure 9.1 The Number of Days a Senate-Confirmed Cabinet Official Served in an "Acting" Capacity During the Trump Administration, January 20, 2017, to February 21, 2020

Source: Aaron Blake, February 21, 2020, "Trump's Government Full of Temps," *The Washington Post*, https://www.washingtonpost.com/politics/2020/02/21/trump-has-had-an-acting-official-cabinet-level-job-1-out-every-9-days/.

reality television show with the signature catch phrase "You're Fired!"[2] the ability to make personnel moves quickly was seen as a virtue, and it came with the added benefit of the reduced congressional scrutiny that comes with avoiding confirmation hearings. Just three years into his administration, Trump's acting officials in the cabinet had already served more than three times as many days as acting officials had served during the eight years that Obama served as president.[3]

The president's use of acting officials to fulfill duties of jobs that supposedly require Senate confirmation was a test for which the Senate had no real response. Perhaps the most significant case was the department of homeland security (see Figure 9.1), where once Kirstjen Nielsen resigned in August 2019, the post was filled by officers whose appointments were found by the Government Accountability Office to be invalid under the Federal Vacancies

---

[2] Before embarking on his political career, Trump was the longtime host of the NBC reality television program "The Apprentice."

[3] Aaron Blake, February 21, 2020, "Trump's Government Full of Temps," *The Washington Post*, https://www.washingtonpost.com/politics/2020/02/21/trump-has-had-an-acting-official-cabinet-level-job-1-out-every-9-days/.

Reform Act of 1998.[4] The Government Accountability Office plays a significant role in adjudicating issues related to the Vacancies Act, including determining when officials have exhausted their authorization to serve in acting capacities in positions normally requiring Senate confirmation, as well as whether the officials designated by departments and agencies should be serving at all.

As the GAO wrote in its determination regarding the Trump appointments at DHS, "Officials who assumed their positions under such amendments, including Chad Wolf and Kenneth Cuccinelli, were named by reference to an invalid order of succession."[5] In this case, the law provided the appropriate process for an order of succession at DHS, but the Trump administration did not follow it and there was no efficient remedy.[6] Cuccinelli's appointment was a rather egregious example of flaunting the advice and consent process because the challenges he would have in getting confirmed by the Senate were well known. The former attorney general of the commonwealth of Virginia, Cuccinnelli was first appointed principal deputy director of US Citizenship and Immigration Services. The USCIS statement announcing his appointment was less precise, saying that he would serve as the "acting director" of the office.[7]

In installing Cuccinnelli, Trump was going against the expressed will of the Senate. "He's spent a fair amount of his career attacking Republicans in the Senate, so it strikes me as an odd position for him to put himself in to seek Senate confirmation," Senator John Cornyn, a Texas Republican, said when the White House was reportedly mulling an actual Cuccinelli nomination, as Politico reported.[8] Years earlier SCF endorsed Matt Bevin's primary challenge to Senate Republican Leader Mitch McConnell (Gerth 2013). Bevin would lose that primary, but he would eventually be elected governor of Kentucky. "Mitch McConnell has filled the Senate with people like Lisa Murkowski, John McCain, Shelley Moore Capito, Lamar Alexander, and Dean Heller who all promised the voters they would repeal Obamacare, but

---

[4] Often referred to as simply the Vacancies Act, 5 U.S.C. § 3345 et seq.

[5] "Department of Homeland Security—Legality of Service of Acting Secretary of Homeland Security and Service of Senior Official Performing the Duties of Deputy Secretary of Homeland Security," Government Accountability Office Decision File B-331650, August 14, 2020, https://www.gao.gov/products/b-331650.

[6] 6 U.S.C. § 113(g).

[7] "Cuccinelli Named Acting Director of USCIS," U.S. Citizenship and Immigration Service press release, June 10, 2019, https://www.uscis.gov/archive/cuccinelli-named-acting-director-of-uscis

[8] Burgess Everett and Elaina Johnson, "Republicans Ready to Quash Cuccinelli," Politico, June 4, 2019, https://www.politico.com/story/2019/06/04/cuccinelli-immigration-nomination-1353314.

when the time came to do it they refused," Cuccinelli wrote in an August 2017 fundraising message for the fund, as CQ Roll Call reported.

Border Security National Emergency

No incident more underscored the challenges of Senate Republicans seeking to impose checks on the unfettered powers than the response to the president's border security national emergency declaration. Trump, who had signed into law a belated fiscal 2019 consolidated appropriations bill on February 15, 2019, did not receive the funding his administration had sought for border wall construction.[9] In response, the president on the same day declared a national emergency, saying that security at the border between the United States and Mexico had reached a "crisis."[10] "Because of the gravity of the current emergency situation, it is necessary for the Armed Forces to provide additional support to address the crisis," Trump said.

Trump invoked a provision of federal law authorizing the use of military personnel and for military construction projects during a national emergency or declared war even when not otherwise authorized. The law says, "the Secretary of Defense, without regard to any other provision of law, may undertake military construction projects, and may authorize the Secretaries of the military departments to undertake military construction projects, not otherwise authorized by law that are necessary to support such use of the armed forces."[11] Here, the Senate tried to respond, but it had a legislative tool that proved insufficient. A March 2019 Senate vote, for instance, saw the adoption of a joint resolution to terminate the border security emergency.[12]

Senator Thom Tillis, a North Carolina Republican, had an unusual odyssey leading up to his opposition to the disapproval measure. He had penned an opinion piece for *The Washington Post* outlining the case for blocking the president's action, even as he said he supported Trump's desire to clamp down on the border. "Although Trump certainly has legitimate

---

[9] PL 116-6.

[10] "Declaring a National Emergency Concerning the Southern Border of the United States," Presidential Proclamation 9844, February 20, 2019, https://www.federalregister.gov/documents/2019/02/20/2019-03011/declaring-a-national-emergency-concerning-the-southern-border-of-the-united-states.

[11] 10 USC § 2808.

[12] Niels Lesniewski, "Senate Learns Pushing Back on Trump Can Be Hard Work," *Roll Call*, March 14, 2019, https://rollcall.com/2019/03/14/senate-learns-pushing-back-on-trump-can-be-hard-work/.

grievances over congressional Democrats' obstruction of border-security funding, his national emergency declaration on Feb. 15 was not the right answer," wrote Tillis, adding that he understood would attempt to implement the policy. "In fact, if I were the leader of the Constitution's Article II branch, I would probably declare an emergency and use all the tools at my disposal as well. Tillis wrote. "But I am not. I am a member of the Senate, and I have grave concerns when our institution looks the other way at the expense of weakening Congress's power."

When it came time for the Senate to vote, Tillis, who was up for reelection in 2020, had a complete change of heart. "The concerns I've raised were never about what President Trump is trying to accomplish but rather with setting a precedent that a future Democratic president would exploit to bypass Congress to implement policies well outside the mainstream," Tillis said in a March 14, 2019, statement. "Over the past several weeks, I've met with the Vice President and senior White House staff to build consensus on amending the National Emergencies Act to prevent a future left-wing president from misusing their authority." No legislation advanced to significantly rein in the scope of the national emergencies act before Trump left office. The Senate vote, which was 59–41, followed House passage the previous month. The measure lacked sufficient support to override a presidential veto, which would have required a two-thirds vote.

Representative Joaquin Castro (D-Texas), who introduced the measure in the House, called the resolution to disapprove of the funding, which became a recurring vote during the Trump presidency, "the most consequential vote we've probably taken in decades that will determine the balance of power between Congress and the president of the United States." In a radio interview, Castro continued: "And if Donald Trump gets his way now, and Congress allows this to stand, it's likely that he'll come back again and try to do the same thing on the border wall issue again, or on other issues, and that future presidents will also do the same thing."[13]

The Washington Post cited the example of Mike Lee, a conservative Utah Republican senator, as among those who expressed concern at the time about the separation of powers, since the spending clearly went against the will of Congress.[14] The problem, as with other kinds of disapproval resolutions,

[13] Joaquin Castro, interviewed by the Texas Standard, Texas Public Radio, February 26, 2019, https://www.texasstandard.org/stories/joaquin-castro-says-voting-to-sop-the-presidents-emerge ncy-declaration-is-the-most-consequential-vote-in-decades/.

[14] Colby Itkowitz, "These 12 Republicans Defied Trump and Voted to Overturn His Declaration of an Emergency at the Border," *The Washington Post*, March 14, 2019,https://www.washingtonpost.

is that bypassing the legislative filibuster itself is not sufficient to reach enactment—the House and Senate would also need to override a presidential veto. It would pass the Senate 59–41, short of the two-thirds. Trump's response, which came in the form of a tweet, was "VETO!"[15]

Confederate Base Name Veto

One case where the president did not prevail over the will of Congress was a veto of a defense authorization over a combination of factors including confederate base naming provisions. As a White House correspondent, I asked then-White House Press Secretary Kayleigh McEnany in a press briefing, "If Congress were to send over, say, the defense authorization with language that were to rename one of these bases for someone who, say, was a general who won the Civil War, would the President veto the defense authorization?" She continued, "The President will not be signing legislation that renames America's forts."[16] The widely reported public display of opposition to proposals to change the name of military bases came, perhaps by happenstance, on the same day the Senate Armed Services Committee was in the middle of marking up the year's defense authorization measure.

Unlike most committees, the Armed Services panel continues to conduct much of its work in closed session, so it was not yet publicly known that the committee had adopted a bipartisan version of an amendment offered by Sen. Elizabeth Warren (D-Massachusetts), to set up a process for renaming military bases and a host of other federal facilities that had been named for prominent supporters of the old Confederacy. "Fort Bragg, North Carolina is named for Major General Braxton Bragg. Bragg was a slaveowner, and like the others, Bragg chose to take up arms against the United States and kill US soldiers, but with an infamously poor record as a military commander, he wasn't very good at it," Warren said in June 30, 2020, floor speech.

---

com/politics/these-12-republicans-defied-trump-and-voted-to-overturn-his-declaration-of-an-emergency-at-the-border/2019/03/14/3fd67890-4682-11e9-90f0-0ccfeec87a61_story.html.

[15] Amanda Becker and Richard Cowan, "Trump Vows 'VETO!' after Bipartisan Senate Rebuke on Wall," *Reuters*, March 14, 2019, https://www.reuters.com/article/us-usa-trump-congress-emerge ncy/trump-vows-veto-after-bipartisan-senate-rebuke-on-wall-idUSKCN1QV1A8.

[16] Niels Lesniewski, "Senate Armed Services on Collision Course with Trump over Confederate Names," *Roll Call*, June 10, 2020, https://rollcall.com/2020/06/10/senate-armed-services-on-collis ion-course-with-trump-over-confederate-names/.

"Widely regarded as the most disliked man in the Confederate army, Bragg commanded forces that were so badly defeated at the Battle of Chattanooga in 1863 that he ultimately resigned."[17]

Language regarding the naming of military bases survived the conference committee process, despite the president's veto threat and the late point in the year at which the bill was being considered. The president gave other subsequent reasons for his veto of the measure, but they were wholly rejected by super majorities in each chamber of Congress, with Trump in lame duck status at the time. For the Senate, overriding the veto involved an usual session on New Year's Day 2021.[18] But, this rebuke came after he had already lost reelection.

National Security Tariffs

Section 232 of the Trade Expansion Act of 1962 was used to impose tariffs on steel and aluminum[19] from European allies and a Senate-led effort to respond went nowhere. And in perhaps the most widely criticized case, in February 2019, Commerce Secretary Wilbur Ross, made a determination that "excessive" imports of automobiles and automobile parts was displacing domestic manufacturers in a way that could have national security risks. The Commerce Department in a report from February 17, 2019 wrote:

> The contraction of the American-owned automotive industry, if continued, will significantly impede the United States' ability to develop technologically advanced products that are essential to our ability to maintain technological superiority to meet defense requirements and cost effective global power projection, as well as provide the necessary R&D and manufacturing base in the event of a national emergency.[20]

[17] Elizabeth Warren, Senate floor speech, June 30, 2020. https://www.warren.senate.gov/newsr oom/press-releases/warren-delivers-floor-speech-on-her-amendment-to-rename-all-bases-and-other-military-assets-honoring-the-confederacy.

[18] Matthew Daly, "In a First, Congress Overrides Trump's Veto of Defense Bill," *The Associated Press*, January 1, 2021. https://apnews.com/article/election-2020-donald-trump-defense-policy-bills-85656704ad9ae1f9cf202ee76d7a14fd.

[19] "Adjusting Imports of Steel Into the United States," Presidential Proclamation 9705, March 8, 2018, https://www.federalregister.gov/documents/2018/03/15/2018-05478/adjusting-impo rts-of-steel-into-the-united-states, and "Adjusting Imports of Aluminum Into the United States, Presidential Proclamation 9704," March 8, 2018, https://www.govinfo.gov/content/pkg/FR-2018-03-15/pdf/2018-05477.pdf.

[20] "THE EFFECT OF IMPORTS OF AUTOMOBILES AND AUTOMOBILE PARTS ON THE NATIONAL SECURITY," Department of Commerce, February 17, 2019, https://www.bis.doc.gov/

But that report justifying imposition of tariffs on automotive imports—including from US allies in NATO member states—was hidden from public view for the entirety of the remainder of the Trump administration. It was among the most egregious examples of the former president disregarding a legal requirement. The *Wall Street Journal* editorial board said in response to the report after its belated release that "one takeaway is that Congress ought to get its act together and revise or repeal Section 232. The law is so expansive that in a 2018 court case the government declined to answer directly when asked if the President could unilaterally tax imported peanut butter."[21]

Senator Patrick Toomey, the top Republican on the Banking Committee, and other concerned lawmakers had actually gone so far as to try to require the report be released through an amendment to a fiscal 2021 appropriations law, which led the Justice Department's Office of Legal Counsel to make a claim of executive privilege. "The Secretary's report is protected by executive privilege. It is a quintessential privileged presidential communication—a report from a Cabinet Secretary to the President advising him of the officer's opinions and recommending decisions by the President. The report is also protected by the deliberative process component of executive privilege, because it reflects a recommendation made in connection with deliberations over the President's final decision. In addition, disclosure of the full report at this time could compromise the United States' position in ongoing international negotiations" (Engel 2020).

Trump also made use of the trade law to impose limits on steel and aluminum imports, including on US allies, under the apparent guise of national security considerations. The president's order recognized the incongruity: "In adopting this tariff, I recognize that our Nation has important security relationships with some countries whose exports of aluminum to the United States weaken our internal economy and thereby threaten to impair the national security. I also recognize our shared concern about global excess capacity, a circumstance that is contributing to the threatened impairment of the national security."[22] Toomey and Mark Warner (D-Virginia), among

index.php/documents/section-232-investigations/2774-redacted-autos-232-final-and-appendix-a-july-2021/file.

[21] "How Trump Nearly Justified Car Tariffs," *The Wall Street Journal*, editorial board, July 19, 2021, https://www.wsj.com/articles/how-trump-nearly-justified-car-tariffs-11626734503?mod=opinion_lead_pos4.

[22] Presidential proclamation 9704.

others, have continued to advocate for changing the trade law, but as of 2022, no legislation has advanced.

The bill spearheaded by Toomey and Warner would narrow the sweeping definition of "national security" for Section 232 tariff justifications that the authors said in fact sheet has been used by the Commerce Department since 2001, long predating Trump's presidency but deployed more aggressively during his tenure. According to a fact sheet regarding the 2019 version of the bill, which identified 11 initial supporters (6 Republicans and 5 Democrats), the measure would have declared, "Congress has 60 days to approve any proposed Section 232 actions. If Congress does not pass an approval resolution, the President's proposed trade actions shall have no force or effect."[23] But, as with the effort that Tillis was involved with regarding the parameters for declaring national emergencies, no such legislation has been enacted.

Impeachment; Twice

Trump was ultimately impeached by the House on two different occasions and for two distinct reasons. For the purposes of this chapter, it is the first impeachment trial that merits more attention, because the grounds for that impeachment—and eventual acquittal by the Senate, since the proximate cause for the impeachment includes charges of abuse of power related to his withholding "the release of $391 million of United States taxpayer funds that Congress had appropriated on a bipartisan basis for the purpose of providing vital military and security assistance to Ukraine to oppose Russian aggression and which President Trump had ordered suspended."[24] It was the infamous "perfect phone call" as the former president would put it,[25] which led to that first impeachment.

The Washington Post reported that Mulvaney, who had gone from being director of the Office of Management and Budget, was told by Trump to withhold the money ahead of a well-documented July 2019 call between Trump and Ukrainian President Volodymyr Zelenskyy. A declassified memo

[23] Summary of the Bicameral Congressional Trade Authority Act of 2019 (S. 287), prepared by the office of Sen. Patrick Toomey, bill introduced January 31, 2019, https://www.toomey.senate.gov/imo/media/doc/232%20one%20pager.pdf.

[24] "IMPEACHMENT OF DONALD J. TRUMP PRESIDENT OF THE UNITED STATES," House Judiciary Committee, House Report 116-346, December 15, 2019.

[25] See, for example, the January 16, 2020 tweet: "I JUST GOT IMPEACHED FOR MAKING A PERFECT PHONE CALL!"

with a rough transcript of that July 25, 2019, call was ultimately released by the White House. Zelenskky relayed that Ukraine was "almost ready to buy more Javelins from the United States for defense purposes," to which Trump responded with a request "to do us a favor though because our country has been through a lot and Ukraine knows a lot about it."[26] Part of that favor involved a request for damaging information about Hunter Biden, a son of the current president who was at the time a potential 2020 adversary of Trump.

According to reporting in *The Washington Post* in the aftermath, the delay in releasing the funds between the summer and the eventual release on September 11, was being described by administration agencies as "interagency process" without much in additional context.[27] The release of the money, belated as it was, drew praise from senators, Senator Ron Portman (R-Ohio), who had been among the lawmakers in both parties advocating for the aid package. "I appreciate President Trump releasing the security funds for Ukraine, and I want to thank him for doing so," Portman said in a statement at the time. "I strongly support the president's position that NATO allies and especially our European countries in the region can and must do more to support Ukraine. Our military aid is crucial to allow Ukraine to defend itself, but increased European security assistance is also crucial, and would make our support more effective."[28]

In the meantime, House Democrats were determined in their estimation that Trump was attempting to extort Ukraine to help support his political objectives back home. Representative Adam Schiff (D-California), chairman of the House Intelligence Committee, said "it reads like a classic organized crime shakedown" at a September 2019 hearing.[29] In addition to his role on the Intelligence panel, Schiff, a senior member of the Judiciary Committee, served as an impeachment manager.

[26] "Telephone conversation with President Zelenskky of Ukraine," Memorandum of telephone conversation, declassified September 24, 2019, https://www.documentcloud.org/documents/6429 034-White-House-memo-on-Trump-call-with-Ukraine.html.

[27] Karoun Demirjian, Josh Dawsey, Ellen Nakashima, and Carol D. Leonnig, "Trump Ordered Hold on Military Aid Days before Calling Ukrainian President, Officials Say," *The Washington Post*, September 23, 2019, https://www.washingtonpost.com/national-security/trump-ordered-hold-on-military-aid-days-before-calling-ukrainian-president-officials-say/2019/09/23/df93a6ca-de38-11e9-8dc8-498eabc129a0_story.html.

[28] Rob Portman, "Portman Welcomes President Trump Decision on Security Assistance & Urges Other NATO Countries to Do More to Help Ukraine," press release, September 12, 2019, https://www.portman.senate.gov/newsroom/press-releases/portman-welcomes-president-trump-decision-security-assistance-urges-other.

[29] "Whistleblower Disclosure, House Intelligence Committee hearing, September 206, 2019, video of statement from Chairman Adam Schiff here: https://www.pbs.org/newshour/politics/watch-schiff-says-whistleblower-complaint-reads-like-crime-shakedown.

The House adopted the articles of impeachment on December 18, 2019, with 230 members supporting the vote on the first article related to the abuse of power and 229 members supporting the second, related to obstruction of Congress itself.[30] The only House lawmaker who was not a Democrat to vote in support was Rep. Justin Amash, a Michigan independent who had previously been a Republican.[31] "Impeachment is like an indictment. We're just issuing the charges. The trial happens in the Senate. There's certainly probable cause to issue charges," Amash said.[32]

The trial in the Senate, the first of its kind since the impeachment of President Bill Clinton, was a national spectacle that came shortly before the attention of the United States would shift to the COVID-19 pandemic, which still a developing story as the trial proceedings to set the ground rules got underway, with Chief Justice John Roberts presiding, on January 21, 2020. Few doubted that Trump would be acquitted by the Senate, with a two-thirds vote needed to convict. As the proceedings got underway that day, that Senator Mitch McConnell, the majority leader, argued against the Senate taking an active role in investigating the president's actions while also sitting as the court of impeachment.

"For example, many senators, including me, have serious concerns about blurring –blurring—the traditional role between the House and the Senate within the impeachment process. The Constitution divides the power to impeach from the power to try. The first belongs solely to the House, and with the power to impeach comes the responsibility to investigate," the majority leader said on the Senate floor. "The Senate agreeing to pick up and carry on the House's inadequate investigation would set a new precedent that could incentivize frequent and hasty impeachments from future House Majorities." McConnell, in arguing that conducting a more robust investigation of the president's actions would be beyond the traditional scope of the Senate's role in the impeachment process, may well have short-circuited any additional investigation of Trump's actions with respect to Ukraine.

---

[30] House roll call votes 696 and 696.

[31] Amash announced his formal departure from the GOP in the summer of 2019, see for ex. Justin Amash, "Our Politics Is in a Partisan Death Spiral. That's Why I'm Leaving the GOP," *The Washington Post*, July 4, 2019, https://www.washingtonpost.com/opinions/justin-amash-our-politics-is-in-a-partisan-death-spiral-thats-why-im-leaving-the-gop/2019/07/04/afbe0480-9e3d-11e9-b27f-ed2 942f73d70_story.html.

[32] Manu Raju and Ali Zaslav, "Independent Lawmaker Says He's Ready to Vote to Impeach Trump," CNN, December 6, 2019, https://www.cnn.com/2019/12/06/politics/justin-amash-supports-impe achment.

Senator Mitt Romney, the Utah Republican who was a former governor of Massachusetts and the GOP presidential nominee in 2012 became the first, and to that point only, senator to vote in favor of removing from office a president from his own party, with President Richard Nixon having resigned the office before facing potential removal. "What he did was not 'perfect'—No, it was a flagrant assault on our electoral rights, our national security interests, and our fundamental values. Corrupting an election to keep oneself in office is perhaps the most abusive and destructive violation of one's oath of office that I can imagine," Romney said in a 2020 floor speech.[33] Romney's remarks were in the context of the first impeachment, though they could have been in relation to the second, as well.

Less than a month after Trump's term as president ended, Romney would no longer be alone among Republicans in voting to convict a member of his own party.[34] Trump was impeached by the House for a second time (on different charges) stemming from his provocations of the mob that attacked the US Capitol on January 6, 2021 and his subsequent delay in responding to help call off his supporters and defend the Capitol. Republican Senators Richard Burr, Bill Cassidy, Susan Collins, Lisa Murkowski, and Ben Sasse, as well as Toomey, would join with Romney in voting to convict.

Some other Republicans, including McConnell, argued that impeachment and removal was not an appropriate remedy in the case of a president who had already left office. *The New York Times* had earlier reported that McConnell was backing the impeachment, at least "privately," citing "people familiar with Mr. McConnell's thinking," but he voted to acquit.[35] "Whatever our ex-President claims he thought might happen that day . . . whatever reaction he says he meant to produce . . . by that afternoon, he was watching the same live television as the rest of the world," McConnell said in a floor speech. "A mob was assaulting the Capitol in his name. These criminals were carrying his banners, hanging his flags, and screaming their loyalty to him." McConnell said that Trump "didn't take steps so federal law could be faithfully executed, and order restored."[36]

[33] Mitt Romney, floor speech on his vote to convict President Donald Trump, February 5, 2020, https://www.romney.senate.gov/romney-delivers-remarks-impeachment-vote/.

[34] Senate vote 59.

[35] Jonathan Martin, Maggie Haberman, and Nicholas Fandos, "McConnell Privately Backs Impeachment as House Moves to Charge Trump," *The New York Times*, January 12, 2021, https://www.nytimes.com/2021/01/12/us/politics/mcconnell-backs-trump-impeachment.html.

[36] Mitch McConnell, Senate floor speech, February 13, 2021, https://www.republicanleader.senate.gov/newsroom/remarks/mcconnell-on-impeachment-disgraceful-dereliction-cannot-lead-senate-to-defy-our-own-constitutional-guardrails.

But McConnell ultimately sided with those who made the argument that the Senate, as a court of impeachment, lacked jurisdiction over Trump once he was a former president. "Brilliant scholars argue both sides of the jurisdictional question. The text is legitimately ambiguous. I respect my colleagues who have reached either conclusion. But after intense reflection, I believe the best constitutional reading shows that Article II, Section 4 exhausts the set of persons who can legitimately be impeached, tried, or convicted. The President, Vice President, and civil officers," McConnell said. "We have no power to convict and disqualify a former officeholder who is now a private citizen."

By the point the second Trump impeachment trial took place, McConnell was the minority leader, with Democrats having taken the narrowest of Senate majorities in the aftermath of Democratic victories in two January run-off elections in Georgia, which combined with Vice President Kamala Harris taking office, left the Senate with a 50-50 split and a Democratic tie-breaker. McConnell and New York Democratic Senator Chuck Schumer, by then the majority leader, had agreed with their colleagues to organize the Senate in much the same way as their predecessors Tom Daschle and Trent Lott had the last time that there was a tie in Senate control.

So, the Democratic caucus could have pressed the argument, prolonged the trial and sought to call witnesses. Internal discussions among Democrats were spirited, but it was a report from Politico that distilled the reality. "The jury is ready to vote," Politico quoted Democratic Senator Chris Coons, a Delaware senator and long-time ally of the now president, as having said in closed-door conversations, "People want to get home for Valentine's Day." Coons had reportedly expressed concern that prolonging the process, which could have further disrupted the regularly scheduled President's Day recess, could also cost the Democratic impeachment managers votes.[37]

More color about that meeting emerged in a 2022 book by Rachael Bade and Karoun Demirjian, with House Democrats responding after Coons left the room with expletives. Representative David Cicilline, (D-Rhode Island) was quoted as saying "Are you fucking kidding me?" about the prospect that a presidential impeachment trial could be affected by the timing of Valentine's Day.[38]

---

[37] Burgess Everett, Heather Cagyle, and Marianne Levine, "Inside Democrats' Witness Fiasco," Politico, February 13, 2021, https://www.politico.com/news/2021/02/13/senate-democrats-impeachment-witnesses-468992.

[38] Quoted in Rachael Bade and Karoun Demirjian. 2022. *Unchecked: The Untold Story Behind Congress's Botched Impeachments of Donald Trump*, William Morrow, 844.

Rules Changes

But, even as the former president on numerous occasions escaped potential checks on his power from a perhaps ill-equipped Senate, he also could not get senators to bend to his will on one of his recurring top priorities: eliminating the legislative filibuster. "Congress must immediately pass Border Legislation, use Nuclear Option if necessary, to stop the massive inflow of Drugs and People," Trump tweeted on April 2, 2018, one of several occasions in which he tried to get McConnell and the rest of the Senate Republicans on board with rules changes.

The "nuclear option" in the parlance of the Senate relates not to nuclear weapons, but to the chamber's internal rules. Generally speaking, using the so-called nuclear option involves using a simple majority vote to establish a new Senate precedent that bypasses the process for changing the rules under regular order. Majority leaders have used the procedures from time-to-time, including McConnell himself on April 6, 2017, in order to eliminate the requirement for 60 senators to support breaking a filibuster of a Supreme Court nominee. But in that case, getting Neil Gorsuch confirmed to the court as an associate justice was in line with the interests of both McConnell and Trump.

Eliminating the legislative filibuster, on the other hand, has long been opposed by McConnell and a majority of his conference. "I recognize it may seem odd that a Senate majority leader opposes a proposal to increase his own power... But my Republican colleagues and I have not and will not vandalize this core tradition for short-term gain," McConnell wrote in a 2019 *New York Times* opinion piece.[39] Trump continued the campaign, as other presidents have, for the Senate with a membership ever so slightly in his favor to change the filibuster rules—but it contrasts with the other cases here precisely because it was the prerogative of the Senate to make the change.

Conclusion

Ultimately, Trump's disregard for the norms of the Senate was an extension of the past tensions between the executive and legislative branches — but

---

[39] Mitch McConnell, "The Filibuster Plays a Crucial Role in Our Constitutional Order," *The New York Times*, August 22, 2019, https://www.nytimes.com/2019/08/22/opinion/mitch-mcconnell-senate-filibuster.html.

taken to new extremes. Past presidents had called for the elimination of the filibuster to achieve their policy objectives, and Trump certainly was not the first or last president to try to stretch the envelope when it comes to federal spending. Trump also was not the first president to face a politically charged impeachment trial and prevail. But, the legislative filibuster endured for another day, and so for as much as Trump's disregard for traditional norms demonstrated the ways in which the chief executive can bypass the Senate, it was more of a profession along the existing path to further executive branch power than a shock that disrupted the body.

10

Senate Communication in the Era of Trump

Annelise Russell

Introduction

Senators can no longer just be the guys in the dark, smoke-filled room forging policy deals. A successful political reputation is increasingly a publicized endeavor, and in the Senate, those choices play out on Twitter where journalists and stakeholders fight to have the first word. The changing digital climate has been evolving in the Senate for more than two decades as senators have used social media and digital to draw the attention of journalists, appeal to advocates and stoke political divisions, but the threat of 3 a.m. tweets by President Donald Trump offered unprecedented fuel to the fire. The Trump election secured a digital era of high-velocity political information, and senators' digital efforts, especially Democrats, became the voice of sustained opposition. If you look at the @SenateDems Twitter account from 2015–2019, it becomes very clear how engagement shifted under the Trump presidency and during the Democratic leadership transfer from the late Harry Reid to Chuck Schumer (see Figure 10.1).

Congressional policymaking is only getting more complex, and paired with that complexity, is a communication crisis of rapid information exchange and constant engagement spurred by social media. Lawmakers and senior staff still plan their message for the week, organizing around new legislation, upcoming votes, and planned events, but they expect to manage a schedule that is at risk of blowing up at any moment and is likely ripe for revisions. As one communications staffer describes it, "Reputation management [and] risk mitigation are two of the most important things that people who work comms and Congress do."[1]

---

[1] Interview. 1/12/22. Former Communications Director.

Annelise Russell, *Senate Communication in the Era of Trump* In: *Disruption?* Edited by: Sean M. Theriault, Oxford University Press. © Oxford University Press 2024. DOI: 10.1093/oso/9780197767832.003.0011

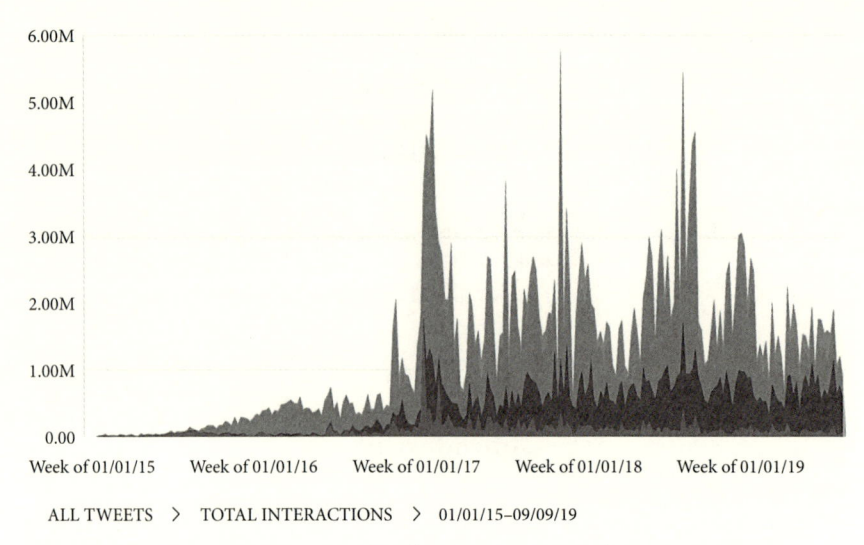

ALL TWEETS > TOTAL INTERACTIONS > 01/01/15–09/09/19

Figure 10.1 Twitter Interactions for the @SenDems Hashtag, 2015–2019
Source: CrowdTangle Intelligence Report for @SenateDems on Twitter.

The shift toward the fast-paced digital information exchange predates President Trump, but the new heights reached and expectations for instantaneous information accelerated the Senate's adoption of a crisis communication operation where the incentives of social media contribute to a high-volume information exchange that has the potential to overwhelm a congressional office. Twitter adds pressure and speed to an already uncontrolled stream of political news, and during the Trump presidency, that news sped up and continued into the night. The folks who work in Congress now adapt their daily routines to the digital dialogue and rapidly cycling narratives such that journalists holding a story for a couple hours for an official lawmaker statement is no longer sufficient. The rise of polarizing rhetoric and deviation from policy realities is made possible on a digital platform that has gained a foothold in Congress because lawmakers can create content, journalists can track minute-by-minute the movement of lawmakers, and staff can monitor the narrative for looming political crises. A shifting media environment is nothing new for an institution that adapted to C-SPAN cameras, normalized TV and satellite trucks, and experienced the erosion of local media in favor of DC-centric press, but the totality of what an office must manage in the digital news climate where senators and their staff have become content creators rather than just facilitators threatens congressional capacity. Lawmakers and their offices were struggling to meet the demand of a Twitter-driven information exchange before Trump was ever elected, but the requirement to be on Twitter rather than the choice and the need to track the political narrative at all hours of the day went from bad to worse during the Trump presidency.

Twitter tests the capacity of the Senate to handle the information flow when the pressures for transparency are high and the demands from stakeholders and advocates continue to increase. Senate offices have organized themselves to not only triage the information flow but also perpetuate the digital exchange as content creators. Fifteen years ago, congressional offices thought of "New Media" as a separate, largely unknown operation to provide outreach to bloggers and a growing digital constituency. Today, new media is part of the digital operation that has evolved to become central to congressional communications operations. The normalization of digital directors and the need for professional media services places even greater emphasis on congressional communications and the need for resources to manage those efforts. Drawing from Senate social media data and congressional staff and political journalist interviews, I explain how the Senate continues to adapt to a Trump-reinforced Twitter environment where misinformation is common, facts are debatable, and news is always being made. President Trump did not induce a new style of communication in Congress, but rather helped to escalate a new era of digital engagement where the institutional and media norms have been altered to match that of a disaster response mitigating the information deluge. The information exchange never stops, meaning that journalists, communications staff, and policy staff are always on alert for new information that disrupts the political agenda and redefines the terms of debate. The Senate adopted a digital advertising platform for governance and continues to grapple with the repercussions.

Trends Toward Digital and Crisis Communication

Many suggest the Trump presidency was a watershed moment for reconsidering presidential performance, and in many ways, this perception holds true because Trump offered a new type of presidential candidate, moving us away from agenda-setting, rhetorical presidencies to ubiquitous leaders with content-creating power on a massive digital scale (Tulis 1987; Scacco and Coe 2021). The president used Twitter early and often to shape

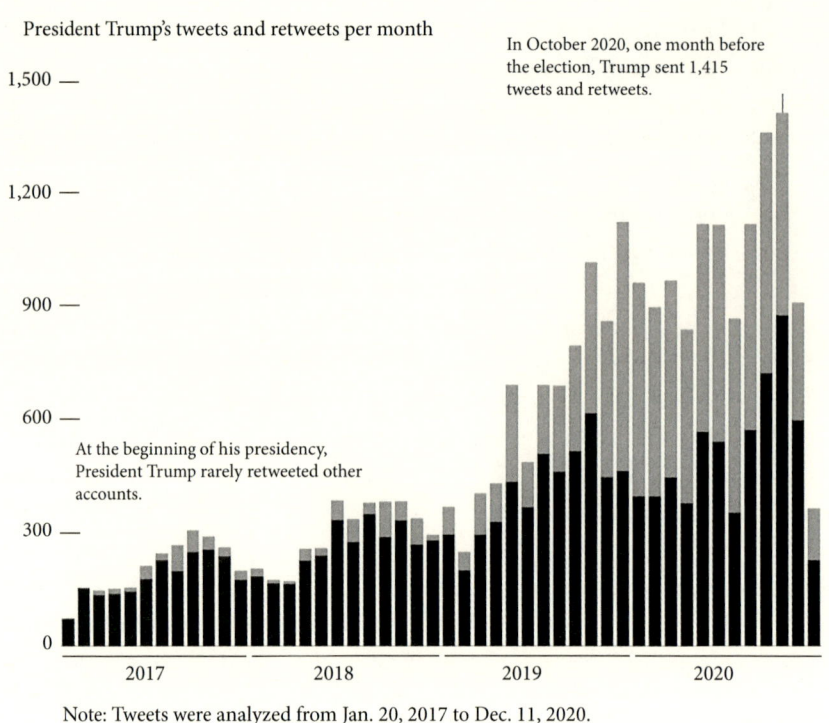

Figure 10.2 President Trump's Twitter Activity During Office
Source: Trump Twitter Archives and CNN's Priya Krishnakumar

the political narrative such that by the time senators and staff were headed into the workday, they were bombarded by questions about the president's statement on Twitter and had lost control of the narrative (Interview 9/12/ 22). President Trump's frequent Twitter activity continued to rise during his time in office, reinforcing the digital culture that extended from the White House to Congress (see Figure 10.2).

Trump changed what we should expect from both a presidential candidate and president in office, often highlighted by the way he interacted—or didn't—with both social and traditional media. One political reporter noted that an adversarial relationship between a president and the press is good for a healthy democracy, but the relationship with President Trump was especially nasty and dangerous at times.[2] While Trump pushed the boundaries for what is acceptable in political and government communication, he wasn't

---

[2] Interview. 11/20/2020. Political Journalist.

building a new strategy out of thin air. The playbook had already been in motion, and one need not look any further than Congress. Rather than thinking about Donald Trump as a fire-starter, it is more useful to think of his time in office as a critical accelerant speeding the development of a combustible communication climate.

The old folkways of the Senate, comradery and collegiality were already disappearing in the digital realm before Trump ever declared his presidential intentions. Even the CODELs—congressional travel often lauded for bipartisanship and friendship—have become susceptible to the norm-breaking partisan warfare in Congress (McGee and Theriault 2022). Senators' legislative behavior and choices about how to approach procedure were already shifting as a new generation of senators drew from the lessons of former House Speaker Newt Gingrich and brought a warrior mentality to the upper chamber (Theriault 2013; Lee 2009). Layered on top of those institutional differences are new digital opportunities that have elevated the role of digital and press operations in the Senate. One former digital media staffer noted that Trump and the rise of political journalism outlets like *Politico* were inflection points, but the general trends extend back to even before the Obama 2008 campaign and decisions the parties made about how to integrate online media.[3] In 2007, many were surprised when former senator and Democratic presidential hopeful John Edwards confirmed via Twitter that his then-wife, Elizabeth Edwards, was facing a cancer reoccurrence. In 2005, former Majority Leader Harry Reid began the "war room" putting together a team to tackle what was then called "new media" to reach both progressives and voters back home. In early 2008, Senator Ed Markey—then chair of the House Energy and Commerce Subcommittee on Telecommunications—hosted a simultaneous virtual hearing in the 3D community Second Life with his own avatar and virtual chairman's seat.

The Senate was already taking turns testing how far you could go on Twitter, who you could call out, and where the line was that you could not cross. During the second term of the Obama presidency, senators were regularly turning to Twitter to call out political opposition, reinforce partisan narratives, and engage in high-stakes blame avoidance (Russell 2018). Former staff confirm Republican Senator John Cornyn was regularly running his own Twitter account on flights home and using his platform to talk about the threat of Hillary Clinton and her missing emails.[4] In 2013 and

---

[3] Interview. 4/5/2022. Former digital communications staff.
[4] https://twitter.com/johncornyn/status/601835558000848896.

2015, Republican senators used Twitter go negative against Democrats—the president in particular—for the Affordable Care Act, immigration, runaway spending, and overall ineffectiveness at the federal level. One-in-seven tweets by Republican senators in 2013 was about something Democrats or the president was doing wrong (Russell 2018). Democrats pulled their own punches and escalated the digital warfare once Trump was elected, but the notion that Trump somehow changed the game isn't quite born out on Twitter because the Senate was already grappling with disappearing folkways and emerging digital trends.

The Trump presidency wasn't the reason congressional communications came to mirror a disaster response, but many still attribute the Twitter-driven attention cycle to his preference for digital communication that could break news at all hours of the night. Lawmakers of both parties faced new challenges about what it meant to have the president making news overnight and operating within an institution where the speed and volume of information was increasing. The shift with President Trump wasn't a directional shift, as Congress had been fighting "for the right to Twitter" since 2008 when the Senate updated its Franking rules.[5] The pressing question this time was about "how low one can go" when it comes to digital communication as blame avoidance and partisan sideswipes gave way to full frontal attacks and distortion of facts.

> The idea of somebody abusing another member of Congress or threatening to start a war on Twitter, you know, that at that point, it wasn't something that we had considered because you just, you know, you had different standards for the President of the United States. So we went from "go, go go to like, trying to figure out, you know . . . what guardrails do we need to put in place?"[6]

Congressional offices adapted to shape their routines around the rapidly cycling narratives, trying to manage the information flow while also managing their own preferred message. Congressional staffers note that in the first few months of the Trump presidency many press secretaries and communications

---

[5] NPR. "Congress Members Fight For The Right To Twitter," https://www.npr.org/transcripts/92398555.
[6] Interview. 2/16/2022. Former Democratic communications staffer.

directors were working at all hours of the night, trying to predict how to respond to the seemingly random pattern of tweets and trying to keep up with the changing rhetoric moving from the White House to congressional leadership. That speed of engagement, and the heightened political rhetoric that accompanied it, meant that many congressional offices were constantly on the defensive and reacting to the president became a central part of how they organized. One former policy staffer described her office's Twitter presence in terms of presidential reaction, especially early in the Trump presidency:[7]

> The biggest change that has happened that I have seen over nearly six years doing press is the rise of Trump, and the changes that follow the rise of Trump. And very specifically, I think about how some in my party very quickly realized that our role was going to be to kind of give voice to the opposition.[8]

The rise of polarizing rhetoric and deviation from political realities is made possible on a digital platform that has gained a foothold in Congress given the ability of lawmakers to create content, for journalists to track minute-by-minute the movement of lawmakers, and for staff to monitor the narrative for looming political crises. Congress has a long history of shifting practices to new media environments, such as the introduction of C-SPAN cameras, the normalization of TV and satellite trucks, the erosion of local media in favor of DC-centric press, or today's digital news climate where senators and their staff have become content creators rather than just facilitators. All of these changes were underway before Trump was ever elected, but the need to be on Twitter and drive the digital narrative at all hours of the day went from bad to worse during the Trump presidency:

> President Trump was sort of a prime example of somebody who . . . gets something at 5:30 in the morning, and temporarily at least throws off a legislative effort . . . And then, you know, he was almost the only one with the power to bring it back online.[9]

---

[7] Interview. 3/19/2021. Former legislative staffer.
[8] Interview. 9/24/2021. Democratic congressional staffer.
[9] Interview. 2/2/2022. Republican communications staffer.

The Twitter to Cable Pipeline

> Cable news is still important, and particularly on the Republican side, where talk radio is still very important. Those are those are still important pieces of infrastructure.[10]

Trump also reinforced an important pipeline for media traction by using social media as a platform to launch onto other, traditional media. As one journalist described it, Twitter is the main thing for reporters on the Hill, because members of Congress all use Twitter. Journalists, politicos, and people who work in Congress are the main audience on Twitter. And this nuanced and niche community on Twitter is where producers, bookers, and those with the power to extend a lawmaker's reach beyond the congressional Twitter ecosystem are looking for information and leads. Whereas senators were increasingly taking to Twitter to air their grievances—a common tactic of minority partisans in both Congress and the White House—that messaging became a signal boost that rocketed them onto evening cable news and spots on CNN.

> You increasingly have lawmakers, I would argue at both sides who care less about legislating and more about like becoming social media stars that that get them on cable news at night.[11]

Ridiculous and bold statements, particularly by Trump and those on the right, ensured new opportunities for those voices on *Fox News* and *Newsmax*, using Twitter to amplify the message and reach new audiences. While Twitter is often thought of a different audience than that of the cable-news watcher, in many ways it became a launching pad for reaching those other voters indirectly and less costly than paid media on the campaign side. During the Trump era, one former communications staffer described how people would often be outraged by the things the former president said, but more often than not, those same people could not distinguish between what the president actually said on Twitter versus what was said on cable news. The two platforms became intertwined during the time of Trump, and many senators capitalized on that relationship between new and traditional media opportunities.

[10] Interview. 2/28/22. Former Republican communications staffer.
[11] Interview. 1/6/22. Republican communications staffer.

There were a lot of times where, and trust me over the years, I learned which things Trump did on Twitter on which one television, and I would like often have to correct them and say, "that actually wasn't a Twitter thing. You know, that didn't he didn't post that to Twitter."[12]

Missouri Senator Josh Hawley offers one notable example of the pipeline connecting senators' digital rhetoric to cable news. On December 30, 2020, just a week before the presidential election certification, the senator announced that he would object to the certification of the presidential election results, claiming election interference and the failure of states to follow election laws. While he issued a traditional press release, that release came packaged on Twitter, using the digital platform for a sort of public relations trifecta — using a traditional press release as the content for a tweet that was then reported as news by cable outlets like *Fox News*. Hawley is one of numerous senators who uses his tweets to build media momentum, propelling them onto the headlines of evening programs and news websites. That same day, Senator Hawley appeared on *Fox News* program "The Story" to talk about his plan to object to states' presidential electors and the "blowback" that he got from Democratic colleagues in the Senate. He noted that while he didn't have any concerns about the election administration in his state, his voters felt disenfranchised by the process in states like Georgia and Pennsylvania.

The social media to cable pattern has become a viable strategy beyond conservative media audiences as progressive Connecticut Senator Chris Murphy has also used his authenticity on Twitter to garner new audiences on other platforms. In the wake of the horrific school shooing in Uvalde, Texas, Senator Murphy was one of the most vocal lawmakers on social media, responding to the heinous attack and insisting that the Senate act to prevent deaths with meaningful legislation. Given that visible and quick response on social media, it was no surprise that he was a headlining spots on *MSNBC*, reiterating many of the same points and arguments that he had been making on Twitter and Instagram in the days before. And the pipeline came full circle as the lawmaker from Connecticut used his appearance on the Sunday show as content for his social media followers, creating his own buzz in ways that senators were not able to do even ten years ago.

Congress communicates as if responding to a crisis where information is constantly changing and people are always looking for new information.

[12] Interview. 2/16/22. Democratic communications staffer.

Stakeholders and staff are using digital to track that information flow, trying to preempt unforeseen problems. The emphasis on digital and rapid response comes with organizational trade-offs in a resource-strained organization like Congress where dollars for digital mean savings elsewhere. As one staffer described, communications rather than legislation have become central to many lawmakers' agendas, and those communication priorities extend from Twitter, to cable news, and back to the self-promotion that members and their staff choose to use:

> For like a rank-and-file member, the fact that we have a growing number on both sides of the aisle who are not really here to legislate, would indicate that there will be an increasing increased importance placed on the ability to message by social media, in addition to the cable news.[13]

Perpetuating Conflict

Twitter has become the most salient and accessible venue for senators to target political opponents and champion party successes, and during the Trump presidency that upward trend continued. Senators' reputation-building on Twitter is complex and dynamic—spanning policy, constituent concerns, crisis response, and holiday greetings—but politics is arguably one of the most visible aspects of that digital branding. Beginning in 2013, every senator has maintained an active Twitter account to use as part of their official messaging in office—long before President Donald Trump expanded the political possibilities of Twitter. The Senate was already undergoing a transition where digital politicking became a vehicle for broadening the scope of political rhetoric, where "DEMOCRATS FAILING" made for good entertainment and further the back-and-forth between partisans. Twitter is an ideal platform for senators to blame political opponents and send party-specific signals—drawing a wide audience that is low cost in terms of human and fiscal resources.

The fiery rhetoric on Twitter began to smolder before Trump, but the slope of its upwards trajectory is linked to President Trump's antagonizing Twitter presences. Senate Twitter data from 2013 to 2017 suggests institutional

---

[13] Interview. 2/28/22. Former Republican congressional staffer.

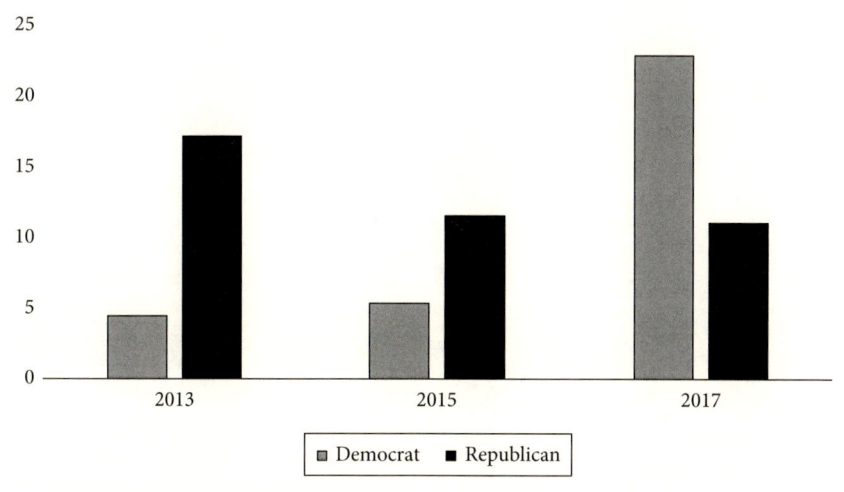

Figure 10.3 Senators' Partisan Rhetoric as a Percent of Total Tweets, January 1–June 30, 2013, 2015, and 2017
Source: Russell (2018).

partisan dynamics were influencing members' social media communications before Trump ever announced his presidential candidacy. Tweets with partisan rhetoric are defined as those that include explicit mentions of either party, such as, "@ GOPHELP . . . bill to overturn Obamacare," or leaders of the party, that is, "Democratic Leadership escorting President." Democrats and Republicans alike have used the president and his party as a lightning rod for the angry digital appeals they use to motivate voters and constituents. During the Obama presidency, Republican senators used Twitter to call out Democratic opposition and bolster the Republican brand, but upon President Trump's election, Democratic senators ratcheted up the political rhetoric (see Figure 10.3). Looking specifically at those negative tweets calling out partisan opposition, Democrats and Republicans flip-flopped in 2017 as Democratic senators took partisan attacks on Twitter to new heights in their loyal opposition to the Trump presidency (see Figure 10.4). Negative digital rhetoric is like "ugly politics" or "party warrior" behavior that criticizes the other party or its representatives (Sinclair 2016; Theriault 2013; Russell 2021). Senators from the president's party—reinforcing the relationship between senators' rhetoric and the presidency—are less likely to use party labels to go negative and that relationship holds even when controlling for their position within the chamber (Russell 2021).

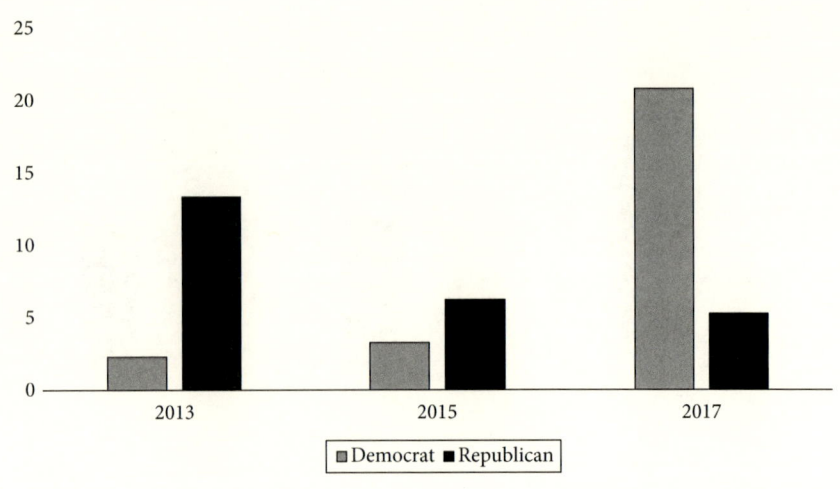

Figure 10.4 Senators' Negative Partisan Tweets as a Percent of Total Tweets, January 1–June 30, 2013, 2015, and 2017
Source: Russell (2018).

We typically think of senators' campaign communications are the primary vehicle for partisan messaging, but even outside of the election context, Twitter emboldens politicians to become advocates of their political brand. Senators have to manage that brand with the limited resources they have, and they use digital tools to signal how they think about public policy, constituent service, and politics. Research shows politics is rarely the primary priority senators convey on Twitter, but how and when senators do choose to engage in party politics is influenced by presidential politics—even beyond the specific individual. The ability to use Twitter with relatively minimal control by the party or media gatekeepers has elevated what began as a tool simply for minority interests to gain traction and turned into a central feature of the information shared in the Senate. Senators' choices about how and when to make partisan appeals to a digital constituency shape both representation and the information supply. Digital shifts and new technology have changed business in Congress incentivizing rapid responses, limiting time for detail-oriented policies, and making it hard to resolve many of the capacity questions that go unanswered (Tromble 2018). Lawmakers' are making an important connection to journalists, special interests, and copartisans on social media, and that relationship is not because of Trump, but rather it was buoyed and accelerated by the social media practices of the former Republican president. Senators multiple, competing priorities lead to strategic behavior that integrates partisan with the rhetorical agendas that lawmakers use to motivate an audience and make them repeat customers on cable news.

The Legacy of Trump Tweets

The impact of Trump's communication style and where he pushed the boundaries of what is acceptable is felt far beyond the Senate, the House, or even the insurrection at the Capitol on January 6, 2021. President Trump capitalized on a ripe political environment and changing communications climate and accelerated what was already an increasingly digital, high-velocity, high-volume information exchange laced with political attacks and misinformation. The president spurred a change in the Senate about what it meant to seek power and how that power could be sought and maintained by carving out space in the digital political climate. In an environment where people are moving at a rapid-response pace with few norms for digital engagement, the boundaries of what is acceptable and how to engage one another are less defined. Trump and the senators took advantage.

Trump fueled a race to be radical online that began during the Obama presidency where early Twitter adopters laid the groundwork for how lawmakers could take advantage of new technology. During the Obama presidency, Republican leaders regularly used Twitter to provide vocal opposition to Democratic policy in Congress and the White House. Republican leader Mitch McConnell made clear that his objective was to thwart the Democratic president's policy proposals and potential successes, and many of the Republican senators were able to do on Twitter daily by shaping the narrative for congressional reporters and political advocates. Twitter was gaining traction as the most visible and accessible tool for slowly chipping away at issues, reframing debates, and engaging in political agenda setting to message on issues and narratives that advantage political allies:

> I mean, before you get your facts out, Twitter's already been retweeted 1000 times. And even if you issue a correction, it's too late.[14]

---

[14] Interview. 1/13/22. Former Republican communication staffer.

When we think about the impact that President Trump and his digital partisan messaging had on the Senate, one need not look any further than Texas Republican John Cornyn. Compared to the junior senator from Texas, Ted Cruz, Senator Cornyn is considered more policy-minded and more willing to work across the aisle. He holds a leadership responsibility and with that comes greater scrutiny and institutional responsibility. In 2013, those differences where on full display when Cornyn balked at Cruz's notion of using a potential government shutdown as leverage to defund Obamacare and, in 2022, when Cornyn worked across the aisle to negotiate a deal on firearm legislation in the wake of the Uvalde Elementary School shooting in Texas.

But when it comes to digital messaging, Cornyn is no shrinking violet, and he operates in a Senate where digital norms incentivize bold and bombastic language more akin to his Texas counterpart. He is traditionally, and expectedly given his role as the party whip, one of the most vocal partisan warriors in terms of the politicization of his messaging and the negative politics he uses to describe partisan opposition (Russell 2021). In 2013, he regularly called out President Obama for perceived failures relating to healthcare. In 2015, he would regularly tweet about the "missing" emails of former Secretary of State and later presidential candidate Hillary Clinton. Twitter gave senators a bully pulpit years before Trump, and Cornyn took advantage. Journalists, politico, and policymakers chalked up Cornyn's behavior to expected partisan messaging from minority opposition to the White House.

But by summer of 2022, the expectations around digital had increased, Trump fueled tension between partisans, and the not-so-real world of Twitter carried even greater consequences for political realities in and outside of Congress. In the wake of the *Roe v. Wade* overturn, Senator Cornyn took an opportunity to take a shot at a familiar foe on Twitter—but doing so in a digital space where people had come to expect toxic partisanship and misinformation. The senator once again used to Twitter to respond to a statement by former President Obama, who was criticizing the Supreme Court's reversal of 50 years of reproductive rights precedent. Cornyn critiqued the former president's statement—as he had done many times before—implying that legislation for racial equality was an example of judicial activism equal to that of the original decision in Roe. Cornyn wasn't talking about "DEMOCRATIC FAILURES" but he linked the words from the first black president to judicial activism through that of high-profile court cases on race. Cornyn wasn't doing anything he hadn't done before, but the Trump presidency had changed just how low we expected lawmakers to go when firing off political attacks. The expectation was not-so-subtle racism because that is what we have come to expect as a normal facet of the digital exchange in Congress.

Regardless of the senator or his digital director's intent, as the senator has brought up the case of *Plessy* on Twitter before, the power of congressional Twitter is that nuance, background, and explanation are never realized. The senator alarmed many people assuming his tweet meant he was in favor of reconsidering segregation legislation, even while congressional insiders and hill journalists dismissed it as irrelevant and a continuation of Cornyn's known frustration with the 1800s decision.

The definition of what was acceptable or "fair game" for politicians on Twitter changed during the Trump presidency as the answer to "is this a suitable response?" was increasingly, "yes." The Senate shifted toward less caution, context and restraint and into a social media frenzy where lawmakers remain less concerned with intentions and implications. It's not that Cornyn himself had crossed a line, though some would argue he was certainly walking a bit close to the sun, but speaks to the fleeting standard of acceptability, truth, or decorum in digital rhetoric. President Trump used his tweets as an on-ramp to cable news, stoking political divisions through digital communication that began in the Senate at least three years before Trump was elected. Senators' within-party variation was already in decline (Rohde and Aldrich 2010; Theriault 2008; McCarty et al. 2006; Cox and McCubbins 2007), and those interparty differences continued to grow at a rapid pace during the Trump era, pushing the chamber in a familiar direction yet arguably past the point of no return.

The era of clickbait-driven content coming out of the Senate coincides with the rise of what was once termed "New Media" because headlines caught attention but nobody was waiting to see how the story played out. The pace of news increased during the Trump era, and the demand for more information fueled both journalists' demand for content and lawmakers' need to supply information that kept up with the digital news cycle. As one former staffer described the transition to digital media, "It became very evident as time went on that, even when things died after 48 hours, there was another crisis."[15] But the Senate's sustained communication crisis, fully emerging during the Trump presidency, is the Twitter-driven information exchange

---

[15] Interview 107. 3/18/2022. Former Democratic Communication Staffer.

and perverse incentives that reward clicks and re-tweets without any deference for the institution or policymaking.

References

Cox, Gary W., and Mathew D. McCubbins. 2007. *Legislative Leviathan: Party Government in the House*. Cambridge: Cambridge University Press.

Lee, Frances E. 2009. *Beyond Ideology: Politics, Principles, and Partisanship in the U.S. Senate*. Chicago: University of Chicago Press.

McCarty, Nolan, Keith T. Poole, and Howard Rosenthal. 2006. *Polarized America: The Dance of Ideology and Unequal Rights*. Cambridge, MA: MIT Press.

McGee, Zac A., and Sean M. Theriault. 2022. "Partisanship in Congressional Travels abroad". *International Politics* 59: 925–954.

Rohde, David W. 1991. *Parties and Leaders in the Postreform House*. Chicago: University of Chicago.

Russell, Annelise. 2018. "US Senators on Twitter: Asymmetric Party Rhetoric in 140 Characters." *American Politics Research* 46(4): 695–723.

Russell, Annelise. 2021. *Tweeting Is Leading: How Senators Communicate and Represent in the Age of Twitter*. Oxford: Oxford University Press.

Scacco, Joshua M., and Kevin Coe. 2021. *The Ubiquitous Presidency: Presidential Communication and Digital Democracy in Tumultuous Times*. Oxford: Oxford University Press.

Sinclair, Barbara. 2016. *Unorthodox lawmaking: New Legislative Processes in the US Congress*. CQ Press.

Theriault, Sean M. 2008. *Party Polarization in Congress*. New York: Cambridge University Press.

Theriault, Sean M. 2013. *The Gingrich Senators: The Roots of Partisan Warfare in Congress*. Oxford: Oxford University Press.

Tromble, Rebekah. 2018. "Thanks for (Actually) Responding! How Citizen Demand Shapes Politicians' Interactive Practices on Twitter." *New Media & Society* 20(2): 676–697.

Tulis, Jeffrey K. 2017. *The Rhetorical Presidency*. Princeton, NJ: Princeton University Press.

11

The Crisis of Senate Legitimacy

Lee Drutman

Introduction

What is the purpose of the United States Senate? One possible response is that the Senate serves no useful purpose anymore in the twenty-first century. "Abolish the Senate" wrote longtime congressman John Dingell in December 2018, after Democrats had taken back the House but not the Senate in the 2018 midterms.[1] Complaining of inevitable Senate obstruction, Dingell wrote: "With my own eyes, I've watched in horror and increasing anger as that imbalance in power has become the primary cause of our national legislative paralysis."

Dingell is not alone. "Abolish the Senate" has become a reliable premise in the Trump-era (and now Biden-era) for left-leaning essayists and columnists. Here's another: "Today's upper chamber has completed its transformation into a smaller version of its more populist sibling, the House—except this one does not come close to reflecting the actual population, or for that matter, the actual population's actual interests."[2] And another: "Thanks to the U.S. Senate, the government still overrepresents the racist and populist parts of the country. It also now overrepresents the rural areas or underpopulated interior regions that are the biggest losers in the global economy—and by no coincidence, it has made easier the rise of Trump."[3] And another: "There's only one conclusion here. Before the Senate kills democracy, we must kill the Senate. That's right. Kill the Senate. It shouldn't exist. Or maybe it can

---

[1] John D. Dingell, "I Served in Congress Longer Than Anyone. Here's How to Fix It," *The Atlantic*, December 4, 2018, https://www.theatlantic.com/ideas/archive/2018/12/john-dingell-how-restore-faith-government/577222/.

[2] Jay Willis, "The Case for Abolishing the Senate," *GQ*, October 16, 2018, https://www.gq.com/story/the-case-for-abolishing-the-senate.

[3] Thomas Geoghegan, "Abolish the Senate: Only the House Is the House of Our Dreams," *The Baffler* 53 (2020): 24–35.

Lee Drutman, *The Crisis of Senate Legitimacy* In: *Disruption?* Edited by: Sean M. Theriault,
Oxford University Press. © Oxford University Press 2024. DOI: 10.1093/oso/9780197767832.003.0012

exist, but only as a toothless and meaningless body, like the British House of Lords."[4]

In a more academic vein, the failures of the Senate to resolve pressing public problems have been well documented by political scientists, who have emphasized partisan procedural warfare as a key driver of dysfunction (Binder 2004, 2015; Smith 2014). As Daniel Wirls (2021) argues in *The Senate: From White Supremacy to Government Gridlock* (a title with knives out), "The contemporary Senate is neither here nor there. It is neither as the framers intended it to be, nor does it meet the requirements of contemporary American government, whether one conceives of it as a republic or a democracy . . . Together, equal representation and supermajority cloture, compounded by the continuing body doctrine, add up to constitutional incoherence."

Because the Senate now has a clear pro-Republican bias, the perceptions of Senate illegitimacy are largely on the political left. The political right, for its part, sees the Senate under attack. "Between the drive to eliminate the legislative filibuster and the campaign to add new states for partisan advantage, the U.S. Senate hasn't been under this much political pressure since the passage of the 17th Amendment (on the direct election of Senators) in 1913," begins the *Wall Street Journal* editorial of April 11, 2021, written on the occasion of House Democrats advancing legislation to make Washington, DC, the 51st state.[5] In the telling of the *Wall Street Journal* editorial board, "The enduring influence and legitimacy of America's legislative upper house has long distinguished the U.S. from many less stable democracies. But a new majoritarian ideology threatens to upend that achievement."

Indeed, the parallels to the 17th Amendment (a product of the Progressive Era) are appropriate. Many of the current criticisms of bicameralism reflect Progressive-era criticisms of the Senate. For example, Progressive Senator George Norris (1935, 54) of Nebraska argued that the Senate made it easier for "special interests, corporations, and monopolies" to "prevent legislation." Norris is the reason Nebraska has a unicameral, nonpartisan legislature.

Similarly, progressive political scientist Lester B. Orfield (1935, 26) complained that "[T]he present system results in too much check and

---

[4] Michael Tomasky, "Yes, Take This Seriously: It's Time to Kill the Senate," *The New Republic*, June 7, 2021, https://newrepublic.com/article/162659/save-democracy-kill-the-senate.

[5] The Editorial Board, "Targeting the U.S. Senate," *Wall Street Journal*, April 11, 2011, sec. Opinion, https://www.wsj.com/articles/targeting-the-u-s-senate-11618175659.

balance. For every poor measure that may be defeated under the bicameral system, it is likely that two or more good measures fail."

The legitimacy crisis of appointed senators in the early twentieth century had many threatening to invoke Article V and call a new constitutional convention. That crisis, of course, was averted by the passage of the 17th Amendment, and the direct election of senators. The crisis of the Senate is different today because it is much more clearly partisan.

To assess the legitimacy crisis of the Senate, this chapter proceeds as follows. First, I document the recent trends in US political development that have fueled this potential legitimacy crisis, and assess their prospects. Then I consider the broader rationale for bicameralism, and assess the US Senate in light of this rationale. Finally, I assess some possibilities for reform, and under what circumstances such reform could actually succeed. Though the challenges to Senate legitimacy have been building for a while, they hit a new pitch in the Trump years and continue to resonate beyond.

The Small-State Bias

The most obvious and common Senate critique is that it over-represents voters in low-population states as compared to voters in high-population states. The commonly voiced complaint is that voters in Wyoming (population 581,813) have 67 times the voting power of voters in California (population 38,959,247). This is obviously disproportionate. It is true that a few US states are disproportionately large, and more US states are disproportionately small, compared to the median state. This feature has been constant for many, many years, and the rough levels of disproportionality have been consistent since the late nineteenth century, when many low-population states joined the Union in a Republican rush to bolster their legislative power (Stewart and Weingast 1992).

The relative distribution of the US population between small and large states has been roughly consistent for 120 years (see Figure 11.1). The Gini coefficient of US state populations, and though individual state populations have changed over time, the relative inequalities of population across the entire nation have remained remarkably consistent, particularly since 1960. That is, the relative voting power of small states versus large states has not changed much over time.

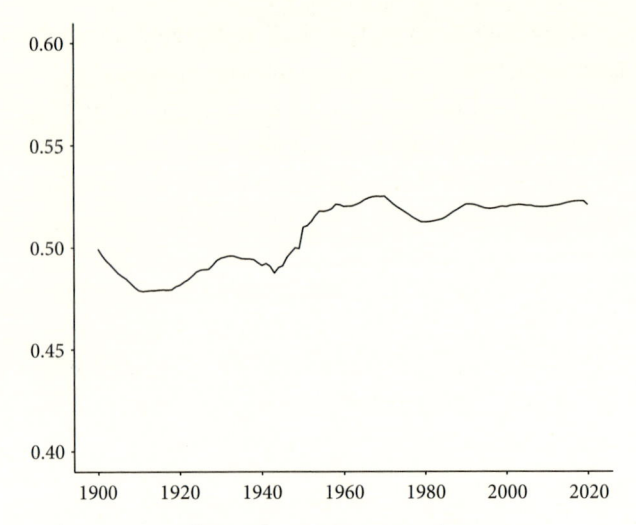

Figure 11.1 The Gini Coefficient for US State Populations

We have well-documented consequences of this small-state bias. Low-population states bring home more federal money per capita than high-population states (Lee and Oppenheimer 1999), and industries concentrated in smaller states tend to get more federal support than industries concentrated in more populous states (Schiller 1999). Because these developments are not new, they are not compelling explanations for the growing attacks on the Senate.

The Republican Bias

What *has changed* is the relationship between state population and state partisanship. Or more specifically, sparsely populated states have become more pro-Republican. From 1900 through about 1948, state population was uncorrelated with Republican presidential vote share. But starting in 1952, the correlation between state population and Republican vote share began to emerge. Though the correlation is still only about −0.25 (or more specifically, −0.28 in 2016, and −0.24 in 2020), the trend is toward increasing correlation. Thus, small states are now different from larger states in a way that is extremely consequential for contemporary US politics: they are more Republican (see Figure 11.2).

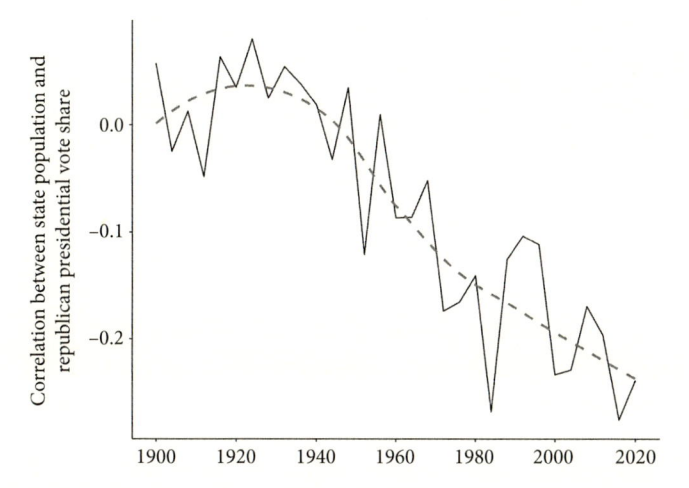

Figure 11.2 Less Populous States are Becoming More Pro-Republican

This shift is a consequence of long-term trends reflecting the realignment of the two major parties along urban-rural divides. For many decades, the Democrats had a sizable conservative wing, allowing them to be much more competitive in less-populous states, which have a tendency to be more rural. But as the parties have realigned along geographical divides over the last several decades, the small-state, conservative bias of the Senate has become a decidedly Republican bias. More populous states tend to be much more urban than less populous states, and liberals disproportionately tend to reside in and around cities (Griffin 2006).[6] This ideological tilt of the Senate has been a consistent feature of American politics for a century, since states with less voting weight became systematically more urban beginning with the 1920 census.[7]

But as the ideological tilt also became a partisan tilt, Republicans came out on top. A more direct way to measure the Republican Senate advantage is to calculate the share of the US population represented by Republican senators as compared to the share of the US population represented by Democratic senators.[8] Though Republicans more frequently controlled a majority of seats

[6] Griffin (2006) concludes that "the residents of states with less-than-average voting weight also tend to be more liberal and to identify with and vote for the candidates of the Democratic Party."

[7] Griffin notes that "states with less voting weight became systematically more urban in 1920. The 1920 census was the first in which the country's urban population outnumbered its rural population."

[8] For split delegations, half of the state's population is considered to be represented by a Republican, half by a Democrat.

in the Senate since 1980, Republican senators have only once represented a very slim majority of the US population (in 1997–1998), when Republican senators represented 50.2 percent of the US population (and 55 seats in the Senate). Prior to that, the last time Republican senators represented a majority of the US population was 1957–1958 (52.5 percent). In the 1950s, the Senate had a slight bias toward Democrats (see Figure 11.3).

Though the Senate has had a pro-Republican bias for many decades, the problem was not as pronounced when the Republican and Democratic parties had some meaningful overlap in their coalitions. Cross-party cooperation was common; Democrats frequently held the majority despite the bias, and few complained. But as cross-partisan compromise and ideological overlap has vanished from Congress, Republicans' small-state advantage has become much more consequential because partisan control of the chamber has become so much more consequential.

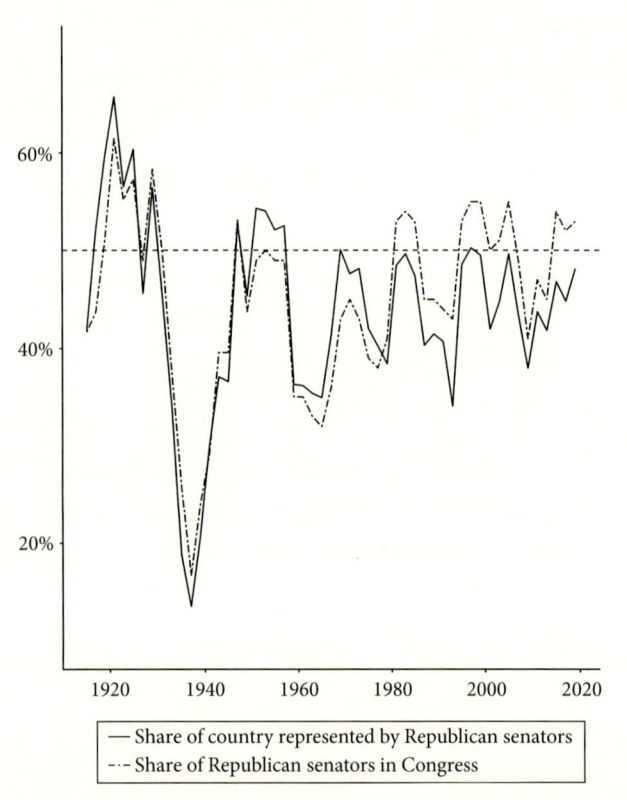

Figure 11.3 Proportion of States and Population Represented by Republican Senators

Will this imbalance continue? The future is always a foreign country, but demographers can certainly make predictions. This takes us to a second aspect of the Senate's legitimacy crisis—race, and in particular, the overrepresentation of the most White states.

The White Bias

The history of the Senate, and especially the use of the filibuster, is also the history of race in America (Jentleson 2021). As Daniel Wirls (2021) has compellingly argued, "The Senate has been uniquely related to the history of race in America, from the depravity of slavery, through the protracted era of racial subjugation, to the post-civil rights decades of inequality and underrepresentation."

Today, in a country that is rapidly diversifying, the Senate remains much whiter than America at large. The underrepresentation of voters of color in the Senate has been well-documented (Malhorta and Raso 2007; Lee and Oppenheimer 1999; Griffin 2006; Baker and Dinkin 1997). As *New York Times* columnist David Leonhardt wrote in a 2018 piece with the provocative title, "The Senate's White-State Bonus." As the column explained, "Because the Senate gives special treatment to the residents of small states—in the form of extra political power—and because small states are overwhelmingly White, the Senate also effectively gives special treatment to White Americans. Yes, it's partly historical accident. But the consequences are huge. The structure of our federal government awards more political representation to one race than to other races."[9]

During a period in which racial issues have become central to American partisan politics, this systematic underrepresentation of voters of color creates yet another legitimacy challenge for the Senate. Over the last two decades, as America has become increasingly racially diverse, much of that diversification has happened in more populous states. Less populous states have always been more White than more populous states, but that trend has accelerated over the last two decades. Thus, the Senate not only overrepresents

---

[9] David Leonhardt, "The Senate: Affirmative Action for White People," *The New York Times*, October 14, 2018, sec. Opinion, https://www.nytimes.com/2018/10/14/opinion/dc-puerto-rico-statehood-senate.html.

Republican voters over Democratic voters; it also overrepresents White voters over voters of color (see Figure 11.4).

Demographers expect that as America becomes more diverse over the next several decades, more populous states will diversify faster (Griffin, Frey, and Teixeira 2020). These trends will exacerbate the White-state bias of the Senate over time, thus adding another dimension to the potential legitimacy crisis of the Senate as unrepresentative of the United States population as a whole.

Trump exacerbates these consequential trends because he expanded Republican support among less well-educated white voters and rural voters. Republicans managed to pick up two seats in the 2018 Senate midterms, even though Democrats won the House by making gains in professional suburbs. Because Trump's rise further elevated divides over race and culture to the center of US politics, the White-state Senate bias is not only more severe, but also more consequential.

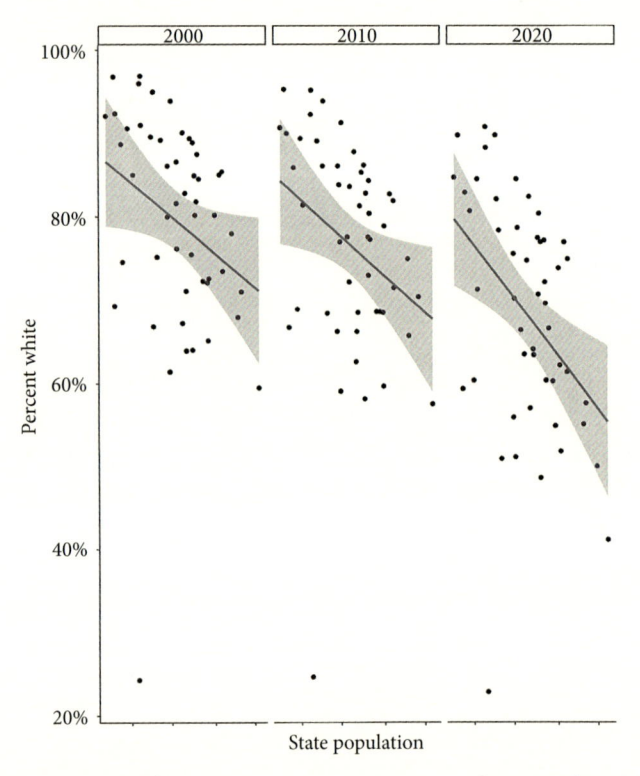

Figure 11.4 More Populous States are More Diverse and Diversifying Faster

Both the pro-Republican bias and the pro-White bias of the Senate are central to the legitimacy challenge of the Senate. But the Senate has its defenders, despite this bias (or perhaps, because of this bias). Let us now turn to the case for the Senate and assess it on its merits.

Why Bicameralism?

While the political left attacks the Senate, the political right typically defends it. As the left argues against the Senate on the grounds of democratic equality, so the right defends the Senate on small-r republican grounds as an institution of restraint and compromise.

Every advanced student of American government knows the apocryphal story in which Virginians George Washington and Thomas Jefferson were discussing the purpose of the Senate while drinking coffee (or perhaps tea). "Why did you pour that coffee into your saucer," Washington asked Jefferson. "To cool it, of course," replied Jefferson. "Even so," Washington said, "We pour legislation into the senatorial saucer to cool it." Apocryphal or not, it does capture one widespread rationale for bicameralism (particularly at the time).

Essentially, the generalized case for bicameralism suggests two main benefits: A "sober second thought" (that the Senate can offer a strategic pause on the sometimes over-heated passing passions of the lower House) and a "second opinion" (that the Senate not only offers a pause, but also a different way of looking at things which comes from its ability to provide a new and different perspective). The more specific case for the US Senate also argues that offers unique benefits in protecting and preserving federalism. Let us now evaluate these claims.

The "Sober Second Thought"—Senate as Moderating Overresponsiveness

How responsive should government be? One compelling argument for a cooling-saucer Senate is that it acts as a kind of dampening mechanism on the ups and downs of public opinion. Majorities are not stable and depend on which issues are salient at a given moment. A certain amount of institutional friction is thus necessary as a guard against arbitrariness. Change should be slow and gradual, or else it cannot be stable and legitimate.[10] While "responsiveness" is a common metric for evaluating government performance in both public discourse and empirical political science, "Political theorists do not, and never have, regarded responsiveness as the central measure of democratic quality. When they have imagined a perfectly responsive regime, they have judged that this would be a bad thing" (Sabl 2015).

Of course, just as *too much* responsiveness to small shifts in electoral tallies can be destabilizing, so *too little* responsiveness to mounting public pressure can also be destabilizing. If legislative institutions are unable to broker solutions and compromises to mounting public problems, growing levels of public frustration can also grow destabilizing. Finding the proper amount disagreement between the two chambers invites a paradox attributed to the Abbé de Sieyes: "If a second chamber dissents from the first, it is mischievous; if it agrees it is superfluous." Herman Finer suggested one answer: "If the two assemblies agree so much the better for our belief in the wisdom and justice of the law; if they disagree, it is time for the people to reconsider their attitude."[11]

The differences between the two chambers have varied over time. In eras in which American politics has been more consensual and defined by moderating, centripetal forces, the differences have not been significant enough to draw ire. But in eras in which American politics is more polarized and narrowly contested, compromise becomes much harder. Narrow majorities also increase the likelihood of gridlock, given that the close contest for power tends to make compromise difficult as party leaders are eager to draw differences they can use in the upcoming elections (Lee 2016; Koger and Lebo 2017). And the combination of the two factors—high polarization and narrow majorities—is especially likely to lead to gridlock.[12]

Unified partisan control has been rare in the modern era (only about 25 percent of the time since 1968), contributing to gridlock. Additionally,

---

[10] Riker (1992, 115) writes: "This instability in policy seems clearly a function of a pure majoritarian system, unsecured against majority tyranny and liable always to the adoption of out-of-equilibrium policies. So I conclude that practically as well as theoretically there is an advantage to stable ground rules for society. And this stability comes in good part from the assurance bicameralism gives that parliamentary majorities are social majorities that cannot be upset."

[11] As quoted in Shell (2001).

[12] Jones (2022, 18) argues: "Higher party polarization increases gridlock, but that the magnitude of this increase diminishes to the extent that a party is closer to having enough seats to thwart filibusters and vetoes. Therefore, unified government is just as prone to gridlock as divided government when parties are highly polarized and neither party has a large majority. On the other hand, divided government is just as productive as unified government when party polarization is low or when one party has a veto-proof, filibuster-proof majority."

split chambers, which contribute even more to gridlock, have also become more common in the last decade. Though relatively rare historically (there were only six split congresses in the entire twentieth century, three of which were in the 1980s), in the 2010s, three of the five Congresses were split. Split congresses make deadlock even more prevalent (Bianco and Smyth 2020). These splits are especially likely when national elections are close (the last time split chambers were common was in the late nineteenth century, another time of close national elections).

One measure disappearing Senate productivity (offered here in Figure 11.5) is to chart the declining number of bills that come up for a "final passage" vote in the Senate. Starting in the 101st Congress, a reasonably productive Congress, the share has steadily declined from 64 to 24 (in the 117th Congress), with a low of 18 in the 115th Congress (2017–2018). To be sure, the Senate passes more bills than this count, because many bills still pass

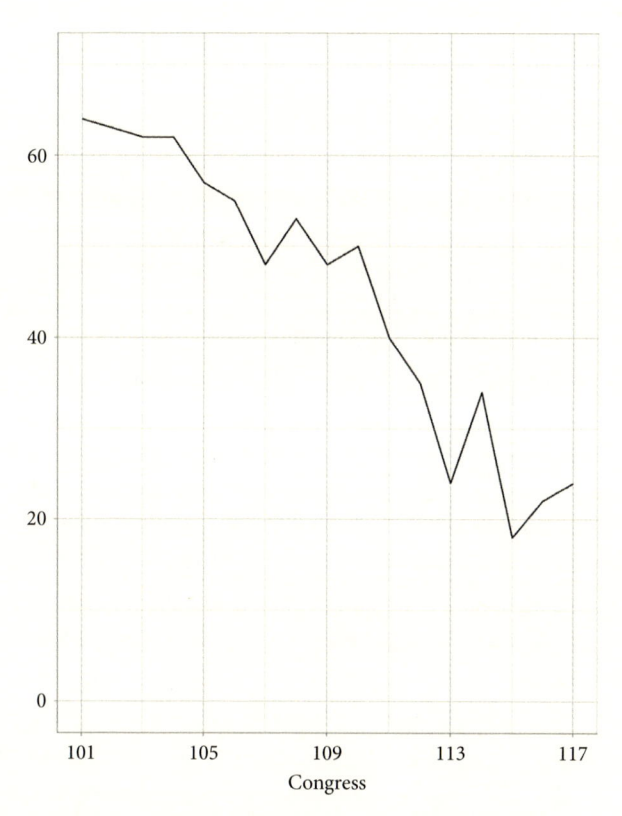

Figure 11.5 The Number of Final Passage Votes in the Senate

by unanimous consent. But the failure of the Senate to vote on more bills that lack unanimous consent reflects the reality that the Senate is simply not dealing all that much. These data document the popular perception that the Senate is indeed a legislative graveyard digging more and more burial plots.

Sarah Binder (2015, 2021) has also documented the increasing failure of Congress to address salient public issues, a failure she blames on gridlock and stalemate and the increased abuse of the filibuster. Steven S. Smith (2022, 585) similarly argues that "the Senate's political environment and senators' political strategies that, in a mutually reinforcing ways, have generated a severe level of obstructionism in Senate legislating in the last two decades." This obstruction "has gravely undermined the institution's responsiveness–far below the level expected by the Framers of the Constitution and warrants serious reform of the way the Senate legislates." Going beyond blaming partisan polarization alone, Smith echoes Binder (and many others) in documenting and critiquing the widespread use of the filibuster. Smith also notes how current Republican senators are very different from their predecessors in respect for the institution, picking up on Sean Theriault's (2013) well-documented argument that a new generation of Republican senators (the "Gingrich Senators") mark a more radical break with tradition. This new, confrontational approach to Senate procedure may be doing more than anything to undermine the legitimacy of the Senate. After all, if the argument for the Senate rests on its ability to foster debate and deliberation (with respect for tradition front and center), the radical populism of the new Republican senators seems to make a mockery of this case.

One possible way that some defend these empirical patterns of obstruction would be to argue that in moments in which American society is polarized and divided (such as the current period), *perhaps* the federal government should do very little. *Perhaps* the Senate should prevent a narrow and quite likely fleeting majority from forcing its preferred policies on the rest of the country. *Perhaps* better to let the individual states make policy in most area. *Perhaps* only if and when there is broad national agreement, only then should Congress legislate.

Perhaps. The consequence of Congress failing to resolve issues over the last two decades is that states have reinforced the national divides by moving in decidedly different policy directions. Over the last several decades, gridlock in Congress has corresponded to increased policy divergence in the states. Put simply, Republican-controlled states are passing extremely conservative policies; Democratic-controlled states are passing extremely liberal policies. These divergences both reflect and reinforce existing national-level polarization. Congressional gridlock, driven largely by a filibuster-happy countermajoritarian Senate, has not fostered compromise. It has just transferred partisan warfare to the states.

If the Senate is supposed to be the deliberative, reasoned institution, then the current moment of hyper-partisan conflict would be *precisely* the moment in which a second chamber could add the most value by offering an entirely different perspective on existing partisan conflicts. Indeed, this is the key selling point of a second chamber—that it offers not only sober reflection, but also a new angle through a process of deliberation.

The Second Opinion

Making public policy is hard, and almost all collective decisions benefit from a diversity of perspectives (Page 2008). In an earlier stage of democratic development, when bicameralism was the norm, the second perspective that a second chamber could offer was that of the most esteemed and learned elites—those worthy of ascending to the heights of the Senate to offer their good counsel to the nation.

Though highly elitist, one could certainly make a case for a second chamber selected solely based on their demonstrated sagacity and wisdom, a kind of council of elders. Certainly, senators have long cultivated this beau ideal of themselves. This more general case for a second opinion, as with the case for some friction and pause in lawmaking, has some solid foundations in normative democratic theory. But again, it sets up a standard on which to evaluate the Senate. Does the Senate offer a genuinely different perspective than the House? If so, what is that perspective?

Until recently, the Senate was at least a more free-wheeling institution, in which entrepreneurial senators had more opportunities to shake things up and perhaps force new solutions. But as Sarah Binder (2021, 671) has recently written, "Today, there are fewer opportunities for rank-and-file senators from either the majority or minority party to participate on the Senate floor. Senators expect instead that their party leaders will aggressively seek to manage the Senate—negotiating compromises, structuring floor votes to advance the electoral interests of their party and individual members of the majority party . . . Intense partisan team play in the Senate often puts legislative deals out of reach." Of course, these developments have been building for decades, as the parties have sorted more clearly along ideological lines (Theriault 2008). The Trump years thus marked a continuation and a calcification.

Senate Democrats vote very much like House Democrats; Senate Republicans vote very much like House Republicans. This pattern has been true for a while, but perhaps it is even truer today. The simplest way to represent it is to compare the difference in chamber median DW-NOMINATE scores for both Democrats and Republicans since 1900 (see Figure 11.6). Though small differences exist (e.g., senators tend to be slightly more moderate than House members), they are tiny. The analysis here echoes an earlier finding by Michael Cutrone and Nolan McCarty (2009), who concludes that "the chambers have been quite congruent in their preferences."

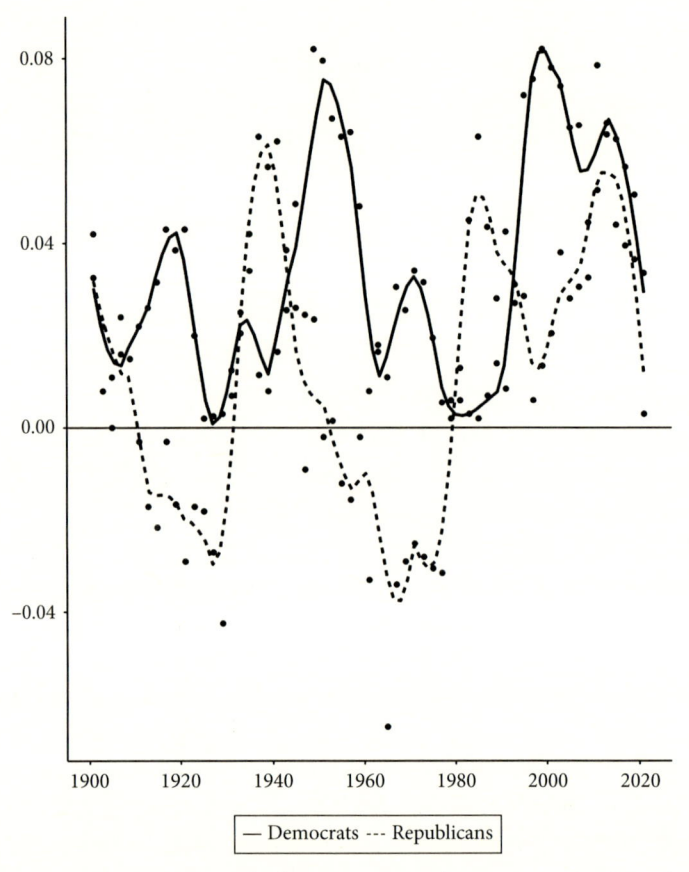

Figure 11.6 Median Senator Ideology Minus Median House Member Ideology

Interestingly, up through 2008, the pattern for Democrats and Republicans appears to move in opposition. When Republican senators become more ideologically extreme, Democratic senators become more ideologically moderate. Presumably particular states flipping back and forth and the changes who comprises the respective party's coalition can explain this trend. Since 2008, though the difference in both parties has begun to fall in tandem, for this first time in the time series. Thus, an already minimal difference between House members and senators is collapsing to zero, which is consistent with the increased partisan polarization of Congress, and the increased leadership-driven approach to voting in both chambers. This further undermines the argument for a second chamber than can provide a fresh take on contemporary public policy problems. If the Senate is just a second House (which has much longer been a top-down, leadership-driven partisan institution), but just with more representation for small states (which tend to be more Republican), it is much harder to see the value of a second chamber other than as an intensifier of partisan gridlock.

Senate as Guarantor of Federalism

A third argument for the American version of a Senate, in which all states get equal representation, is that equal representation as a powerful bulwark in defense of federalism, which in and of itself is a crucial piece of the American republic.[13]

The most common claim on behalf of the Senate as a bulwark of federalism is that states have unique political cultures and circumstances, and that large states would impose their values on small states if they had the chance. This argument actually makes two claims. The first is that states have meaningfully different political cultures. The second is that small states have distinct interests separate from large states.

---

[13] Duncan (2018, 17). argues: "For example, as conservative legal scholar Richard F. Duncan argues, "the Constitution creates the Senate to check national power and to advance federalism by ensuring that each state in the union has an equal voice in one branch of the national government. . . . Each Senator elected to represent Wyoming in the Senate is a resident of Wyoming and was elected by the people of Wyoming. Thus, she is more likely to reflect the regional and cultural values of her electorate—the people of Wyoming—than would be the case if Senators were elected by a national electorate . . . Thus, rather than contradict the fundamental values of the American Constitution, the Senate's embrace of federalism and state equality in one house of Congress reflects and embodies the checks and balances that protect the liberty of we the people of the several states."

Let's start with the first claim, that states have meaningfully different political cultures that must be preserved and that they accordingly take a wide range of approaches across a wide range of policy areas. Yet, when one looks at state level policy, one is struck by how much Republican-controlled states have similar polices everywhere across a wide range of issues, and Democratic-controlled states have similar policies everywhere across a wide range of issues. If the states are still laboratories of democracy, the illusion of 50 laboratories belies the fact that two mega-research institutes are supplying and controlling all the experiments (Grumbach 2022; Kettl 2020). The increasing nationalization of US politics has effectively wiped out regional policy and partisan variety (Hopkins 2018; Hopkins, Schickler, and Azizi 2022).

Putting aside normative debates about the value of federalism (particularly today), an even bigger challenge to the Senate-as-guarantor-of-federalism is the fact that the Senate has never actually performed this function in US political history. If the Senate is actually a guarantor of federalism, we should expect the House to be much more aggressive in preemption policies. In reality, we see no difference by chamber. Nor do we see any meaningful difference by party, other than that Democrats tend to be more for federal floors of citizen protection and Republicans more for ceilings on government regulations.[14] Even in an earlier era when both parties were more ideologically mixed, federalism votes were mostly defined by ideology, and the Senate was no more a guarantor of federalism than the House (Hero 1989).

Never in American political history has a substantive policy issue divided small states from large states. Studies generally conclude that "no major issue has divided small states from large states per se at any point in United States history" (Lee and Oppenheimer 1999; Griffin 2006).[15] Partisanship and ideology of elected representatives have always been much more significant determinants of their votes on all issues, including those related to federalism.

Whatever theoretical claims exist on behalf of the Senate, it is hard to find evidence for them in practice. And though this chapter focuses on the US

---

[14] As SoRelle and Walker (2016) report, "Since the 1960s, both parties appear to have contributed in relatively equal measure to the dramatic increase in federal preemption across an array of policy issues. For example, President Bill Clinton, a Democrat, and President George W. Bush, a Republican, each signed sixty-four preemption statutes into law during their respective eight years in office; indeed, President Bush failed to veto a single preemption bill." See also Zimmerman (2009).

[15] Though, to be sure, large and small states have disagreed consistently over process issues that would change their relative power in the early republic (Zagarri 1986).

Senate specifically, the same could be said more broadly about bicameralism in democracies around the world. Indeed, as Cutrone and McCarty (2009) conclude in a review of the literature "the case for bicameralism seems less than overwhelming. Even in models where bicameralism might have an effect, we find that the necessary conditions for such an effect are empirically rare."

Can the Senate Be Reformed?

Despite theoretical and historical arguments in favor of American bicameralism, the empirical reality is that the Senate no longer offers a distinct second thought or second opinion, if it ever did. Nor is there any evidence that it is a friend of federalism, other than by indirectly leaving many issues to the states from its own failure to resolve them at a national level—a pattern that has worsened (not healed) divisions in the United States. It is enough to make one wonder what purpose a second chamber serves.

In the current global era of "democratic stress," seven European democracies singled out upper chambers for their unrepresentativeness, their unaccountability (many are still unelected), and their extensive veto powers—all of which are considered to be vestigial elitist chambers of an earlier transition to democracy, and thus antidemocratic by modern standards (Vercesi 2022). In the twenty-first century, Belgium, Germany, Ireland, Italy, Romania, Spain, and the United Kingdom have all considered major reforms to their second chamber, either involving reduction of powers, a change in selection method (many upper chambers are still appointed), or outright abolition. Upper-chamber reform, though, is hard. Of these countries, only Belgium (2011) and Germany (2006) succeeded (Vercesi 2022). Senate reform has also been a perennial issue in Canada, which like many countries, has a vestigial appointed Senate that lacks legitimacy.

The German case is particularly intriguing. Germany's upper chamber, the Bundestrat, represents German states (Lander). Under the 1948 German constitution (which Americans helped to draft), the Bundestrat was given more limited powers. At the time, it was expected that only 10 percent of federal laws would require Bundestrat approval. By the late 1990s, the Bundestrat had claimed jurisdiction over much more legislation and had become an obstructionist body as the relationship between state and national authorities grew entangled. Germans increasingly blamed high unemployment, low growth, and growing budget deficits on the bicameral gridlock (Stecker 2016). But because of the complexity of the legislative process, German voters didn't know who to blame or hold accountable. In 2003, Germany set out to form a "Joint Commission on the Modernization of the Federal State." The commission laid out reforms that drew clearer distinctions between federal and state authority, and in exchange, reduced the power of the Bundestrat to only legislation that mandates specific implementation instructions. By most accounts, the reform appears to have been moderately successful — at least in reducing the ability of the Bundestrat to stonewall legislation (Stecker 2015; Zolnhofer 2008).

The Belgian Senate reform also came after an extended period of gridlock, and similar to Germany, the reform reduced the powers of the Senate in exchange for a devolution of authority to the federated entities. The reforms turned the Belgian Senate into "a nonpermanent body," which currently holds a plenary meeting eight times a year. The monocameral procedure, in which the legislative power is vested in the Chamber of Representatives without involvement of the Senate, has become the standard legislative procedure" (Goossens 2017; Goossens and Cannoot 2015).

Could the United States navigate a similar more-federalism-for-less-Senate-power reform? Perhaps the German process could serve as a model. Consider the current impasse. The political left generally views the Senate as illegitimate because of its anti-majoritarian tendencies. The political right generally views the Senate as the last defense against an overreaching national government and as a defender of federalism. But as discussed above, the Senate hasn't actually protected federalism very well. Nor is it likely to do so. Rather, it has protected conservative power, but conservative power has been as likely as liberal power to use the authority of Washington, DC, to undermine state and local authority.

Sketching out the contours of such a deal are obviously beyond this chapter. But the basic arguments for attempting to work out such a compromise might be as follows.

First, the growing legitimacy crisis of the Senate threatens the entire foundations of American government, and the increasingly minoritarian tilt of the Senate—and the gridlock it imposes on the entire system—is likely to persist for the foreseeable future.

Second, because we have almost certainly reached the end of what Don Kettl (2020) calls the "Fourth Generation" of Federalism, now might be an opportune time to reevaluate. Kettle argues that "fierce cross-pressures" and "deep fissures" have emerged as polarizing states have attempted to administer vast federal programs, especially those dealing with healthcare.

Third, given the both the rapid response needed to public problems in certain cases, and the increasing complexity and range of public problems in others, it may make more sense to rethink bicameralism in a way that allows the national legislature to respond more quickly, and also give states more freedom to respond quickly and independently. Certain policy responses may demand fast action, in which one chamber can move quickly. Other policy actions may require slower responses that deal with complexity. By limiting the issues on which the Senate has jurisdiction, Senators could specialize their expertise more narrowly. The Senate already has certain powers that the House lacks, such as oversight of political and judiciary appointments, and foreign treaties, consistent with the expectation that it should be a wiser, more deliberative body.

Fourth, the best moment for a compromise is when two sides have fought to a stalemate over an extended period and neither side sees a clear path to victory and both sides feel they are fighting a defensive war. Carving out certain powers and autonomy for conservative states in exchange for limiting some powers of the Senate might offer a reasonable peace treaty. As a diversifying America continues to split into deep red and deep blue, with increasing gridlock at the national level, the conditions that have produced reform in other federalized democracies such as Germany and Belgium are increasing.

The Trump years added to the pressure on the US political system in distinct ways. The Trump years accelerated both the partisan polarization of US politics, and the pro-White, pro-Republican bias of the Senate. The Trump administration also led many Democrats to rediscover the values of federalism as ways to resist a far-right national government. These trends have further deepened the crisis of representation and governance, putting more pressure on the Senate, but also perhaps opened some possibilities on the left for delegating more powers to the states in exchange for a less powerful Senate.

Does the US Senate Have a Future?

Bicameralism has a long history. Does it have a future in America? Political institutions evolve and change and find new purposes under new circumstances. Bicameralism evolved from the Aristotelean idea of mixed government that balanced democracy, aristocracy, and monarchism. But few today think the aristocracy should have an equal role to the democracy (the people). There is still value in an upper house that can bring a sober "second thought" to certain complex problems and offer a different set of perspectives than a lower house that is more connected to the people. There is also still value in the principles of federalism, localism, and subsidiarity.

Still, absent a complete revolution in the American system of government akin to 1787 Constitution replacing the Articles of Confederation, the United States Senate will not be abolished. Instead, it must be reimagined for the twenty-first century, in a political, social, cultural, and economic time that is far different from any the Framers could have possibly imagined. Indeed, the Senate is under the greatest threat to its legitimacy since 1913, when the demand for direct elections of senators forced the 17th Amendment. How it responds is unclear, but few institutions can persist for long without any reserve of popular support.

Senate dysfunction during the Trump years demonstrates how important it is to reimagine the American political system for the twenty-first century—a political, social, cultural, and economic time that is far different from any the Framers could have possibly imagined. Moments of major political change are moments in which institutions appear deeply dysfunctional and entirely incapable of self-correction. We are likely in such a moment now. While Trump was not the sole cause, the Trump years brought us to the brink. Where we go from here is up to us.

References

Baker, Lynn A., and Samuel H. Dinkin. 1997. "The Senate: An Institution Whose Time Has Gone." *Journal of Law & Politics* 13: 21.

Bianco, William, and Regina Smyth. 2020. "The Bicameral Roots of Congressional Deadlock: Analyzing Divided Government Through the Lens of Majority Rule." *Social Science Quarterly* 101(5): 1712–1727, https://doi.org/10.1111/ssqu.12811.

Binder, Sarah. 2021. "Marching (Senate Style) Towards Majority Rule." *The Forum* 19(4): 663–684, https://doi.org/10.1515/for-2022-2039.

Binder, Sarah. 2015. "The Dysfunctional Congress." *Annual Review of Political Science* 18, no. 1: 85–101.

Binder, Sarah A. 2004. *Stalemate: Causes and Consequences of Legislative Gridlock.* Washington DC: Brookings Institution Press.

Cutrone, Michael, and Nolan McCarty. 2009. *Does Bicameralism Matter?* Donald A. Wittman and Barry R. Weingast, eds. Vol. 1. Oxford: Oxford University Press, https://doi.org/10.1093/oxfordhb/9780199548477.003.0010.

Duncan, Richard F. 2018. "Electoral Votes, the Senate, and Article V: How the Architecture of the Constitution Promotes Federalism and Government by Consensus." *Nebraska Law Review* 96(4): 799–828.

Goossens, Jurgen. 2017. "Electoral Reforms in Belgium's Sixth State Reform: Historic Split of Electoral Constituency BHV, Reform of the Senate, and Coincident Elections." *Election Law Journal: Rules, Politics, and Policy* 16(2): 316–324, https://doi.org/10.1089/elj.2016.0420.

Goossens, Jurgen, and Pieter Cannoot. 2015. "Belgian Federalism after the Sixth State Reform." *Perspectives on Federalism* 7(2): 29–55, https://doi.org/10.1515/pof-2015-0009.

Griffin, John D. 2006. "Senate Apportionment as a Source of Political Inequality," *Legislative Studies Quarterly* 31(3): 405–432, https://doi.org/10.3162/036298006X201869.

Griffin, Robert, William H. Frey, and Ruy Teixeira. 2020. America's Electoral Future. Washington DC: States of Change Project.

Grumbach, Jacob M. 2022. *Laboratories against Democracy*. Princeton, NJ: Princeton University Press.

Hero, Rodney E. 1989. "The US Congress and American Federalism: Are 'Subnational' Governments Protected?" *Western Political Quarterly* 42(1): 93–106.

Hopkins, Daniel J., Eric Schickler, and David L. Azizi. "From Many Divides, One? The Polarization and Nationalization of American State Party Platforms, 1918–2017." *Studies in American Political Development* 36: 1–20.

Hopkins, Daniel J. 2018. *The Increasingly United States: How and Why American Political Behavior Nationalized.* Chicago: University of Chicago Press.

Hopkins, Daniel J., Eric Schickler, and David L. Azizi. 2022. "From Many Divides, One? The Polarization and Nationalization of American State Party Platforms, 1918–2017." *Studies in American Political Development* 36(1): 1–20. https://doi.org/10.1017/S0898588X22000013.

Jentleson, Adam. 2021. *Kill Switch: The Rise of the Modern Senate and the Crippling of American Democracy.* New York: Liveright Publishing Corporation.

Jones, David R. 2022. "Party Polarization and Legislative Gridlock." *Political Research Quarterly* 18(1): 125–141.

Kettl, Donald F. 2020. *The Divided States of America: Why Federalism Doesn't Work.* Princeton, NJ: Princeton University Press.

Koger, Gregory, and Matthew J. Lebo. 2017. *Strategic Party Government: Why Winning Trumps Ideology.* Chicago: University of Chicago Press.

Lee, Frances E. 2016. *Insecure Majorities: Congress and the Perpetual Campaign.* Chicago: University of Chicago Press.

Lee, Frances E., and Bruce I. Oppenheimer. 1999. *Sizing Up the Senate: The Unequal Consequences of Equal Representation.* Chicago: University of Chicago Press.

Malhotra, Neil, and Connor Raso. 2007. "Racial Representation and U.S. Senate Apportionment." *Social Science Quarterly* 88(4): 1038–1048, https://doi.org/10.1111/j.1540-6237.2007.00517.x.

Norris, George W. 1935. "The One-House Legislature." *The ANNALS of the American Academy of Political and Social Science* 181 (1): 50–58.

Orfield, Lester B. 1935. "The Unicameral Legislature in Nebraska." *Michigan Law Review* 34(1): 26, https://doi.org/10.2307/1281882.

Page, Scott E. 2008. *The Difference: How the Power of Diversity Creates Better Groups, Firms, Schools, and Societies*. Princeton, NJ: Princeton University Press.

Riker, William H. 1992. "The Justification of Bicameralism." *International Political Science Review* 13(1): 101–116, https://doi.org/10.1177/019251219201300107.

Sabl, Andrew. 2015. "The Two Cultures of Democratic Theory: Responsiveness, Democratic Quality, and the Empirical-Normative Divide." *Perspectives on Politics* 13(2): 345–365, https://doi.org/10.1017/S1537592715000079.

Schiller, Wendy J. 1999. "Trade Politics in the American Congress: A Study of the Interaction of Political Geography and Interest Group Behavior." *Political Geography* 18(7): 769–789.

Shell, Donald. 2001. "The History of Bicameralism." *The Journal of Legislative Studies* 7(1): 5–18, https://doi.org/10.1080/714003862.

Smith, Steven S. 2014. *The Senate Syndrome: The Evolution of Procedural Warfare in the Modern U.S. Senate*. Norman: University of Oklahoma Press.

Smith, Steven S. 2022. "Senate Republican Radicalism and the Need for Filibuster Reform." *The Forum* 19(4): 585–602, https://doi.org/10.1515/for-2021-2032.

SoRelle, Mallory E., and Alexis N. Walker. 2016. "Partisan Preemption: The Strategic Use of Federal Preemption Legislation." *Publius: The Journal of Federalism* 46(4): 486–509.

Stecker, Christian. 2016. "The Effects of Federalism Reform on the Legislative Process in Germany." *Regional & Federal Studies* 26(5): 603–624, https://doi.org/10.1080/13597 566.2016.1236334.

Stecker, J. Broschek. 2015. "Pathways of Federal Reform: Australia, Canada, Germany, and Switzerland." *Publius: The Journal of Federalism* 45(1): 51–76, https://doi.org/ 10.1093/publius/pju030.

Stewart, Charles, and Barry R. Weingast. 1992. "Stacking the Senate, Changing the Nation: Republican Rotten Boroughs, Statehood Politics, and American Political Development." *Studies in American Political Development* 6(2): 223–271, https://doi. org/10.1017/S0898588X00000985.

Theriault, Sean M. 2008. *Party Polarization in Congress*. Cambridge: Cambridge University Press.

Theriault, Sean M. 2013. *The Gingrich Senators: The Roots of Partisan Warfare in Congress*, 1 ed. Oxford: Oxford University Press.

Vercesi, Michelangelo. 2022. "Democratic Stress and Political Institutions: Drives of Reforms of Bicameralism in Times of Crisis." *Representation* 58(1): 85–102, https://doi. org/10.1080/00344893.2019.1635195.

Wirls, Daniel. 2021. *The Senate: From White Supremacy to Governmental Gridlock*. Charlottesville: University of Virginia Press, http://ebookcentral.proquest.com/lib/ jhu/detail.action?docID=6562289.

Zagarri, Rosemarie. 1986. *The Politics of Size: Representation in the United States, 1776–1850*. Ithaca, NY: Cornell University Press.

Zimmerman, Joseph F. 2009. *Contemporary American Federalism: The Growth of National Power*. New York: SUNY Press.

Zolnhöfer, Reimut. 2008. "An End to the Reform Logjam? The Reform of German Federalism and Economic Policy-Making." *German Politics* 17(4): 457–469, https:// doi.org/10.1080/09644000802490444.

12

The End of the Institutionalist

Christina Bellantoni[*]

Introduction

It was a scenario that surprised Joe Lieberman at the time. A Republican senator was working closely with him on two issues they both cared deeply about. The first was legislation related to climate change and the economy, with lawmakers working behind the scenes at the same time as some negotiated a sweeping immigration plan that would finally provide a pathway to citizenship for millions and include sensible border security measures. But back home, people on the far-right of that senator's party were having a meltdown, and he pulled away from the climate effort.

It was April 2010. Republican Senator Lindsey Graham of South Carolina had been at the table for both the climate measure sponsored by Lieberman and Senator John Kerry and an immigration policy overhaul being negotiated by Republicans and Democrats. Graham abandoned Kerry and Lieberman, despite attending 183 meetings and devoting more than 120 hours of scheduled Senate time to the climate effort, according to a 2010 *New York Times Magazine* profile by Robert Draper.[1]

Lieberman said in a 2022 interview with me that he remembers Graham telling him, "I can't do this anymore. I'm just taking so much crap at home for the work I'm doing on immigration, I simply can't do two big things like this at once." *The New York Times* had reported a few months before the pullout that Graham's cross-party cooperation had "clearly come at a price":[2]

[*] The author acknowledges Owen Foster, Tawfiq Othman, Marcel Lacey, and Marie Chantal Marauta of the USC Annenberg Center for Communication Leadership and Policy provided excellent research.

[1] Robert Draper, "Lindsey Graham, This Year's Maverick," *The New York Times*, July 1, 2010, https://www.nytimes.com/2010/07/04/magazine/04graham-t.html.

[2] Sheryl Gay Stolberg, "The White House's G.O.P. Mainstay? Maybe Not," *The New York Times*, April 27, 2010, https://www.nytimes.com/2010/04/27/us/politics/27graham.html.

Christina Bellantoni, *The End of the Institutionalist* In: *Disruption?* Edited by: Sean M. Theriault,
Oxford University Press. © Oxford University Press 2024. DOI: 10.1093/oso/9780197767832.003.0013

At home, passions are running high. Locals derisively call him 'Graham-nesty' for his work on immigration. He has been censured by three chapters of the South Carolina Republican Party. At a townhall-style meeting in Greenville last fall, constituents angrily shouted him down.

"You and Obama—guilty of treason!" one hollered.

"Why do you think it's necessary to get in bed with people like John Kerry?" demanded another, referring to Mr. Graham's Democratic co-sponsor on the energy bill.

Rush Limbaugh and the talk radio right, echoed by Fox News and the newspaper I worked for at the time, *The Washington Times*, propelled immigration and border security to be something that split the Republican Party. Congressional switchboards would light up around the clock when the immigration issue got hot on the right, with people flooding offices across the Hill with calls demanding Congress fund and build the border wall.

This episode was nearly a decade before Trump would make building the wall a campaign cry. The movement was there, waiting for a political leader. The threat of a serious challenge from the right in a primary also has always been there for Republicans. The late Senator Robert Bennett was the first in the age of the Tea Party, defeated at the Utah Republican Convention in 2010 thanks to activists who were angry he supported the Troubled Assets Relief Program, created and run by the Obama administration to stabilize the country's financial system, restore economic growth, and mitigate foreclosures in the wake of the 2008 financial crisis. Soon Tea Party favorites were ushered into congressional seats, two years later Senator Richard Lugar was defeated for siding with Democrats on major issues, and the angsty far right was earning increasing power and attention at every level of government.

While back in 2010 Lieberman was glad Graham was still working on immigration, the Democrat took note, worrying even then that the right was gaining disproportionate power over Republicans.

Lieberman couldn't have predicted a dozen years ago that the scenario would soon become the norm, only to be exacerbated by Donald Trump's unique and, in his view, dangerous influence over the Republican Party. "Trump . . . remains the leader of the largest single component, certainly the activist component, of the Republican Party," said Lieberman, now serving as senior counsel at law firm Kasowitz Benson Torres after spending 24 years in the US Senate. "And if you take him on, you risk the enmity of that group,"

Lieberman said. "His disruption did stand in the way of the resolution of some big national problems that really need to be resolved."

As Lieberman's story makes clear, the political divisions that make it difficult to solve a crisis certainly did not begin when Trump took the oath of office. What his presidency did was accelerate what had been slowly happening in the Senate. People from both parties who had been willing to work together had increasingly less incentive to do so, even institutionalists who had always revered traditions and decorum over combative politics.

At the same time, the Washington ecosystem and especially the news media did nothing but fan the flames.

Immigration Compromise Seemed Possible, Until It Wasn't

Trump's Lucy-and-the-football behavior over immigration is perhaps the clearest example of how Senate Republicans were jerked around during the 115th and 116th Congresses. Graham and others returned to negotiations in 2017 facing an early 2018 deadline on the DREAM Act allowing people brought to the country as minors to legally remain and work in the United States. The president had said he had "great love" for the so-called dreamers, and at first seemed to be working with the bipartisan group in good faith. But as the talks grew more serious, Trump demanded what Politico dubbed "politically toxic reforms to the diversity lottery and family migration that Democrats could never get behind."[3]

"The administration made it difficult for some [Republicans] to try to publicly support anything," one Republican senator said, according to Politico.[4] Senator James Lankford was in the initial group, which at one point had boasted high-profile lawmakers from both parties and Senator Angus King, an independent who participates in the Democratic Caucus. Lankford ultimately voted against the plan. The Oklahoma Republican told reporters at the time the plan had gone too far to the left. Others who were part of the bipartisan talks questioned if the pullout from Lankford, Thom Tillis of North

---

[3] Burgess Everett and Elana Schor, "Inside the Senate's Ugly Immigration Breakdown," *Politico*, 2018, https://www.politico.com/story/2018/02/16/senate-immigration-daca-dreamers-breakdown-415629.

[4] Everett and Schor, "Inside the Senate's Ugly Immigration Breakdown."

Carolina, Bob Corker of Tennessee, Dean Heller of Nevada and Orrin Hatch of Utah was thanks to Trump's schizophrenia over the proposal.[5]

Inconsistent messaging from the White House directly led to dwindling numbers of Republicans in the room, said one Democrat who was a part of the negotiations. It seemed to them that one week Trump would support efforts to help dreamers and the next he would tweet in ways that signaled the Republicans would be anything but politically protected if they worked with Democrats on the issue. On one day in January 2018, for example, Trump issued scathing tweets about the "so-called bipartisan DACA deal," calling it "a big step backwards." He didn't directly criticize Republicans, but took aim at the Democrats as "shutting down our military," causing a "setback" and "not being interested in life and safety."

The senator who was part of the negotiations said the message was clear to Trump's supporters: He would ensure that Republicans backing this effort and working with Democrats would become losers in every sense of the word. "Republican senators felt they had the rug pulled out from them," said the senator, who requested anonymity to be able to speak candidly about private discussions. "Absolutely a single tweet by Trump on immigration reform could chase Republicans at a negotiating table with Democrats out of the room," agrees Lieberman, who maintained close friendships with Senator John McCain and other Republicans long after leaving the Senate.

As for Graham, who once proclaimed the Tea Party would "die out" because "they can never come up with a coherent vision for governing the country,"[6] he found himself the target of the Trump administration, by tweet and even from Trump's Department of Homeland Security as officials "anonymously bashed him in a phone call with reporters," as the February 2018 vote approached, Politico reported.

DHS issued a statement that Politico labeled as dousing any hope of securing the 60 votes needed to get past an expected filibuster.[7] It said the measure would turn the United States into "a sanctuary nation where ignoring the rule of law is encouraged." And that was that. "The DHS release was like nothing I've ever seen from a government agency. It was more like

[5] Everett and Schor, "Inside the Senate's Ugly Immigration Breakdown."
[6] Draper, "Lindsey Graham, This Year's Maverick."
[7] "Schumer-Rounds-Collins Destroys Ability of DHS to Enforce Immigration Laws, Creating a Mass Amnesty for over 10 Million Illegal Aliens, Including Criminals," U.S. Department of Homeland Security, https://www.dhs.gov/news/2018/02/15/schumer-rounds-collins-destroys-abil ity-dhs-enforce-immigration-laws-creating-mass.

from a political campaign. And it wasn't very accurate. And that's putting it mildly," King told Politico.

Dan Diller, policy director of the Lugar Center, called immigration the issue most amenable to compromise by its structure, especially considering a bipartisan effort in 2013 had passed the Senate with more than 60 votes only to go nowhere in the GOP-controlled House. "That's what makes all the demagogic shenanigans around it so dispiriting," he said.

The bipartisan group that had once numbered more than 20 continued to lose support from Republicans. The legislation (informally dubbed the "common sense" bill) the group ultimately crafted would have provided a pathway to citizenship for the dreamers, but not their parents, and would have provided $25 billion for border security.[8]

In the end, the legislation attracted only eight Republican "Yes" votes.[9] Graham, Lisa Murkowski of Alaska, Susan Collins of Maine, and Mike Rounds of South Dakota were the only supporters of the plan who were still serving in 2022. The others have either retired or were later defeated for reelection. Senator Lamar Alexander, who served 18 years in the Senate and had long lamented the decline in working across the aisle, was among those who retired. When announcing the decision, he told Politico, "I still think it's possible to get a lot done. I just wish it were easier."[10]

In further testament to the schizophrenic nature of the Trump White House on the immigration issue, new reporting suggests that as policy discussions were unfolding on the Hill, the president was continuing to push issues that appealed to the far right such as revoking birthright citizenship that welcomes anyone born on US soil.[11] His Attorney General Bill Barr worked to block him, according to *Peril*, by Bob Woodward and Robert Costa, "He was enabling President Trump, but he was also, on issues like birthright citizenship, trying to pull him away from the more far right

[8] Dyland Scott and Tara Golshan, "The Senate's Failed Votes on DACA and Immigration: What We Know," *Vox*, February 12, 2018, https://www.vox.com/policy-and-politics/2018/2/12/17003552/senate-immigration-bill-floor-debate.

[9] "Roll Call Vote 115th Congress—2nd Session." *U.S. Senate: U.S. Senate Roll Call Votes 115th Congress—2nd Session*, May 26, 2021, https://www.senate.gov/legislative/LIS/roll_call_votes/vote1152/vote_115_2_00035.htm.

[10] Burges Everett, "Lamar Alexander to Exit Polarized Senate: 'I Just Wish It Were Easier,'" *Politico*, https://www.politico.com/story/2018/12/17/sen-lamar-alexander-will-not-run-for-reelection-1067254.

[11] "How America faced 'Peril' in final days of Trump presidency," PBS NewsHour, September 22, 2021, https://www.pbs.org/newshour/show/how-america-faced-peril-in-final-days-of-trump-presidency.

elements of the Republican Party," Costa said on PBS in September 2021 when discussing the book.

The Few in the Middle

The initial concept for this chapter was that the idea of moderate Republicans is a myth—that what once was is no longer. There were Republicans in the middle serving in the Trump-era Senate: McCain, Collins, and Murkowski, along with Jeff Flake of Arizona, Mitt Romney of Utah, Rob Portman of Ohio, and Bob Corker of Tennessee. If this cast of characters sounds familiar, it's probably because their names were elevated by a media that feeds on tension, division, and conflict. They are just that: characters designed for storytelling but not necessarily in accurate fashion.

Those are the names that appeared in the middle again and again from 2017 until 2021, ranked by a variety of legislative votes, how frequently the lawmaker sided with the president and what bills they authored or co-sponsored. The measurement of moderation is inconsistent, though the scorekeepers are plentiful.

I left *The Los Angeles Times* for academia just before the 2018 midterm elections, and my own perception as a news consumer no longer tasked with running political coverage is that most indexes have little meaning when the news media is constantly holding lawmakers up as foils of the villains and heroes they have created as a frame for coverage.

Former *Roll Call* reporter Meredith Shiner wrote for *The New Republic* that Collins has actually been "cast" by the press as a "dutiful moderate" to "create tension in their stories and to avoid facing the reality that the Washington they once knew—a Washington defined by a pragmatic centrism—had completely disintegrated, if it ever existed at all":[12]

> But the truth is that her persona is mostly a myth concocted by a media unable to grasp the new reality of a bitterly divided politics. Congressional reporters have a conforming lexicon that guides their coverage. Perhaps no approach to writing about Congress has been more commonly accepted and less useful than framing its work as "political theater." This was never a

---

[12] Meredith Shiner, "How the Media Created the 'Moderate' Susan Collins," *The New Republic*, December 12, 2022, https://newrepublic.com/article/156781/media-created-myth-moderate-susan-collins.

particularly compelling approach to covering the halls of power, but it has become especially damaging in an era when GOP politicians are unbound by the conventions of truth. Over the past 10 years, endless brinksmanship on funding the government or averting a default on the credit of the United States has been as predictable as it has been irresponsible.

When I first read this piece from Shiner—a former colleague and someone I consider a close friend—it stung. I thought of all the times I'd done just that while performing as a pundit on cable news or finding something sexy for the top of my morning newsletters at the PBS NewsHour and *The Los Angeles Times*.

Collins, Flake, and McCain were the most prominent "moderate" voices in my day as a congressional reporter, and I came back to them repeatedly as a way to make my writing interesting with those elements of "theater." Sure, Collins is frequently at the table for negotiations on policy that lawmakers attempt to craft in a bipartisan fashion. She has been a go-to for Republican and Democratic presidents.

Despite those rankings showing her in the middle, it's a mistake to consider Collins Democratic-leaning, and it's always been foolhardy for the left to count on her, one senator told me. "Anyone that knows her would never think this is someone who would ever switch, or this is someone who would reflexively be more progressive on every issue. She is a classic centrist Republican but still a tried and true Republican," the senator said.

Whether they were inflated with outsized importance or purely fulfilling a role as media creations didn't really matter for the people disappointed when Collins and Flake supported Brett Kavanaugh during the ugly saga that was his nomination and confirmation. For the passive observer of politics in Washington, that 2018 fight punctured perception and cost Collins Democratic support in her home state. The overturning of *Roe v. Wade* less than four years later prompted Collins to say she was the one who "felt misled."[13]

Supreme Court nominations provide clear markers of just how partisan things have grown over the last few decades. Diller noted that his former boss (Lugar) was the last Republican senator from a red state who was not a lame duck to vote for a Democratic-nominated Supreme Court justice. The steady

---

[13] Carl Hulse, "Kavanaugh Gave Private Assurances. Collins Says He 'Misled' Her," *The New York Times*, June 25, 2022, https://www.nytimes.com/2022/06/24/us/roe-kavanaugh-collins-notes.html.

erosion of bipartisan votes for nominees to the nation's highest court reflects poorly on both Republicans and Democrats, Diller said.

"Everyone is just voting to save their skin," Diller told me. Over 14 years, Lugar, Graham, and Lamar Alexander were the only senators not from a blue state or lame ducks to support a justice from the other party before Biden nominated Kentanji Brown Jackson in 2022. Romney was joined by Collins and Murkowski, who also happened to be fellow party defiers on Trump's second impeachment. The searing image of Romney staying in the chamber as the lone Republican to applaud for the first female Black Supreme Court justice's confirmation says everything, to me at least, about where moderation is these days.[14]

The Lugar Center pulled together its research in March 2022, just before Brown was confirmed 53-47, and reading their long analysis really drove home just how much things had changed in a relatively short amount of time. Most justices received support from senators of the opposite party of the president, well past the politicized Robert Bork episode. Justices Kennedy (1988), Souter (1990), Ginsberg (1993), and Breyer (1994) were all confirmed with fewer than 10 dissenting votes, researchers point out, and even Clarence Thomas ultimately had 11 Democratic senators supporting him in 1991. Chief Justice John Roberts earned 23 Democratic supporters in 2005. The next six nomination battles from 2006 until 2020 are when the strong partisan trend began to develop in defiance of historical precedent. In fact, "Graham is the only current Republican [s]enator from a red state who cast a vote for an Obama SCOTUS nominee. No Democratic [s]enator from a blue state—current or retired—cast a vote for any of the four Republican SCOTUS nominees that followed John Roberts in 2005."

Working Together

Mark Warner of Virginia arrived in the Senate in 2009, just as Barack Obama was leaving to become president. Warner was a former southern governor with a reputation for working with Republicans to solve problems. The label he gave himself on the campaign trail was "radical centrist," which he admits

[14] Patricia McKnight, "Watch: Mitt Romney Applauds Jackson Alone While GOP Senators Leave Chambers," *Newsweek*, April 8, 2022, https://www.newsweek.com/watch-mitt-romney-applauds-jackson-alone-while-gop-senators-leave-chambers-1696219.

earned him snickers from the press. Warner said when approaching his own legislation he would find a good Republican partner whenever he could, even facing pushback from the left. His observation having served before, during and after Trump's tenure in the White House is that "the universe of people who would do a big bipartisan deal has always gotten a little bit smaller."

While Warner blames both sides, he said the ratio of potential Democrats who would go into a bipartisan deal versus potential Republicans has almost always been 2-to-1 Democrats over Republicans. This was particularly the case, Warner said, during the Trump era. "If being part of the bipartisan deal meant you had to go against Trump, there was a real reluctance of Republican senators to do that," he said in an interview. There was "lots and lots of eye rolling from the Republicans I was working with as Trump would tweet out or spout out on a daily basis," Warner added. Warner said there really was no major effort to try to put a tax deal together in 2017 that would ever get 10 Democratic senators. And the Trump administration at that point was unwilling to seriously negotiate, he said.

A student of politics could argue there are moderate Democrats who could have been courted to join the tax cut effort, but the Trump White House didn't seem interested. As Reuters reported in December 2017, "The framework for both the Senate and House bills was developed in secret over a few months by a half-dozen Republican congressional leaders and Trump advisers, with little input from the party's rank-and-file and none from Democrats."[15] Tim Hogan, a spokesman for the anti-tax-cut group Tax March, told *The Washington Post* there was never "a serious proposition that could attract Democratic senators."[16]

Warner did note some exceptions to the divided Trump-era Senate: his own work with the Intelligence panel and the Russian interference in the 2016 election and hammering out details with then-Treasury Secretary Steve Mnuchin on COVID relief funding. Bipartisanship "could still exist even under Trump," he said.

A datapoint that's available now, of course, is what the Senate gets done during Joe Biden's presidency. One indicator that would suggest progress is

---

[15] David Morgan and Amanda Becker, "Senate Approves Major Tax Cuts in Victory for Trump," *Reuters*, December 1, 2017, https://www.reuters.com/article/us-usa-tax/senate-approves-major-tax-cuts-in-victory-for-trump-idUSKBN1DV4K2.

[16] David Weigel, "Democrats Once Seen as Potential Yes Votes on Tax Cuts Appear to Walk Away," *The Washington Post*, October 28, 2021, https://www.washingtonpost.com/news/powerpost/wp/2017/11/28/democrats-once-seen-as-potential-yes-votes-on-tax-cuts-appear-to-walk-away/.

the gun measure passed in summer 2022 following a series of devastating and deadly mass shootings. It was a 65–33 vote, with 15 Republicans joining every Democrat. The Senate also worked together to lift the debt ceiling, passing a bipartisan measure 63–36 in May 2023.

Rewarding Bombast

Senators reject opportunities to be better at every turn, but much of the blame should rightly fall to my industry: the media. That "political theater" of Washington always made it fun to cover, but quickly becomes a shorthand that degrades the conversation down into winners and losers. It leaves the consumers of news about the people making decisions in the federal government wondering about substance but quite familiar with gaffes, barbs, and labels such as moderate.

That's unhealthy, but it's also not where the people are. Gallup found that on average in 2021, 37 percent of Americans described their political views as moderate, 36 percent as conservative and 25 percent as liberal. Once you parse the numbers further, it's clear that most of those are left-leaning moderates. Gallup drilled down into the sharp decline in the number of Republicans who identify as moderate today since 1994 and the Republican Revolution—from 33 percent then to 22 percent in the latest survey. "Republicans' right-leaning stance held firm last year, with 74 percent identifying as conservative, 22 percent as moderate and just 4 percent as liberal," the firm's 2022 analysis reads. "Roughly three in four Republicans have identified as conservative each year since 2018 after the proportion rose from 70 percent in 2016 and from 58 percent in 1994."

David Lauter, of *The Los Angeles Times*, writing for "The Essential Politics" newsletter in September 2022, observed that although the so-called moderates don't engage in politics as intensively as more partisan voters, they have a strong ability to sway elections. He cited Fowler, Hill, Lewis, Tausanovitch, Vavreck, and Warshaw (2022), who found candidates benefit electorally from ideological moderation; yet many studies conclude that vote choices are highly partisan. "We find that the moderate subset of the electorate responds to moderation and to candidate experience. As the old saying goes, ideologues may vote for a 'blue dog' as long as that dog shares their views. But, the moderates in our analyses seem to care that the candidate is, in fact, a dog," the authors wrote.

Since I've been out of newsrooms full time, and with a little distance from Washington, I've realized the way journalists handle politics has been one of the most destructive forces over the last decade. When the media goes back to the same people, who are better known for throwing bombs than solving problems, again and again because they get clicks and ratings, that sends a clear message to politicians: there's little incentive for you to work together. We will reward the loudest in the room. It's not that compromise is getting more elusive, it's that journalists are more attracted to conflict.

Airtime and headlines lead to national name recognition, which translates to money and ultimately that brings power. You don't even have to sit for the vote, pay attention in the hearing or talk with your constituents. Why would anyone bother to forge partnerships with the other side, especially if there's a reporter who can break news with the speed of their thumbs waiting outside the room where deals could be negotiated. Those who do want to do public good, find compromise and, you know, actually legislate, each year have fewer people to work with, fewer to try and gather in the room.

During the Trump years, Senate Republicans who tried to get there did so at great peril. Not only might they risk a primary election back home, but if they dared to raise Trump's ire he would back their GOP challengers with gusto. Previous loyalty didn't even seem to matter. Just consider the more than two dozen tweets he sent attacking his one-time attorney general Jeff Sessions in the span of a scant few months when he tried to reclaim his Senate seat in 2018. The attack was even more ironic because Sessions was the first senator to endorse Trump when he sought the 2016 Republican nomination for president.

As I worked on this chapter, two former Senate Republicans died. Biden's statements about them illustrated to me how much things have changed. In honoring Bob Dole, Biden cited major policy victories the senator had made a reality, including the Americans with Disabilities Act, a federal holiday in the name of Martin Luther King, Jr., and improvements to Social Security and child nutrition. "This work, for Bob, was about more than passing laws. It was written on his heart," Biden stated. When Orrin Hatch died soon after, Biden lauded his longtime colleague as someone "who looked out for the people who often didn't have a voice in our laws and our country."

I'm not sure anyone serving in the US Senate could be worthy of such praise today. And that to me feels like the ultimate disruption, particularly because the 2022 midterms kept it going for what appears to be the foreseeable future.

It's not actually Trump's fault—his presidency just accelerated the already in progress erosion of norms and bipartisanship.

Trump Lit the Match and Threw It on the Fire

The president's nastiness, disdain for procedure and decorum, and governing by tweet couldn't have been a surprise to anyone paying attention. And he inherited a Senate already deeply divided with a lack of interest in coming together for the good of the country. "His personal actions and words have been so extreme in breaking norms," said Diller of the Lugar Center. "He has been this actor who has changed things by just his own being [and] he did so many things that are helping to break American politics." Diller said the Lugar Center found something counterintuitive in their research, especially related to legislation Trump may not have been following as closely as immigration, taxes, his Supreme Court nominees, and impeachment (Branegan, Diller, and Spitz 2020).

The Bipartisan Index is a nonpartisan ranking produced by the Lugar Center and Georgetown University's McCourt School of Public Policy. It ranks all lawmakers not on votes but bill sponsorships and co-sponsorships. Researchers found that under the radar Senate Republicans tried to build alliances with Democrats on matters such as opioids or invasive species in our lakes or roadbuilding. Republican senators dominated the highest rankings of their index during the first three years of the Trump era when there was a proliferation of these Republican bipartisan initiatives. "We dub this the Trump effect," Diller said. The center placed responsibility squarely on electoral politics:

> Most Republican [s]enators face potential threats to their re-election both from elements within their party and from their Democratic opponent. Before the Trump era, [s]enators rarely experienced this type of dual vulnerability. With their party being led by a polarizing [p]resident whose public approval percentage has usually hovered in the 40s, Republicans from competitive states have concerns about his potential impact on their general election prospects. The Republican loss of the House in 2018 underscored the risk to individual Senate seats. Yet verbally distancing oneself from the [p]resident or voting against one of his priorities or appointments carries

extreme political risks for any Republican legislator. Such members may be the object of angry presidential tweets, draw a primary challenger, lose election funding, or suffer other forms of political excommunication. In this atmosphere, the details of legislative work have offered Republican [s]enators an avenue to express subtle independence and broaden their appeal without reference to the daily media focus on President Trump. As long as their legislative efforts avoid contradicting Trump on the few topics receiving his close attention, such as immigration and trade, they have substantial room to engage with Democrats on bipartisan legislative approaches that might appeal to the political center.

After Biden took office, Republican scores on the index tanked.

Warner said he has found principled conservatives in today's Senate who are willing to call out Trump, but that doesn't mean they're going to suddenly want to go do business with Democrats. "The press got caught up in that as much as anybody," Warner said. "Trump was so far out of the mainstream and so reckless in so many ways that Democrats almost presumed that anyone who spoke up against Trump or his antics must be then willing to work with Dems on issue positions and that's just not the case."

He doesn't see much improving, especially as "Trump's presence still lurks out there." Lieberman, a founder of the political group "No Labels," which strives to find consensus across party divides, identifies a host of factors leading to this perilous moment. Changes in values, demography, media, gerrymandering, and money in politics are at the top of his list. "All those things which conspired to make it very difficult for members of both parties to come to the center to talk to each other about a problem or national problem, to negotiate, to compromise, to get something done. Which is the way we've almost always made big steps forward legislatively in this country," Lieberman said. "Though President Trump was unique, unconventional, disruptive, in many ways disgusting, certainly he didn't create the problems in Congress and the workings of Congress and the White House together," he said, adding, "but he made them worse and in some ways he still is."

Lieberman tried to sound a hopeful note, telling me he has "no doubt" the country can rebound: "We can still get out of it." Writing most of this chapter as the January 6 hearings raged on Capitol Hill and revising it after the midterm elections swept Republicans narrowly back into power in the House to further divide Washington, I am less sure.

A Journalist's View

My own perceptions of the US Senate are completely warped by the things I had the good fortune to experience over the course of my time covering politics on Capitol Hill.

One of the first things that happened to me as a cub congressional reporter, it turns out, was a tradition in its final days. Senate Majority Leader Bill Frist gathered a handful of journalists for a pen-and-pad briefing on the Senate floor. His predecessors had been doing it weekly, a special privilege away from the television cameras. The Senate Press Gallery says it hasn't been done in at least a decade, perhaps longer. Frist, a Tennessee Republican, stood in the well and talked about major bipartisan legislation on highways and a compromise on judicial nominees. There was a sense of honor and privilege to get to hear from one of the nation's most important political leaders about how things get done on Capitol Hill, from both the press and the politicians.

Around that time, not long after Tom Daschle lost his seat thanks in part to spending so much time in Washington instead of his home state of South Dakota, things started to shift. Every retirement meant one less Senate family dining in bipartisan fashion with Capitol Hill neighbors, a trend that would eventually bleed into lawmakers sleeping in their offices and valuing Twitter followers more than getting to know their peers.

I'd been covering Congress and campaigns for about a year when the most extraordinary thing I've ever witnessed on the Senate floor began. The Republicans had lost both the House and the Senate and the post-"thumping" 2006 lame duck session was in full swing. I watched a lot of C-Span at the time.[17] I lived only a few blocks from the Capitol building, and I could keep an eye on the Senate floor and know when to run over for votes, the time when reporters had the best chance of catching senators for interviews in the hallways.

I kept hearing Mike DeWine at odd hours talking about soldiers who had died in Iraq and Afghanistan. The Ohio Republican was one of those moderates, if you will, who had just lost his seat in the midterms thanks to George W. Bush and deep dissatisfaction with the two wars DeWine had supported.

---

[17] *National Archives and Records Administration,* National Archives and Records Administration, https://georgewbush-whitehouse.archives.gov/news/releases/2006/11/20061108-2.html.

"I rise today," he would say, to honor this person, someone who had been a friend, a son, a devoted patriot. It followed his somber formula for the speeches, 153 in all to mark the men and women who had been killed serving in Iraq and Afghanistan from his home state of Ohio since the start of those wars. The floor remarks took on a new urgency in the lame duck session once DeWine's days in Washington were numbered. While other Republicans who had been ousted in the midterm elections were giving VIP tours to friends or lining up cable news contracts, DeWine stood on the Senate floor, often alone, in tribute to the troops. "I will think about them until the day I die," he told colleagues in his farewell address.

There were days DeWine came to the microphone at his desk after Senate business had concluded and stayed on the floor past midnight, describing a young person whose life was lost in battle, perhaps his seventh speech of the day. DeWine had started the task in 2002, when an Ohioan became the first serviceman killed in Afghanistan. He told me in 2006 that he pledged to finish the tributes before leaving after 12 years in the Senate and more than two decades on Capitol Hill. Most lasted several minutes and included details, such as how 27-year-old Sgt. Justin Hoffman teased "the love of his life," girl-friend Teri Price, that he would propose "as soon as he stepped off the plane on his way back from Iraq." Or how Pvt. Samuel Bowen's sister, Consuella, had not erased messages he left on her answering machine. DeWine remembered Pvt. Adam R. Shepherd as "someone who could brighten any day," and lauded the 1993 wrestling championship that made Maj. Ramon J. Mendoza Jr. a Buckeyes sports legend. Then there was Army Sgt. Daniel Michael Shephard of O'Leary Ohio, killed in Iraq when his vehicle was hit by a bomb on August 15, 2004. He was 23. DeWine's floor speech honored him as a great athlete and a reliable friend. "Danny was more concerned for the lives of others than he was for his own. I don't think any of us could think of anything more honorable," the senator said. He went on to describe a high school romance with Kassie, and shared that the sergeant never met his son, his namesake.

The narratives were crafted through detailed research, much of which was done during funeral services that the senator—whose own daughter had been killed in a car wreck 13 years earlier—regularly attended. Aides said he never jumped the line to pay his respects, but he always took notes to be able to craft his speeches later. The tributes often included direct quotes from family, friends, and teachers. "The story is not about me," DeWine said then. "Every day for the rest of their lives, these families will think of their lost father, their lost son, their lost husband." For most of the fallen troops, "their lives had just begun," he said. The speeches are a permanent record of the United States Senate, and "if the family members 100 years from now want to look it up, it's there. It won't go away," he said. DeWine staffers sent each family the congressional record and video or DVD copies of the floor speech. In total he would spend a dozen hours of floor time, most in the last four days of the lame duck session, a race to honor everyone Ohio had lost. One aide helping him even crashed on the office couch after pulling an all-nighter to write. "We had to get it done," the aide told me in 2019. "I am so glad we did."

I wrote a story about it, and I always felt like it didn't capture just how extraordinary the moment was.[18]

I've been telling this story ever since because I found it moving. There. I can say it now that I'm not a practicing political journalist. DeWine's words made me cry, and it was one of the few moments of valor I ever witnessed on Capitol Hill. A loser, doing something important in the wee hours when no one was listening, because it mattered to him. It stood out amid the pettiness of Washington. Anyone would have forgiven him for giving one big speech and naming the dead. And no one else had made anything close to such a visible effort.

Reading the story itself 12 years later when I started teaching journalism students about narrative writing, I realized I'd gone about it all wrong. I briefly entertained the idea of going back for a do-over, of describing DeWine's speeches with the emotion I felt that reporters were supposed to suppress. Someone had told me that he'd gotten the information from the families to be able to read the resolutions into the official congressional record. That the details were important to him. For some reason, I didn't put that in the story.

I used my regret in a journalism class lesson plan, explaining to students what I would have done instead. I even re-interviewed DeWine, now serving as governor, and someone who had worked high up in his Senate office at the time. That aide told me that no one realized how torn the senator had been over his 2002 vote in favor of the Iraq War, an issue that would contribute to his defeat by Democrat Sherrod Brown.

DeWine's Ohio, of course, is less a swing state than it used to be. Democrats had high hopes in 2022 of capturing the seat vacated by the retiring Portman, cited by so many as a reasonable lawmaker squarely in the middle. Instead, Ohio voters chose Republican J.D. Vance, a Trump loyalist on the far right. Portman endorsed Vance a few months before the election, arguing in part that he would have the political will to make "sensible policy changes to re-gain operational control of the border, including supporting an overwhelmed Border Patrol and ensuring they have the tools and resources they need to do their job effectively."[19]

So what do DeWine's outgoing floor speeches honoring fallen troops have to do with the Trump-era Senate? Maybe nothing, but I can't stop thinking about it. DeWine said he worked with leadership to get floor time where he could. An hour here, 20 minutes there. That they understood it was impor-tant to him.

I simply can't imagine this happening between 2017 and 2021. Think about those years. Senator John McCain's July 28, 2017, thumbs down to save the Affordable Care Act is perhaps the only moment that stands out, and even that is overshadowed by the image of the guy in horns at the dais on January 6, 2021.

A Bleak Future

The premise of this chapter started out as the myth of the moderate Senate Republican. Over the course of discussions with academics and political observers closer to the Senate today than I am, I started to question what it was really about. Are we talking about moderation in tone? Moderation in policy position? Simply being in the middle? Or coming together to make deals across party lines as the Senate was intended to do?

Diller of the Lugar Center said people forget that bipartisanship is not cen-trism. "Bipartisanship can be practiced by people who are very progressive and very conservative, it's almost more an attitude of openness or willing-ness to cooperate with the other side," Diller said. "Moderation is something different altogether," he said, and finds senators "pulling punches" because harsh rhetoric or constant partisan posturing makes governance very diffi-cult. Moderation is signaling "you are open to compromise" by not poisoning

---

[19] Rob Portman, August 30, 2022, "Portman: Vance Win in Ohio Essential to GOP-controlled Senate," Cincinnati Enquirer, https://www.cincinnati.com/story/opinion/contributors/2022/08/30/portman-vance-win-in-ohio-essential-to-gop-controlled-senate/65417009007/.

the well, by suspending the pursuit of partisan advantage by asking "if it's good for me, or good for the country," Diller said.

He added that Lugar, of course, was someone who notably did just that on major issues such as the DREAM Act and the new START treaty on nuclear proliferation. Taking a political risk for bipartisanship is "so rare today," Diller said.

Perhaps during the Trump presidency the idea of moderation among Senate Republicans had simply come to translate as "not Trump."

I stumbled on what Lindsey Graham told graduates at Lander University in Greenwood, South Carolina, in 2010, not long after abandoning the bipartisan climate deal facing pressure back home. "Try to be part of the solution, not the problem," he said, according to Draper in *The New York Times Magazine*. "[T]he only way we're going to solve these problems is working together."[20]

That was the point, I had always thought. Why does it seem harder than ever today?

I set out to ask this question of the many Republican sources I've worked with over the course of my more than two decades covering politics. I was open to the possibility my premise was wrong. Call after call over months came up with nothing. Republican after Republican just didn't want to talk about it. One Senate office insisted the boss wasn't a moderate and the conversation was over. Great topic, one said, we're too busy. Others who I had counted on as trusted contacts completely ghosted me. I tried harder. I started to realize it's not me, it's them.

This is simply not a conversation anyone wants to have anymore.

The people I have talked with pointed me to senators crucial to the question: Graham, Portman, Ben Sasse of Nebraska, Pat Toomey of Pennsylvania, along with the obvious, measurably moderate female senators actually in the middle: Collins and Murkowski. The Sasse office would surely be open to a conversation after he announced he is giving up politics for academia as a university president in Florida. No luck. (Not that I will stop trying.)

Sasse did, however, talk with the National Review's John McCormack, saying that his Nebraska constituents had never expected him to stay in

---

[20] Draper, "Lindsey Graham, This Year's Maverick."

politics "as a lifelong calling." He pointedly noted that, "The best picture in the dome of the U.S. Capitol is Washington surrendering power."[21]

> During his first term, Sasse often expressed disillusionment with politics and sometimes his own party, leaving many to wonder why he was even pursuing a second term in 2020. Sasse told me in 2019 one reason he was seeking another term was that he had a "calling" as "a Tocquevillian or a principled pluralist or a constitutionalist" to fight on behalf of that faction within the conservative coalition, which he had come to realize was smaller than he once thought. Asked how he squares that 2019 comment with his early departure from the Senate, Sasse said on Thursday that "Tocquevillian society is about building things. The center of America really isn't political power ... I think the University of Florida is better positioned to build than any university in America right now."
>
> "The Senate is a very important institution, and I'm incredibly grateful for a lot of the people that I get to serve alongside here," Sasse said. "But frankly, I think one of the most basic things we can do to reinvigorate this place is to say that people ought to only be here for a time and then get back to building stuff."

That's a rare sentiment in the US Congress, especially from someone born after the Baby Boom.

Every Senate is different, and the 2022 midterms ushered in new voices across the political spectrum. I can predict with certainty the media will find someone to elevate as the "key vote" or "critical voice" on policy issues, probably before the senator even takes the oath of office. There is such power in the middle. Just ask Democratic Senators Joe Manchin and Kyrsten Sinema. Matthew Yglesias and Steven M. Teles argued in *The Atlantic* in 2021 that if a cross-party group of moderate senators worked together, "it could dominate the Senate, and with it the operation of the entire political system." They write:[22]

---

[21] John McCormack, "Ben Sasse Explains His Decision to Leave Senate to Serve as University of Florida President." *National Review*, October 6, 2022, https://www.nationalreview.com/2022/10/ben-sasse-explains-his-decision-to-leave-senate-to-serve-as-university-of-florida-president/.

[22] Matthew Yglesisas and Steven M. Teles, "A Moderate Proposal," *The Atlantic*, November 4, 2021, https://www.theatlantic.com/ideas/archive/2021/11/how-moderates-could-actually-take-control-washington/620599/.

Imagine, as a start, that somewhere from six to nine senators agreed to work together, either as a formally separate party or through an agreement of factions in either party. The moderate bloc would enter into a coalition with whichever party's leaders offered it the best deal to change the rules under which the body operates. Today, the majority party makes sure that Senate floor time is consumed with proposals that unite its coalition. Various bills with bipartisan groups of co-sponsors get written all the time, but this kind of legislation gets a hearing only when it serves the majority leader's designs . . .

A moderate bloc could demand rules that prioritize bipartisan bills. The lack of space for this kind of legislation is a primary complaint of a huge share of senators, including fairly ideological ones. But the bulk of members prioritize partisan solidarity over dreams of a more open Senate.

The majority party would have strong incentives to support at least a vote on the bills supported by the moderate bloc, because its control of Congress would depend on keeping the moderates in the fold. And if a concerted bloc of moderates forced a more open process onto party leaders, many members would be quietly happy.

A moderate bloc that exerted agenda-setting power could shift legislative time and attention away from the hobbyhorses of each party's activist class and onto the most fundamental problems faced by the country. With a more open legislative process, Congress could begin to address these issues—not with proposals that would generate unanimous support within either caucus but with bills that could garner majorities in both the House and the Senate, even as they violated the pieties of one party or another.

Yglesias and Teles define the stakes: "Moderates have the power—if they choose to use it—to protect the future of American democracy."

I keep coming back to that *Atlantic* essay, mourning a bit about what is possible. As Lieberman had told me, Trump didn't create this problem.

As he was about to leave office, President Barack Obama had an off the record session with some progressive reporters and shared his view that anything the incoming president did would not do irreversible harm to the country. The transcript remained private for years, but was released through a Freedom of Information Act request to a *Bloomberg News* reporter in 2022. "On balance that leads to me to say I think that four years is okay," Obama told the group three days before Trump was to take office, according to the transcript released by the FOIA. "Take on some water, but we can kind of bail fast enough to be okay. Eight years would be a problem. I would be concerned about a sustained period in which some of these norms have broken down and started to corrode."[23]

The transcript came out as I was finishing this chapter, and even though Obama wasn't talking specifically about the Senate, it felt like the right frame for these questions. The Senate continued on after Trump—and has even accomplished big, bipartisan things under President Joe Biden. But it's broken. Shattered, even. Trump's time in office gave no one the incentive to pick up the pieces.

And it provoked senators like Romney to head for the exits. Timed as Romney announced his retirement in September 2023, the Atlantic's McKay Coppins published an essay revealing explicitly why Romney was leaving. It's a damning account adapted from Coppins' book about the senator.

"A very large portion of my party," [Romney] told me one day, "really doesn't believe in the Constitution." He'd realized this only recently, he said. We were a few months removed from an attempted coup instigated by Republican leaders, and he was wrestling with some difficult questions. Was the authoritarian element of the GOP a product of President Trump, or had it always been there, just waiting to be activated by a sufficiently shameless demagogue? And what role had the members of the mainstream establishment—people like him, the reasonable Republicans—played in allowing the rot on the right to fester?

To Coppins, Romney also offered an extraordinarily candid view of how senators view Trump.

Perhaps Romney's most surprising discovery upon entering the Senate was that his disgust with Trump was not unique among his Republican colleagues. "Almost without exception," he told me, "they shared my view of the president." In public, of course, they played their parts as Trump loyalists, often contorting themselves rhetorically to defend the president's most indefensible behavior. But in private, they ridiculed his ignorance, rolled their eyes at his antics, and made incisive observations about his warped, toddlerlike psyche. Romney recalled one senior Republican senator frankly admitting, "He has none of the qualities you would want in a president, and all of the qualities you wouldn't."

---

[23] Jason Leopold, "Obama on Trump: 1 Presidential Term Is Okay, but 8 Years Would Be a Problem." *Bloomberg*, September 30, 2022, https://www.bloomberg.com/news/articles/2022-09-30/obama-on-trump-1-presidential-term-is-okay-but-8-years-would-be-a-problem-l8t1lk89.

Stepping back to evaluate all the interviews I've done and the research I've found, I decided it's not about the myth of the moderate Republican at all, but the end of the institutionalist. The purpose of the Senate as the cooling saucer for the House has steadily eroded, or, some even argued to me in their interviews, disintegrated entirely.

If that's the case, I am left wondering just how alarmed we should be about the health of our democracy? Democrats sound hopeful, if a little skeptical. And, Republicans have continued being silent. I'll let you know if any of them get back to me.

Reference

Fowler, Anthony, Seth J. Hill, Jeffrey B. Lewis, Chris Tausonovitch, Lynn Vavreck, and Christopher Warshaw. 2022. "Moderates." *American Political Science Review* 117(2): 643–660.

13

Presidents, Congress, and the Politics of Unilateral Action

William G. Howell and Terry M. Moe

Introduction

In the American system of government, lawmaking through the normal legislative process is extremely difficult. There should be no mystery as to why this is so. The Constitution's byzantine separation of powers combined with Congress's complex committee systems, the Senate filibuster, bicameralism, and numerous opportunities for blocking and delay have generated a legislative process that gives special interests, entrepreneurial legislators, and the minority party countless opportunities to interfere and obstruct. Which they regularly do, particularly in our polarized political world. As a result, the modern Congress is prone to gridlock; and judged by its inability to solve modern challenges, it is plainly dysfunctional.

Presidents have no choice, of course, but to find a way of dealing with Congress. It sits at the center of government lawmaking—and presidents, driven as they are to burnish their policy legacies, need to pursue legislative victories as a path to greatness. As a result, whatever happens within Congress, however pathological it may be, invariably informs the strategies and behaviors of presidents.

The resulting interbranch entanglements are reasonably familiar, as presidents and their surrogates work alongside members of Congress in efforts to cobble together enough support to see their policy agendas, or at least some parts of them, passed into law. Even if a president's party has complete control of Congress, the path to victory is strewn with obstacles that threaten to derail much of what presidents seek to do. The prospects of going the legislative route are much worse, moreover, when divided government and polarization take hold, as they have with rising frequency in the modern era. During the last six years of Barack Obama's presidency, Republicans controlled at

William G. Howell and Terry M. Moe, *Presidents, Congress, and the Politics of Unilateral Action*
In: *Disruption?* Edited by: Sean M. Theriault, Oxford University Press. © Oxford University Press 2024.
DOI: 10.1093/oso/9780197767832.003.0014

least one chamber of Congress. Was Obama in a position to "work" with Congress to get core aspects of his liberal agenda passed? Hardly. Similarly, Donald Trump spent the last two years of his presidency putting up with a Democratic House. Was he in a position to persuade Congress to support core aspects of his conservative agenda? Not a chance.

When presidents face little prospect of gaining the necessary support from Congress, particularly in this present period of polarized parties and narrow and unstable majorities, they have little reason to seek mutual accommodation and coordination with its members. Instead, presidents have incentives to simply work around Congress, using their powers of unilateral action—deriving, for example, from the vesting and commander-in-chief clauses of the Constitution, and from the many statutes delegating them (or executive agencies) vast discretion—to make policy on their own. Almost always, Congress cannot bring itself to support, or even expressly oppose, these directives. But because of its internal pathologies, Congress also is usually incapable of taking any coherent action to overturn the presidents' unilateral policies—and as a consequence, they remain on the books unless a subsequent president, also acting unilaterally, removes them.

Such are the politics of unilateral action (for reviews, see Howell 2005; Lowande and Rogowski 2021), which underscore the larger repercussions of congressional gridlock and dysfunction. They don't just affect the efficacy of Congress itself. They reverberate throughout the political system, with particular consequences for the strategies that presidents pursue, the policies that the executive branch produces, the primacy of presidential policymaking, and the growing dominance of presidential power in a constitutional system that was designed to ensure that no single individual would rule by fiat (Moe and Howell 1999).

In this chapter, we spotlight the exercise of unilateral power during the Trump presidency: first, by inventorying the many actions Trump undertook; and second, by taking a closer look at one particular episode that reveals how presidents can unilaterally advance policy change even in the face of explicit congressional opposition. Lest one infer that these powers apply uniquely to the Trump presidency, we subsequently consider the rather extraordinary actions undertaken by his predecessor, Barack Obama, to refashion nation's education policy.

In these short studies, we see presidents who dislodge status quo policies protected by some mix of congressional intransigence and gridlock; who make policy on their own through administrative means; and who thereby shift the locus of government decision-making away from an already troubled legislative branch and into the hands of the executive.

Trump's Unilateral Activities

When the histories are written of Congress during the Trump years, they will not feature extensive lists of landmark laws enacted at the behest of presidential initiative. To be sure, these years were not altogether devoid of legislative accomplishments. While Trump occupied the White House, Congress lowered taxes, increased military spending, and, as Frances Lee's contribution this volume makes clear, spent extraordinary sums of money to combat the coronavirus pandemic. The impetus for these actions, however, came largely from within Congress. Trump was willing to sign these bills into laws, but he provided very little leadership in their construction or passage.

Repeatedly, meanwhile, Congress refused to act on the priorities that mattered most to the Trump administration. Most significantly, it neither adopted comprehensive immigration reform nor overturned the Affordable Care Act, both of which were singular commitments of Trump's campaign for office. Those failures, meanwhile, were just the start of Trump's frustrations with Congress. Even though Republicans held majorities in both chambers during Trump's first two years in office, Congress refused to pass laws that would reduce the offshoring of US jobs, improve infrastructure, expand school choice, permit tax deductions on childcare and eldercare, reduce government corruption, or address rising crime rates—policies that Trump had pledged to quickly pursue upon assuming office. Several years later, as he sought a second term, *The Washington Post* could report that, "Despite Trump's reelection campaign refrain of 'promises made, promises kept,' almost none of his proposed 100-day legislative agenda has seen the light of day, even 1,000 days into his presidency."[1]

But whereas Congress delivered hardly any major legislative victories for the president, Trump did manage to advance an astounding number of policy changes through executive orders, memoranda, proclamations, and other directives (Potter et al. 2022). These policy changes covered the gambit

---

[1] Philip Bump, "Three Years Later, Evaluating the 10 Laws Trump Said He'd Pass in His First 100 Days," *Washington Post*, October 25, 2019, https://www.washingtonpost.com/politics/2019/10/25/three-years-later-evaluating-laws-trump-said-hed-pass-his-first-days/.

from foreign to domestic, from economic to social, from controversial to mundane. Some were of broad salience and significance, others catered to narrower interests and concerned more technical matters. Most *would not have happened* had Congress been the exclusive venue of policy change.

Immigration was a hotbed of unilateral activity under the Trump Administration. As soon as he assumed office, Trump issued an executive order imposing a moratorium on migration from seven countries deemed to be harboring "radical Islamic terrorists" (Iran, Iraq, Libya, Somalia, Sudan, Syria, and Yemen) and suspended the US Refugee Admissions Program. He expanded the power of the Department of Homeland Security to deport un-documented immigrants through "expedited removal." He threatened finan-cial and legal consequences for any sub-national jurisdiction that refused to volunteer persons or information to federal immigration officials. He sus-pended Obama's Deferred Action for Childhood Arrivals (DACA), a pro-gram designed to protect undocumented immigrants who had come to the United States as children (Milkis and Jacobs 2017; Waslin 2020).

And that was just the start. Over the course of his presidency, Trump also issued an executive order that prioritized the removal of aliens who had been convicted or charged with a crime, committed acts that constitute a charge-able criminal offense, abused any public welfare program, had an order of protection against them, or posed a risk to public safety or national secu-rity. He empowered local law enforcement to perform the functions of im-migration officers, denied federal grants to sanctuary cities, made public a list of criminal actions by aliens, provided reports on the immigration status of all aliens incarcerated in state and federal prisons, and established an office within Immigration and Customs Enforcement to provide serv-ices to victims of crimes by undocumented individuals (Lens 2018). He is-sued memoranda that limited US travel to Cuba and disavowed policies that encouraged Cubans to travel to the United States (Turek 2022). He issued an executive order requiring that all departments and agencies work together to ensure that the decennial Census compile data on the citizenship status of all those living within the United States. He required that states and local governments provide written consent authorizing the initial resettlement of refugees into their respective communities. He lowered the refugee ceiling by more than 80 percent (Darrow and Scholl 2020).

Not all of these directives, of course, delivered on their initial promise. Some, notably those involving the so-called Muslim ban, had to be amended after the courts ruled them unconstitutional. Others, including the proposed changes to the census, were never ultimately implemented. And still, both symbolically and substantively, the Trump administration's immigration orders constituted a sharp departure from an immigration status quo that Democrats and Republicans in Congress universally opposed but could not find a way to fix.

Trump's presidency was also a bonanza of deregulatory activity. During his time in office, he issued an executive order requiring executive departments and agencies to identify two existing regulations to repeal for every new regulation it proposed; and furthermore, to calculate the fiscal effect of these proposals to ensure that they did not increase regulatory burdens on the American economy. Trump issued another order requiring each agency to establish a Regulatory Reform Task Force using existing agency resources, with the goal of removing regulations that his people concluded were outdated, inefficient, or excessively costly. He reversed previous executive orders (and rescinded their relevant regulations) that disclosed violations of workplace protections regarding wages and hours, safety and health, collective bargaining, family and medical leave, and civil rights. He directed the Environmental Protection Agency to narrow its regulatory activities associated with the Clean Water Act. He required executive agencies to revise or repeal rules that burdened the development or use of domestically produced energy resources, including oil, natural gas, coal, and nuclear energy resources (Milkis and Jacobs 2017; Lens 2018).

And so it went in policy domain and after policy domain. On energy policy and climate change, Trump reinstated federal approval for the controversial Keystone and North Dakota pipelines, withdrew the United States from the 2015 Paris Climate Accord, lowered fuel efficiency requirements for automakers, repealed Obama's Clean Power Plan rules, and issued proposals that would limit the Endangered Species Act and weaken the Mercury and Air Toxic Standards under the EPA.[2] On health care policy, Trump reinstated the ban on US aid to foreign nongovernmental organizations that perform abortions, withdrew from the World Health Organization, declared a national emergency over coronavirus, and established a batch of associated

---

[2] Discussions of these orders can be found in Milkis and Jacobs; Stephen Ansolabehere and Jon Rogowski, "Unilateral Action and Presidential Accountability," *Presidential Studies Quarterly*, 50 (2020): 129–145; Cayli Baker, "The Trump Administration's Major Environmental Deregulations," *Brookings Institution*, December 15, 2020, https://www.brookings.edu/blog/up-front/2020/12/15/the-trump-administrations-major-environmental-deregulations/; Helier Cheung, "What Does Trump Actually Believe on Climate Change?" *BBC News*, 2020, https://www.bbc.com/news/world-us-canada-51213003.

relief measures.[3] On foreign policy, he imposed sweeping tariffs on imported goods from China, directed executive agencies to monitor, enforce, and comply with "buy American" laws, recognized Jerusalem as the capital of Israel, and withdrew the United States from the Trans Pacific Partnership Trade Agreement, the Joint Comprehensive Plan of Action, and the UN Human Rights Council (Lens 2018; Ansolabehere and Rogowski 2020; Ali, Bibi, and Ashraf 2020).

Amid all this activity, what was Congress doing in response? For the most part, very little. Individual members registered support or opposition. Some of the more controversial orders were the subjects of hearings in the House or Senate. And funds for the president's initiatives were either allocated or withheld. But the details of these policies were crafted within the executive branch; the impetus for their adoption came, nearly always, from members of or allies to the president's team; and limits to their ambitions were defined not by the need to assemble supermajoritarian coalitions in support of new laws—since such coalitions were unnecessary—but by the much easier task of preventing Congress from doing anything of consequence to alter the new policy or its implementation.

Unilateral action, of course, comes with obvious downsides. All else equal, the president would prefer that elements of his policy agenda be adopted legislatively, if only because statutes tend to outlast unilateral directives and rest upon firmer legal footing. Moreover, unilateral actions usually take the form of targeted policy adjustments rather than wholesale, systematic change, a fact that further constrains the president's policy ambitions. Still, by any reasonable metric, Trump managed to deploy his unilateral powers to considerable effect. He did things, lots and lots of things, that Congress would not (and could not) replicate on its own. Moreover, and this is the key point, the same dynamics that kept Congress from legislating also help explain both the political strategies behind and policy significance of the president's unilateral actions.

---

[3] J. B. Bingenheimer, and P. Skuster, "The Foreseeable Harms of Trump's Global Gag Rule. Studies in Family Planning," 48 (2017): 279–290; M. Haberman, E. Cochrane, and J. Tankersley, "Sidestepping Congress, Trump Signs Executive Measures for Pandemic Relief," *New York Times*, August 8, 2020; Katie Rogers and Apoorva Mandavilli, "Trump Administration Signals Formal Withdrawal from W.H.O.," *New York Times*, July 7, 2020; S. Holland, J. Mason, and M. Brice, "Trump Declares Coronavirus National Emergency, Says He Will Most Likely Be Tested,"https://www.reuters.com/arti cle/us-health-coronavirus-usa-emergency/trump-declares-coronavirus-national-emergency-says-he-will-most-likely-be-tested-idUSKBN2102G3.

A Closer Look at Trump's Border Wall

Routinely, the backdrop to unilateral activity is legislative gridlock. When Congress is immobilized, presidents will often act unilaterally to pave a pathway forward. In some instances, though, presidents deploy their unilateral powers even in the face of Congress's expressed opposition. Trump's declaration of emergency on the nation's border with Mexico provides a case in point.

To fix a broken immigration system and a country overrun with what he called "illegals," Trump promised during his 2016 campaign to build a "big, beautiful" wall on the country's southern border.[4] So doing, he insisted, he would finally put a halt to the influx of "drug dealers, rapists, and other criminals" pouring into our country. More than any other policy initiative, the construction of a wall spanning the nearly 2,000-mile border between the United States and Mexico stood as the centerpiece of Trump's presidential campaign. And once elected, he expected Congress to step forward and appropriate the funds needed to build it.

Just five days after his inauguration, President Trump issued Executive Order 13767, which directed the federal government to begin construction. But to secure the funds necessary to launch the project, he needed congressional support. As part of the 2018 federal budget, therefore, he requested a $2.8 billion increase in discretionary funding for the Department of Homeland Security (DHS). During a hearing of the Senate Homeland Security and Governmental Affairs Committee, DHS Secretary John Kelly made clear that these funds would be used to "design and construct the border wall."[5]

Members of Congress were not universally enthusiastic. Though Trump rather quickly secured the support of Speaker Paul Ryan and House Homeland Security Committee Chair Michael McCaul, he faced opposition from numerous other Senate Republicans who expressed concerns about the national debt, as well as Senate Democrats who saw the project as a wasteful, xenophobic political gambit. That summer, funds for the wall were stricken from the budget.

---

[4] Donald Trump Presidential Campaign Announcement, June 16, 2015. Available at: https://www.c-span.org/video/?326473-1/donald-trump-presidential-campaign-announcement

[5] Senate Committee on Homeland Security and Governmental Affairs, "Improving Border Security and Public Safety," Hearing, April 5, 2017, https://www.dhs.gov/news/2017/04/05/written-testimony-dhs-secretary-kelly-senate-committee-homeland-security-and.

Undeterred, the following January the president called for $18 billion in border-wall funding to be distributed over ten years. And later that year, he ratcheted up the request to $23.4 billion as part of his proposed *Build the Wall, Enforce the Law Act*. When Congress still refused to act, Trump promised to veto any appropriations bill for the 2019 fiscal year that did not include at least $5 billion in funding for a border wall, a promise that led to a government shutdown from December 22, 2018, to January 25, 2019. To finally end the shutdown, Trump ultimately signed a bipartisan funding bill in early 2019 that provided just a fraction of the funds he had previously demanded.

With his legislative options effectively exhausted, Trump shifted tack. On February 15, 2019, even as illegal border crossings declined, the president declared a national emergency. Using the emergency powers granted to him—vaguely and questionably—by the National Emergencies Act of 1976, he then diverted roughly $8 billion in funds previously appropriated to the Departments of Defense and Treasury for military construction and the prevention of cross-border smuggling. Trump's declaration met with fierce opposition in Congress, as House Speaker Nancy Pelosi and Senate Minority Leader Chuck Schumer jointly decried it as "a lawless act [and] a gross abuse of the power of the presidency."[6] A number of congressional Republicans raised similar concerns, joining with Democrats in the House and Senate in voting twice to end the national emergency—first in February 2019 and again in September of the same year. Trump vetoed both bills, and Congress lacked the votes to override. For the remainder of Trump's term in office, progress on border wall construction proceeded, albeit haltingly, amidst lawsuits and administrative challenges.

Throughout this period, Congress never managed to stop Trump in his tracks, despite bi-partisan opposition to the ill-conceived and politically polarizing public works project, and despite Congress's exclusive constitutional power over appropriations. Its members could not muster the support needed to retract the president's emergency declaration. They did not so much as even try to pass new legislation that would redirect the funds back to their original purpose. And despite fielding numerous lawsuits from human rights and environmental groups, the courts could not put an end to this charade.

---

[6] Senate Democrats, "Schumer and Pelosi Joint Statement on the Possibility of President Trump Declaring a National Emergency." February 14, 2019, https://www.democrats.senate.gov/es/sala-de-prensa/schumer-pelosi-joint-statement-on-the-possibility-of-president-trump-declaring-a-national-emergency

It wasn't until Trump left office that construction finally drew to a close. But by then, $11 billion in government funds had been spent on the construction of 455 miles of a border wall (most of it simply a reconstruction of existing barriers), with a private organization, *We Build the Wall*, adding 5 more miles on private property in El Paso, Texas.[7]

Recalling Obama's Race to the Top and NCLB Waivers

In lots of ways, Trump's presidency was exceptional—for its demagoguery, populism, incessant lies, and autocratic trashing of democratic norms, practices, and the rule of law. His willingness to exercise unilateral powers, however, does not in itself set him apart from other modern presidents. To the contrary, the overall production of unilateral directives has been steadily increasing for decades (Kaufman and Rogowski 2022), just as the politics that define unilateral action took hold long before Trump. To appreciate both their broader policy significance and the ingenuity with which presidents engage them, we need look no further than Trump's immediate predecessor.

When Barack Obama assumed office in 2008, he inherited an education accountability system administered by the federal government that was rapidly deteriorating. The signature domestic policy achievement of his predecessor George W. Bush, No Child Left Behind (NCLB), established protocols for measuring the "adequate yearly progress" of public schools across the nation and assigning increasingly draconian punishments for failing to meet them. Because of its design, which required students as a whole as well as specified subgroups to meet ever increasing standards of proficiency, it was not long before the preponderance of public schools were deemed failing, teachers and administrators were railing against the verdicts, and Democrats and Republicans alike were calling for the accountability system's overhaul.

What did Congress do in response? Hardly anything. It did not hold hearings on how best to fix the statute. It did not debate the merits of promising reforms. It did not introduce bills intended to fix a system that, all could see, was simply unsustainable. Indeed, year after year, Congress could not even muster the collective will to reauthorize NCLB, even though it was obligated to do so starting in 2007.

---

[7] David Montanaro, "Privately Funded Organization 'We Build the Wall' Starts Construction of Border Barrier in El Paso Area," *Fox News*, May 27, 2019

During his first couple of years in office, Obama periodically called upon Congress to meets its responsibilities and fix the law. But in truth, he spent very little time or political capital trying to jumpstart the legislative process. Instead, he undertook two major initiatives that would redefine the practice of education policy nationwide, even as NCLB formally remained the law of the land.

Obama's first foray into education policymaking came in the form of his "Race to the Top" competition (RttT). Drawing upon $4.5 billion set aside for it in the 2009 American Recovery and Reinvestment Act (ARRA), Obama used this grant competition to stimulate state adoptions of education policies intended to improve college readiness, create new data systems, support teacher effectiveness, and address persistently low performing schools. The ARRA offered very little guidance for how funds should be disbursed. Beyond requiring states to pass along at least 50 percent of the funding received under the RttT competition to local education agencies, the federal Department of Education (DoE) retained broad discretion over the competition's design and operation.[8] Within each category of educational priorities, the Obama Administration freely chose which specific reforms would be rewarded under the RttT competition and by how much; how many states would receive financial rewards and by what amount; and what kinds of oversight mechanisms would be used to ensure compliance.[9] From an operational standpoint, RttT was almost entirely the handiwork of Obama's DoE—and a presidential creation.

With RttT, the president looked past Congress to state legislatures, which he hoped would adopt policies that aligned with his education priorities. As he noted in his July 2009 speech announcing RttT, Obama intended to "incentivize excellence and spur reform and launch a race to the top in America's public schools."[10] Secretary of Education Arne Duncan called the competition "a once-in-a-lifetime opportunity for the federal government to create incentives for far-reaching improvement in our nation's schools . . . ,

---

[8] As the statute notes, "The Secretary shall determine which States receive grants under this section, and the amount of those grants, on the basis of information provided in State applications under section 14005 and such other criteria as the Secretary determines appropriate." American Recovery and Reinvestment Act of 2009, 2012, https://www.govinfo.gov/content/pkg/PLAW-111publ5/html/PLAW-111publ5.htm.

[9] The lack of congressional oversight became a partisan point of contention. Republicans on the House Education and Workforce Committee wrote, "The U.S. Secretary of Education Arne Duncan has been granted control over a multibillion-dollar slush fund to be awarded to states as he sees fit." Smith, Lauren. (2012). Duncan Shows Congress the Way Around Gridlock. *Congressional Quarterly*.

[10] Retrieved from: https://obamawhitehouse.archives.gov/blog/2009/07/24/president-race-top.

the equivalent of education reform's moon shot.'"[11] Media coverage echoed such sentiments, with *The Christian Science Monitor* calling RttT a "massive incentive for school reform," and *The New York Times* subsequently arguing that participating states "would never have attempted reform on this scale without the promise of federal help."[12]

Judged on its own terms, RttT proved to be an extraordinary success. At a time when Congress was incapable of passing nearly any education policy of consequence, state legislatures quickly adopted the president's education agenda as their own. As the advocacy group Education Sector wrote in 2010, "With a relatively modest outlay of money—$4 billion in a $600 billion industry—US Secretary of Education Arne Duncan has dramatically reshaped education policy across the country."[13]

The president's second effort to change education policy through administrative channels came in the form of a new program for granting NCLB waivers. Announced in August 2011, the Obama Administration's waiver program was called, "the most sweeping use of executive authority to rewrite federal education law since Washington expanded its involvement in education in the 1960s."[14] Though the authority to grant waivers was written into the original Elementary and Secondary Education Act, no president had yet required that states agree to a roster of specific policy measures in return for the flexibility that came with a waiver. Obama used waivers not just to unwind previous education commitments at the federal level. He used them to promulgate altogether new ones at the state level (Levesque 2019).

The president recognized that states were clamoring for relief from NCLB, and he used this desire to pressure them to enact policies favored by his administration, including, not surprisingly, many of the same policies rewarded by RttT. To qualify for a waiver, states were expected to implement

---

[11] Arne Duncan, "Education Reform's Moon Shot." *Washington Post*, July 24, 2009. Later, in remarks announcing the finalists of the first phase of the competition, Duncan claimed that RttT was part of a "quiet revolution" in education reform and that the competition had "unleashed an avalanche of pent-up education reform activity at the state and local level." http://www.ed.gov/news/speeches/quiet-revolution-secretary-arne-duncans-remarks-national-press-club.

[12] Gail Chaddock, "Obama's $4 Billion Is Massive Incentive for School Reform." *Christian Science Monitor,* July 24, 2009; Editorial, "Continue the Race," *New York Times,* August 28, 2010.

[13] Chad Aldeman, "How Race to the Top Could Inform ESEA Reauthorization," *Education Week,* June 29, 2010. For some rather exhaustive examinations of this claim, see William Howell, "Results of President Obama's Race to the Top," *Education Next,* August 2015; William Howell and Asya Magazinnik. 2017. "Presidential Prescriptions for State Policy: Obama's Race to the Top Initiative," *Journal of Policy Analysis and Management* 36(3): 502–531; William Howell and Asya Magazinnik. 2020. "Financial Incentives in Vertical Diffusion: How Obama's Race to the Top Initiative Refashioned State Policymaking," *State Politics and Policy Quarterly* 20(2): 185–212.

[14] Sam Dillon, "Overriding a Key Education Law," *New York Times,* August 8, 2011.

new teacher and administrator evaluation systems that took into account student achievement data, adopted college and career-ready curriculum standards, and designed new accountability measures for schools.[15] Within just a couple of years, nearly every state in the Union had passed the policies needed to acquire a waiver. And while scholars debated the merits of these policy changes for student achievement,[16] the imprints left by this waiver program on state laws were plain to see.

Eight years after it was meant to reauthorize NCLB, Congress passed the 2015 Every Student Succeeds Act, which put an end to NCLB and thus to Obama's waiver program. ESSA returned significant amounts of discretion back to the states, which, by that time, had already reoriented their oversight and operations of schools around Obama's education priorities. In important respects, the passage of ESSA represented a repudiation of Obama's education policies, federally imposed accountability, and (alleged) federal "overreach" in general. But ESSA did not boldly reassert congressional prerogatives over education, nor did it directly overturn the changes that Obama had made to the education policy landscape. Rather, Congress shifted the locus of education policymaking back to the states where the president, amidst prolonged congressional gridlock, had just enjoyed immense success.

Conclusion

What happens in Congress does not stay in Congress. Its performance, procedures, and rules affect more than just the insiders directly affected by them. Embedded in a larger system of separated powers, congressional activity (and inactivity) emanates outwards and informs the strategies and initiatives of presidents, who have ambition, capacity, authority, and policy objectives of their own. Look beyond the legislative process and one begins to appreciate how the politics of unilateral action are informed by Congress itself, as presidents take the measure of the first branch of government when deciding how to engineer the behavior of the second.

---

[15] For more on these requirements, see: http://www2.ed.gov/policy/elsec/guid/esea-flexibility/index.html.

[16] Compare, for instance, Hemelt, Steven and Brian Jacob. 2017. "Differentiated Accountability and Education Production: Evidence from NCLB Waivers." NBER Working Papers 23461, National Bureau of Economic Research; and Bonilla, Sade and Thomas Dee. 2020. "The Effects of School Reform under NCLB Waivers: Evidence from Focus Schools in Kentucky." *Education Finance and Policy*. 15(1): 75–103.

There are lots of reasons why Congress did not enact most of Trump's policy priorities. And Trump, surely, carries a fair bit of the blame. The story of these proposals, however, does not end on the cutting floors of Capitol Hill. After failing to pass significant legislation, and in many instances before he even tried, Trump looked to write and implement all kinds of domestic and foreign policies through administrative channels. With executive orders, memoranda, and other unilateral directives, the Trump administration made massive changes in immigration, deregulation, health care, foreign trade, energy, and climate change—often in the face of legislative ambivalence, sometimes confronting steadfast opposition, but routinely yielding policy outcomes that Congress would not have enacted on its own.

In this regard, Trump is not distinctive among modern presidents. As Obama's Race to the Top competition and his conditional waivers to No Child Left Behind make clear, Trump's actions are indicative of something larger. Presidents—all presidents—refuse to sit idly by while their policy priorities languish in Congress. When they have the requisite authority, and when they think they can get away with it,[17] presidents do for themselves what Congress will not.

Congress, of course, is not entirely excluded from these politics. When contemplating unilateral actions, presidents must anticipate how Congress (as well as the judiciary, the federal bureaucracy, and the broader public) will respond to their directives. But Congress's role in these politics is decidedly weak. Rather than being the driving force behind the federal government's efforts to address pressing national problems, its members are left to keep watch over and clean up—if they can—policy directives conceived, written, and implemented in the executive branch.

The travails of the legislative process, as such, do not banish all policy proposals to a neglected purgatory. Often, instead, they displace policymaking activities from Congress to the presidency and thereby shift the balance of power in the president's favor. If you want to gauge the significance of Congress, then, do not focus narrowly on what its members say or do. Look to the adaptive responses of presidents.

---

[17] For more on the dynamics between presidential authority and action, see William Howell, Kenneth Shepsle, and Stephane Wolton. Forthcoming. "Executive Absolutism: The Dynamics of Authority Acquisition in a System of Separated Powers," *Quarterly Journal of Political Science*; William Howell and Stephane Wolton. 2018. "The Politician's Province," *Quarterly Journal of Political Science* 13(2): 119–146.

References

Ali, A. A., BiBi, F., and M.I. Ashraf. 2020. "Trump's Middle East Peace Plan: Prospects and Challenges." *Global Strategic & Security Studies Review* V(II): 1–11.

Ansolabehere, Stephen and Jon Rogowski. 2020. "Unilateral Action and Presidential Accountability." *Presidential Studies Quarterly* 50: 129–145.

Darrow, Jessica, and Jess Howsam Scholl. 2020. "Chaos and Confusion: Impacts of the Trump Administration Executive Orders on the US Refugee Resettlement System." *Human Service Organizations: Management, Leadership & Governance* 44(4): 362–380.

Howell, W., and A. Magazinnik. 2017. "Presidential Prescriptions for State Policy: Obama's Race to the Top Initiative." *Journal of Policy Analysis and Management* 36(3): 502–531.

Howell, W., and A. Magazinnik. 2020. "Financial Incentives in Vertical Diffusion: How Obama's Race to the Top Initiative Refashioned State Policymaking." *State Politics and Policy Quarterly* 20(2): 185–212.

Howell, William, and Stephane Wolton. 2018. "The Politician's Province." *Quarterly Journal of Political Science* 13(2): 119–146.

Howell, William, Kenneth Shepsle, and Stephane Wolton. Forthcoming. "Executive Absolutism: The Dynamics of Authority Acquisition in a System of Separated Powers." *Quarterly Journal of Political Science* 18(2): 243–275.

Howell, William. 2005. "Unilateral Powers: A Brief Overview." *Presidential Studies Quarterly* 35(3): 417–439.

Kaufman, Aaron R., and Jon C. Rogowski. 2022. "Presidential Policymaking, 1877–2020." University of Chicago, mimeo.

Lens, V. 2018. "Executive Orders and the Trump Administration: A Guide for Social Workers." *Social Work* 63(3): 210–221.

Levesque, Elizabeth Mann. 2019. "Waving Goodbye to Congressional Constraints: Presidents and Subnational Policy Making." *Presidential Studies Quarterly* 49(2): 358–93.

Lowande, Kenneth, and Jon Rogowski. 2021. "Presidential Unilateral Power." *Annual Review of Political Science* 24: 21–43.

Milkis, Sidney M., and Nicholas Jacobs. 2017. "'I Alone Can Fix It': Donald Trump, the Administrative Presidency, and Hazards of Executive-Centered Partisanship." *The Forum* 15(3): 583–613.

Moe, Terry M., and William G. Howell. 1999. "The Presidential Power of Unilateral Action." *Journal of Law, Economics, and Organization* 15(1): 132–179.

Potter, Rachel, Andrew Rudalevige, Sharece Thrower, and Adam Warber. 2022. "Not by the Numbers: Evaluating Trump's Administrative Presidency." *Presidential Studies Quarterly* 52(3): 596–625.

Smith, Lauren. 2012. "Duncan Shows Congress the Way Around Gridlock." *Congressional Quarterly* March 12: 490–494.

Turek, Maciej. 2022. "Unilateral Powers and Donald Trump Presidency." *Przegląd Prawa Konstytucyjnego* 2(66): 269–282.

Waslin Michele. 2020. "The Use of Executive Orders and Proclamations to Create Immigration Policy: Trump in Historical Perspective." *Journal on Migration and Human Security* 8(1): 54–67.

Afterword

The Future of the Senate

Sean M. Theriault

As the book developed, I asked the authors to answer the question of how much the Trump presidency disrupted the Senate. The book contains thirteen substantive chapters and thirteen distinct answers to that question. Had all the authors arrived at the same conclusion, I am not sure that a book on the subject would be necessary. I view the different answers as a strength of this book rather than as a weakness. Indeed, it is the diversity of answers that makes them so interesting.

Even the authors offering the two most contrasting answers agree at some fundamental level. Bellantoni suggests that the Trump administration may have pounded the final nail in the coffin of the institutional Senate. While arguing that Trump took the baton handed to him from Obama, Wallner recognized that the partisanship that Trump interjected into the whole system made legislating harder. From Bellantoni to Wallner, the authors' resounding answer is that Trump left his mark on the Senate, although most would say he did not change it *that* much. Rather than trying to put a common mantra on these disparate answers, I would ask the reader to relish in the different opinions expressed by these authors. Instead of encapsulating this edited volume with a concise bumper sticker about disruption or change, I invite the reader to hear the different answers and appreciate the nuance that they provide in understanding how the current Senate operates. It turns out that assessing the extent of change in the Senate resulting from the presidency of Donald Trump is a complicated task.

Perhaps Trump's most significant effect on the Senate was after he lost the 2020 election. His behavior postelection is largely credited with putting the two Georgia Senate seats on the Democratic side of the aisle. His rally on January 6 is widely blamed for inciting an insurrection at the US Capitol that had senators literally running for their lives. Even after Trump

Sean M. Theriault, *Afterword* In: *Disruption?* Edited by: Sean M. Theriault, Oxford University Press.
© Oxford University Press 2024. DOI: 10.1093/oso/9780197767832.003.0015

stoked the insurrection, eight senators—Ted Cruz (Texas), Josh Hawley (Missouri), Cindy Hyde-Smith (Mississippi), John Kennedy (Louisiana), Cynthia Lummis (Wyoming), Roger Marshall (Kansas), Rick Scott (Florida), and Tommy Tuberville (Alabama)—voted to perpetuate Trump's "Big Lie" by challenging the electoral college votes of either Arizona or Pennsylvania. While some senators in his party perpetuated his falsehoods, others rebuked him. Though acquitted of the impeachment charges after he moved back to Mar-a-Lago, the vote, as Zelizer explains, had the most same-party conviction votes on impeachment in the history of the United States.

Indeed, Trump changed the Senate. The extent of that change is either "a great deal" or "a bit" depending upon where along the Bellantoni-Wallner continuum one sits. In this afterward, I ask the next natural question—to what extent did the Senate snap back to its pre-Trump operations? Or, is the Senate that endured January 6, 2021, the new normal from which future changes will happen?

Some of the authors have already given us glimpses into the post-Trump Senate. Wallner shows that the Senate has continued along the same path it was on during Obama and Trump. Ritchie would argue that the same rules are still in place even as Bellantoni waits for Republican senators to return her phone calls. A unified Democratic government, however small, certainly changed the reliance upon unorthodox lawmaking discussed by Reynolds and the strategic circumstances that Volden and Wiseman suggested Democratic senators were able to use during the Trump years. No one expects President Biden to flagrantly violate democratic norms, as Lesniewski documents under Trump, and no one expects Biden to put senators on their back foot by sending inflammatory or incoherent Tweets in the middle of the night, as Russell documented.

Clearly, President Biden interacts with senators differently than President Trump. Instead of Tweets criticizing "Crying Chuck," Biden reached out to the opposition. The first two senators he met with in the Oval Office were both Republican (Susan Collins and Lisa Murkowski). The next group he met included those two, plus eight additional Republicans. It was only after that meeting that he met with his first Democratic senators—the two from his home state of Delaware (Tom Carper and Chris Coons). Only after that meeting did he finally meet with the Democratic Party leadership in the Senate.[1] It would seem Biden's instincts sitting behind the Resolute Desk are

---

[1] Luke Broadwater, February 16, 2021, "Biden Works to Leverage Senate Ties to Power his Agenda," *The New York Times*, https://www.nytimes.com/2021/02/16/us/politics/biden-congress-senate.html?.

the same as when he sat behind the spindle desks in the Senate: when possible, find a senator from the other side of the aisle to get something done.

Biden's early approach may have paid off. Biden's cabinet nominations garnered more cross-party support than Trump's nominations. Each of his nominees to the cabinet got at least one Republican vote; and all but three got more than 10. In contrast, two of Trump's nominees got zero Democratic votes (not including Andrew Putzer's nomination for the secretary of labor, which was pulled due to insufficient support to even be confirmed). On average, Biden's nominees received 23 Republican votes compared to Trump's nominees who received only 19 Democratic votes (see Table AF.1).

The greater cross-party support may have other causes beyond Biden's more congenial approach such as the quality of the nominees or the nominees' adherence to the nomination process. Even if these other causes are more consequential than Biden's approach, it suggests that the Senate returned to more normal operations after the Trump presidency, at least as far as cabinet nominations are concerned.

Not only did Biden's nominees receive greater cross-party support, but also they stayed in office longer. The first to leave Biden's cabinet was Marty Walsh, secretary of labor, more than 2 years after Biden's inauguration. In contrast, more than half of Trump's cabinet left in his first two years. Whereas Biden had just the 15 cabinet secretaries confirmed by the Senate, Trump had 20 confirmed cabinet secretaries and 10 acting secretaries during his first two years.

While we could imagine that an afterward on a book like this might metaphorically "turn the page" on the history of the Senate, it should be stated explicitly that it is hard to think of a political world as being "post-Trump" in any way. While he no longer sits behind the Resolute Desk (but rather his custom-made fake Resolute Desk in Mar-a-Lago) and while he no longer flies on Air Force One (but rather his custom-named Trump Force One), he still influences the news of the day and, certainly by extension, the Senate. In the more than two years since he left the White House, he has been a more popular Google search term than the current president (see Figure AF.1).

Over the first two years of Biden's presidency, Trump was a more popular search term than Biden by 11 percent. In the first four months of the Biden's third year in office once the indictments were handed down and as the race for the Republican nomination heated up, Trump searches more than double Biden (113 percent more to be precise). To appreciate how truly unusual it is that the former president is searched more than the current president,

Table AF.1 Cross-Party Support for Trump's and Biden's Cabinet Nominees

Department	Trump Nominee	Total Vote Yes	No	Dem. Vote Yes	No	Biden Nominee	Total Vote Yes	No	Rep. Vote Yes	No
State	Tillerson	56	43	3	43	Blinken	78	22	28	22
Treasury	Mnuchin	53	47	1	46	Yellen	84	15	34	15
Defense	Mattis	98	1	46	1	Austin	93	2	43	2
Justice	Sessions	52	47	1	46	Garland	70	30	20	30
Interior	Zinke	68	31	15	31	Haaland	51	40	4	40
Agriculture	Perdue	87	11	46	1	Vilsack	92	7	44	6
Commerce	Ross	72	27	20	27	Raimondo	84	15	34	15
Labor	Acosta	60	38	8	38	Walsh	68	29	18	29
HHS	Price	52	47	0	46	Becerra	50	49	1	49
HUD	Carson	58	41	7	40	Fudge	66	34	16	34
Transportation	Chao	93	6	42	5	Buttigieg	86	13	36	13
Energy	Perry	62	37	10	37	Granholm	64	35	14	35
Education	DeVos	50	50	0	47	Cardona	64	33	14	35
Veterans Affairs	Shulkin	100	0	47	0	McDonough	87	7	37	7
Homeland Security	Kelly	88	11	36	11	Mayorkas	56	43	6	43
Average		**73**	**25**	**23**	**25**		**70**	**29**	**19**	**28**

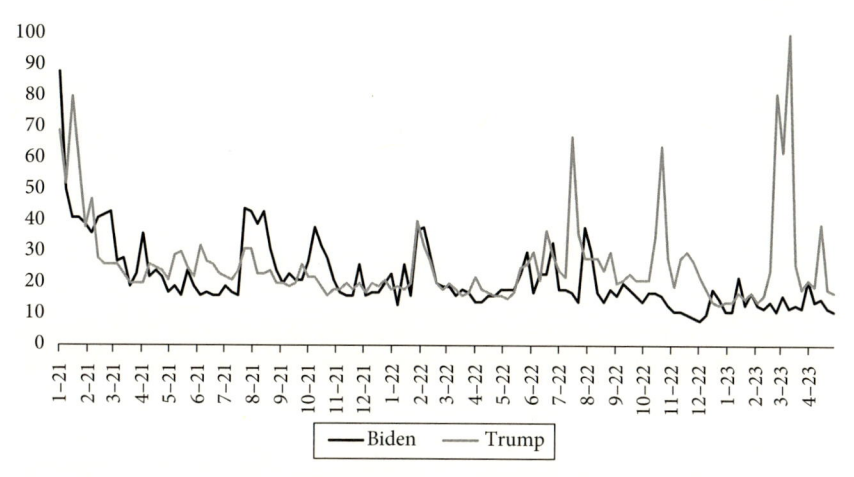

Figure AF.1 Google Searches for "Biden" and "Trump" during Biden's Administration, 2021–2023

Note: Data are computed by week. The most popular search term ("Trump" during the week of his indictment by the Manhattan grand jury) is recorded at 100; all other searches by week are a portion of that maximum amount.

consider that Trump was searched 6.75 more times that Obama from 2017–2019, and Obama was searched 7.75 more times than Bush from 2009–2011.

What may have broken the Trump-induced fever on the Senate even more than his defeat in 2020 and the two Republican losses in the Georgia Senate runoff elections in January 2021 was the resounding defeat of his preferred candidates in the 2022 elections. The best analysis suggests that Trump's candidates faired 5 points worse than the establishment Republicans.[2] That worse showing was felt particularly among Senate Republicans, who remained in the minority during the second two years of the Biden administration. In a hardly veiled attack on those candidates, three months before the election, McConnell warned that Republicans might not take back the Senate because "candidate quality has a lot to do with the outcome."[3] While his candidates ultimately won in Ohio and North Carolina, Trump was roundly criticized for pushing candidates in the primaries who lost very winnable

[2] Nate Cohn, November 29, 2022, "Trump's Drag on Republicans Quantified: A Five-Point Penalty," *The New York Times*, https://www.nytimes.com/2022/11/16/upshot/trump-effect-midterm-election.html.

[3] Sahil Kapur and Frank Thorp V, August 18, 2022, "McConnell Says Republicans May Not Win Senate Control, Citing 'Candidate Quality,'" *NBC News*.

races, including Blake Masters in Arizona, Mehmet Oz in Pennsylvania, and Hershel Walker in Georgia.

The fallout after the dismal results from the Republicans in the Senate was swift. The week after the election, Trump in a speech laced with lies about the 2016 election announced that he would seek the Republican nomination for president in 2024. The contents of the speech and the official announcement landed with a thud in the Senate. Senator Mike Rounds (R-South Dakota) reacted by saying that he wanted "a reasonable person who would unite the party." Senator Kevin Cramer (R-North Dakota) offered, "I think we're all better if there's more of them up on the stage." Senator John Thune (R-South Dakota), the second-ranking Republican, reasoned that "relitigating the 2020 election is not a winning strategy." Senator Shelley Moore Capito (R-West Virginia) agreed, "I think looking forward is always a better campaign strategy."[4] It should be noted that none of these four were included on Bellantoni's call list as "moderates" in the Senate.

Trump attempted to shift blame from his endorsement of flawed candidates to McConnell's August statement about them. He even pushed Senator Rick Scott (R-Florida), the chair of the National Republican Senatorial Committee, to make an unprecedented run against McConnell for his leadership position.[5] While gleeful in winning that race 37–10, McConnell faces a Republican conference that includes fewer senators who are loyal to him and more who are loyal to Trump, though not nearly as much as if Trump's flawed candidates had won in those winnable races. I suspect that four of the six new Republican senators in the 118th Congress are much more loyal to Trump than their predecessors and the other two are at least as loyal to him (see table AF.2). The other Republican senator who is not returning to the 118th Congress, Pat Toomey, voted to convict Trump in the second impeachment trial; John Fetterman, the sitting Democratic lieutenant governor, won the election to replace him.

It should also be noted that all eight senators who voted to challenge the electoral college slates in Arizona or Pennsylvania remained in the Senate during the 118th Congress. We can only presume through their declarations during the campaign that Trump's victorious candidates would have joined their ranks. At this point, it is unclear if that marginal increase would further

---

[4] All quotes come from Manu Raju, Melanie Zanona, and Ted Barrett, November 15, 2022, "Trump's 2024 Bid Gets Harsh Reaction among Hill Republicans."

[5] Alexander Bolton, November 8, 2022, "Trump Touts Scott as 'Likely Candidate' to Replace McConnell as Senate Leader," *The Hill*.

Table AF.2 The Six Changes in the Republican Conferences in the 118th Congress

State	Old Senator	New Senator	Change in Loyalty to Trump
Alabama	Richard Shelby	Katie Britt	Neither Shelby nor Britt had a close association with Trump.
Missouri	Roy Blunt	Eric Schmitt	Blunt was a sometimes Trump critic; Schmitt was one of two Senate candidates in Missouri to receive a Trump endorsement in 2022.
Nebraska	Ben Sasse	Pete Ricketts	Sasse was a frequent Trump critic; Rickets does not have a particularly close association with Trump.
North Carolina	Richard Burr	Ted Budd	Burr voted to convict Trump in the second impeachment; Trump's endorsement of Budd was crucial for his primary victory.
Ohio	Rob Portman	J.D. Vance	Portman was a sometimes Trump critic; Trump's endorsement of Vance was crucial for his victory.
Oklahoma	Jim Inhofe	Markwayne Mullin	Neither Inhofe nor Mullin had a particularly close association with Trump.

disrupt the Senate, but these trends have a way of building upon themselves (Theriault 2013). At the very least, the changes brought about by the 2022 elections suggest that the Republican conference in the Senate is less cohesive than it was following the 2020 election. And with a looming Republican presidential nomination contest and a House Republican conference that is sufficiently divided that it took 15 votes to elect a speaker and then ousted him less than 10 months later, the cohesiveness is only likely to deteriorate as the congress proceeds.

As the 2024 elections heat up and Biden's first term eventually wraps up, we can be certain that Biden's attempt to restore the Senate to the chamber that it was when he served in it will continue, just as Trump's attempt to disrupt it.

Reference

Theriault, Sean M. 2013. *The Gingrich Senators: The Roots of Partisan Warfare in Congress*, New York: Oxford University Press.

Index

For the benefit of digital users, indexed terms that span two pages (e.g., 52–53) may, on occasion, appear on only one of those pages.

Tables and figures are indicated by *t* and *f* following the page number

The manufacturer's authorised representative in the EU for product safety is Oxford
University Press España S.A. of El Parque Empresarial San Fernando de Henares,
Avenida de Castilla, 2 – 28830 Madrid (www.oup.es/en or product.safety@oup.com).
OUP España S.A. also acts as importer into Spain of products made by the manufacturer.

Printed in the USA/Agawam, MA
July 30, 2025

891003.002